# *Industrialization in Sandinista Nicaragua*

## *Series in Political Economy and Economic Development in Latin America*

Series Editor
Andrew Zimbalist
*Smith College*

*Industrialization in Sandinista Nicaragua: Policy and Practice in a Mixed Economy,* Geske Dijkstra

† *The Making of Social Movements in Latin America: Identity, Strategy, and Democracy,* edited by Arturo Escobar and Sonia E. Alvarez

*The Latin American Development Debate: Neostructuralism, Neomonetarism, and Adjustment Processes,* edited by Patricio Meller

*Peasants in Distress: Poverty and Unemployment in the Dominican Republic,* Rosemary Vargas-Lundius

*Distorted Development: Mexico in the World Economy,* David Barkin

*State and Capital in Mexico: Development Policy Since 1940,* James M. Cypher

*Central America: The Future of Economic Integration,* edited by George Irvin and Stuart Holland

*Struggle Against Dependence: Nontraditional Export Growth in Central America and the Caribbean,* edited by Eva Paus

*The Peruvian Mining Industry: Growth, Stagnation, and Crisis,* Elizabeth Dore

*Cuban Political Economy: Controversies in Cubanology,* edited by Andrew Zimbalist

† *Rural Women and State Policy: Feminist Perspectives in Latin American Agricultural Development,* edited by Carmen Diana Deere and Magdalena León

†Available in hardcover and paperback.

# *Industrialization in Sandinista Nicaragua*

## Policy and Practice in a Mixed Economy

Routledge
Taylor & Francis Group
LONDON AND NEW YORK

First published 1992 by Westview Press, Inc.

Published 2018 by Routledge
52 Vanderbilt Avenue, New York, NY 10017
2 Park Square, Milton Park, Abingdon, Oxon OX14 4RN

*Routledge is an imprint of the Taylor & Francis Group, an informa business*



**A CIP catalog record for this book is available from the Library of Congress.**
ISBN 13: 978-0-367-01344-8 (hbK)
ISBN 13: 978-0-367-16331-0 (pbK)

# Contents

*List of Tables* vii
*Preface* xi

1 **Introduction** 1

The Mixed Economy, 3
Industrialization, 7
Outline for This Book, 10
Notes, 12

2 **The New Economic Policy** 15

The USSR, 1917–1925, 16
The Industrialization Debate, 20
The End of the NEP, 24
Conclusion and Comparison, 31
Notes, 32

3 **Industrialization Before 1979** 33

The Central American Industrialization Model, 33
Interpretations of the Central American Model, 38
Perspectives on the Central American Model, 41
Economic Control in Nicaragua, 58
Notes, 67

4 **The Mixed Economy** 69

Ideology, 71
The Mixed Economy in Practice, 76
Notes, 106

**5 Accumulation and Sources for Accumulation** 109

Reactivation and Accumulation: An Overview, 111
Sources for State Accumulation, 115
The Distribution of Income, 128
The 1988 Change, 136
Notes, 141

**6 The Mixed Economy and Industrialization** 143

The Industrialization Strategy, 143
Cooperation in the Private Sector, 164
Notes, 180

**7 Summary and Conclusion** 183

Notes, 190

**Epilogue** 191

*Appendix 1: The Methodology for the Fieldwork* 195
*The Research Questions,* 195
*The Interviews,* 197
*The Sample,* 199
*Agroindustry,* 203
*Appendix 2: List of Questions* 205
*List of Acronyms* 209
*Bibliography* 211
*Index* 221

# Tables


| | | |
|---|---|---|
| 1.1 | Types of economic order | 4 |
| 1.2 | Sectoral structure of GDP and employment, 1950–1984 | 11 |
| 2.1 | USSR: Gross turnover in trade per type of ownership, 1923/24–1925/26 | 19 |
| 2.2 | USSR: Gross industrial production per type of ownership, 1923/24–1925/26 | 20 |
| 2.3 | USSR: Gross industrial production, 1913–1933 | 26 |
| 3.1 | Growth rates of manufacturing in Central America, 1960-1979 | 36 |
| 3.2 | Growth rates of manufacturing industry in Nicaragua per branch, 1960–1977 | 37 |
| 3.3 | Structure of imports by economic use | 41 |
| 3.4 | Nicaragua's balance of payments, 1960–1979 | 43 |
| 3.5 | Exports of Nicaragua and structure of exports, 1960–1979 | 44 |
| 3.6 | Structure of value added per branch of manufacturing, 1960–1983 | 46 |
| 3.7 | Destination of the industrial product per branch | 47 |
| 3.8 | Nicaragua: Import substitution at the regional level per branch, 1960–1980 | 48 |
| 3.9 | Static terms-of-trade effect on Central America, 1960–1979 | 51 |
| 3.10 | Nicaragua's trade cycles, 1963–1979: Some indicators | 56 |
| 3.11 | Government revenue and expenditure, 1960–1979: Some indicators | 57 |
| 3.12 | Nicaragua: Weight in production of major strata of producers before 1979 | 63 |
| 4.1 | Nicaragua: Balance of public and private ownership, 1978 and 1980 | 77 |
| 4.2 | Land tenure in Nicaragua, 1978–1988 | 80 |
| 4.3 | Sample of enterprises: Assignment of foreign exchange for imports of raw materials and inputs | 90 |
| 4.4 | Sample of enterprises: Application of economization | 91 |

4.5 Sample enterprises in need of imported spare parts: Assignment of foreign exchange 92
4.6 Sample of enterprises: Decisions on prices 96
4.7 Sample of enterprises: Decisions on domestic sales 97
4.8 Sample of enterprises: Application of incentive system and MITRAB approval 102
4.9 Sample of enterprises: Investment and assignment of foreign exchange since 1979 103

5.1 Macroeconomic indicators for Nicaragua, 1979–1988 112
5.2 Accumulation balance for Nicaragua, 1977–1985 113
5.3 Property damage and production losses due to armed conflict 114
5.4 Indicators of agricultural production 116
5.5 Indexes of manufacturing value added, 1978–1983 117
5.6 Exports of goods, 1976-1985 119
5.7 Exchange rates in Nicaragua, 1979–1989 121
5.8 Indicators of government finance, 1981–1988 124
5.9 Composition of current government income 125
5.10 Distribution of credit by production sector 126
5.11 Consumption and investment, 1981–1986 128
5.12 Wages and prices, 1980–1984 129
5.13 State and private trade of foodstuffs, 1982–1983 132
5.14 Purchasing power of salaries and inflation rate, February 1988–February 1989 138

6.1 Private ownership in manufacturing industry per branch, 1980–1987 144
6.2 Investment program, 1983–1987 147
6.3 Manufacturing industry: Value added, 1983, and investment, 1980–1984 149
6.4 Sources of financing for manufacturing investment 151
6.5 Imports of raw materials, inputs, and spare parts for manufacturing, 1977 and 1980–1987 153
6.6 Indexes of manufacturing value added, 1980–1987 154
6.7 Sample of enterprises: Capacity use 155
6.8 Sample of enterprises: Evaluation of existing equipment 157
6.9 Sample of enterprises: Origin of the equipment 158
6.10 Sample of enterprises: Problems with labor recruitment 158
6.11 Sample of enterprises: Profits 159
6.12 Sample of enterprises: Reasons for export reduction 162

6.13 Sample of enterprises: Export markets 163
6.14 Sample of enterprises: Opinions on the assignment of foreign exchange for raw materials, inputs, and spare parts 166
6.15 Sample of enterprises: Expectations to receive foreign exchange next year 167
6.16 Private enterprises of the sample: Opinions on the revolutionary process 168
6.17 Industrial investment, 1980–1984, per ownership area 169
6.18 Sample of enterprises: Investment plans and expectations to receive foreign exchange 170
6.19 Private enterprises of the sample: Opinions of shareholders 172
6.20 Private enterprises of the sample: Position of shareholders and alternatives 173

A.1 Comparison of sample and population by type of ownership 201
A.2 Comparison of sample and population by stratum: Categories 1–4; and state or private 201
A.3 Comparison of sample and population: Gross production, employment, and productivity of state and private enterprises 202

# Preface

The subject of this book gripped me from the start, and I never lost my fascination. It gave me the opportunity to combine theoretical reflection with concrete investigation in a country that had just experienced a revolution. From May 1984 to June 1985 I lived in Nicaragua and had many interviews with government officials and directors of state and private manufacturing enterprises. After that, I visited Nicaragua several times and was thus able to include the results of policy adjustments of 1985 and 1988 and the reversals brought about by the 1990 elections.

The main question I address is whether the Sandinista "mixed economy"—a "transitional" mixed economy—could have been stable if the Sandinistas had been able to pursue their industrialization strategy for a longer period of time. Obviously, the instability of the economy was reflected in the FSLN's defeat in the 1990 elections. Although most observers had expected the mixed economy to be unstable, none had foreseen that elections would bring it to an end.

The pessimists expected a U.S. invasion or a military coup that would re-establish a capitalist system. Others were convinced that the mixed economy was only a tactical maneuver of the FSLN and would be substituted by a socialist economy as soon as possible. And many people thought that a mixed economy would by necessity evolve toward a centrally planned economy because of its internal contradictions and the impossibility of achieving industrialization.

The last supposition was the starting point for this book. I wanted to investigate the internal contradictions and policy errors that might have made the introduction of central planning inevitable. For that reason, I compared Nicaragua's mixed economy with the first and longest-maintained mixed economy of this kind in history, that of the USSR under the New Economic Policy (NEP) (1921–1928/29). Although in the end Nicaragua did not evolve toward a centrally planned system but toward capitalism through elections, the comparison of Nicaragua's policy and practice with the NEP still leads to relevant conclusions. On the one hand, this book explains why Nicaragua's mixed economy was remarkably stable for almost eleven years. On the other, it can help to explain the FSLN election defeat in

1990. For example, my conclusion that the Sandinista price and accumulation policies endangered the stability of the mixed economy is still valid: These policies, along with the economic destabilization caused by the *contras*, produced the disastrous economic situation that was to a great extent responsible for the loss of support for the FSLN government.

The great achievement of the Sandinistas is that they enhanced democracy in Nicaragua not only by permitting free elections but also by creating and expanding the physical and institutional conditions for popular participation on many levels. But in the end, their economic policies impeded a continuation of these achievements. In this sense, studying the Sandinista economic experience is crucial for all who favor democratic socialism.

Many people and institutions provided helpful support during the process of carrying out the research and writing this book. I gratefully acknowledge the hospitality of the Instituto de Investigaciones Económicas y Sociales (INIES) in Nicaragua and its then director Xabier Gorostiaga. I wish to thank all other institutions and persons who cooperated in my investigation: the functionaries of the Ministry of Industry and the directors of state and private enterprises. So many of them were kindly willing to receive me and frankly answer my questions.

From the beginning of the research project, I enjoyed the critical and stimulating support of Hans-Jürgen Wagener and Valpy FitzGerald; to both I wish to express my deep gratitude. The book also benefited from the comments of Michael Ellman and Andrew Zimbalist, and from the editorial corrections given by Joy Hackel, Sara Henley, Diane Hess, Gerry Paster, and Millie Thayer. Of course, I am alone responsible for the final contents. Rob Baltussen and Maurice Evers carried out most of the painstaking work of making this book camera-ready.

Financial support for the research was provided by the Foundation for Scientific Research in the Tropics (WOTRO) and later by the State University of Groningen—both in The Netherlands. Subsequently, my then employer, the Instituto de Investigaciones Económicas (INVE) of the University of El Salvador allowed me to work on the updating of the research conclusions. I am particularly grateful to its then coordinator, Flora de Grajeda, for her tolerance and patience during that phase. Finally, I wish to thank my partner, Tom Groot, for his many-sided support during this project.

*Geske Dijkstra*

# 1

# Introduction

With the victory of the FSLN (Frente Sandinista para la Liberación Nacional; Sandinista Front for National Liberation) on July 19, 1979, Nicaragua's new government opted for a "mixed economy": state ownership of the means of production would coexist with private ownership, and the market would operate alongside state planning. The revolutionary government drew lessons from the Cuban example and avoided a premature state control of the economy.

The government began by nationalizing the property of former dictator Somoza, which brought the economic potential of about a quarter of the gross domestic product (GDP) into state hands. In addition, the foreign-owned mining companies were expropriated, and the government took control of foreign trade and the banking system. The rest of the economy, accounting for 60 percent of GDP, remained in private hands. The private sector consisted of small-scale handicraft producers, small traders, and peasants and of large-scale producers in agriculture and industry. The market was still the dominant coordinating mechanism, but the government had decided influence on the economy through its control over the allocation of foreign exchange and finance.

When the Sandinistas seized power the country's economic situation was disastrous. Of the 2.5 million inhabitants about 50,000 people had lost their lives during the liberation war and 100,000 had been wounded. Hardly any food crops had been planted, and many industrial plants were severely damaged. During the eighteen months before the Sandinista victory, an enormous capital flight had taken place: \$220 million in 1978 and \$315 million in the first six months of 1979 (ECLAC 1979:1026). In July 1979 there was only \$3.5 million left in the banks.

The Sandinista government inherited not only the consequences of the war but a country that had developed very unevenly. During the 1950s and 1960s Nicaragua had had high growth rates based on extensive agricultural production for export. But growth had not "trickled down" to the majority of the population. The income distribution was very skewed: Fifty percent of the population earned only 15 percent of national income in 1977 (FIDA 1980:53). Social services such as health and education hardly existed.

In the 1970s economic growth slowed down. Despite a rapid industrialization process in the 1960s and 1970s, the agricultural sector accounted for most exports and absorbed half the labor force in 1979. The industrial sector was to a significant extent dependent on imports of capital goods and raw materials.

The revolutionary government's first objective was to consolidate state power. The FSLN succeeded in establishing control over domestic policies. However, from 1981 onward the country suffered from military destabilization by former members of Somoza's National Guard, the counterrevolutionaries or *contras*. The contras' numbers grew as US government funding for their forces increased. Although they never became powerful enough to overthrow the Sandinista government, their actions brought about severe damage to the economy and forced the government to spend heavily on defense. The need to maintain a well-organized defense was even more pressing because there always was the threat of a direct invasion by U.S. forces.

The government attempted to reactivate the economy, at the same time seeking to change the structure of production. The objective was to make the economy less dependent on foreign trade and to direct production more to the interests and needs of the "poor majority" (MIPLAN 1980 and 1981). The government developed a strategy for state-directed accumulation—that is, the use of resources to increase production—, aimed at fulfilling the basic needs of the population and achieving more international independence.

The agricultural sector was to take priority in the development strategy. The Sandinistas stimulated agricultural exports because foreign exchange was necessary to import capital goods and raw materials. At the same time the Sandinista government stimulated food production for the domestic market in order to begin to fulfill the objective of redistributing goods and services throughout the population. It fostered manufacturing only to meet basic needs, provide intermediate goods for other important sectors like agriculture and construction, and process agricultural products (agroindustry). From 1981 onward state investment projects were initiated, mainly in physical infrastructure, agriculture, and agroindustry.

Although manufacturing proper was not a high priority in Nicaragua's development strategy, I refer to this strategy as "industrial." Although most investment aimed at or supported the expansion of agricultural production in the short term, in the long term it was directed toward an agroindustrialization of the country.

Generally, the economic order—state-controlled, market oriented, or mixed—influences a country's industrialization strategy. A country's industrialization strategy also influences its economic order. This book focuses on Nicaragua's industrialization strategy, examining the relationship between the country's economic order and its opportunities for industrialization. It is hoped that the Nicaraguan experience will provide lessons to other developing countries pursuing industrialization in a mixed economy.

The Nicaraguan economy from 1983 to 1990 must be characterized as a war economy. This raises the question of the relevance of analyzing possibilities for industrialization. In spite of the war, however, the Sandinista government clearly pursued an industrialization strategy. At least until 1988, it maintained a fairly high accumulation rate (the shar of accumulation in the GDP). In addition, for a small country like Nicaragua, the war situation did not fundamentally alter sectoral priorities within the industrialization strategy. In larger and more developed countries, increased demand as a result of war can stimulate economic production in general and lead to a buildup of heavy industry in particular. In Nicaragua, this increased demand only created imbalances such as inflation and a balance-of-payments deficit, because the war also reduced domestic supply. So although the war had a negative influence on industrialization possibilities, this influence mainly related to the speed of industrialization and rarely led to changes in the allocation decisions.

One would expect the war also to limit the comparability of Sandinista Nicaragua with other countries. But in practice, all developing countries that establish a noncapitalist economic system need to defend themselves against attacks or threats of attacks of at least one capitalist power.[1] Even in the context of war, then, developing countries generally design strategies for development, including industrialization.

## The Mixed Economy

The economic order, or economic system, is the institutional structure that determines who makes decisions about production, distribution, and consumption (see also Bornstein 1989:4; Wagener 1980:70). The institutional structure is the more or less stable pattern of juridical norms and social behavior. The main determinants of the institutional structure are the ownership of the means of production (private or collective) and the coordination mechanism that links economic

TABLE 1.1 Types of Economic Order

| | *Ownership* | |
|---|---|---|
| *Coordinating Mechanism* | *Private* | *State* |
| Market | I | II |
| Planning | III | IV |

*Source:* Author's elaboration of Wagener, H.-J. 1980. *Economische systemen: Theorieën, instituties en doelstellingen*. Alphen aan de Rijn: Samson, p. 219.

entities (market or planning).[2] This classification leads, in principle, to four types of economic order (see Table 1.1):[3] a capitalist order, with private ownership of the means of production and use of the market as a coordinating mechanism (I); a socialist order, with state ownership of the means of production and use of planning as a coordinating mechanism (IV); a market economy with state ownership of the means of production (II); and a planned economy with private ownership (III).

Although in type II the state is juridical owner of all means of production, decisions on production and, to some degree, investment, are decentralized and made by the enterprises. The state determines only part of investment. This type exists in Yugoslavia to a certain extent. The combination of central planning with predominance of private ownership of large-scale means of production (type III) seems feasible only in wartime.[4]

The Sandinista mixed economy is "mixed" regarding both ownership and the coordination mechanism. But in actuality, all existing economic systems are "mixed." Countries such as France, The Netherlands, and even the United States have some state enterprises, apply price regulations and (anti) monopoly laws, and have social insurance. We can call these systems "Keynesian-mixed economies," in which the state acts to correct some undesired consequences of the market system and to provide infrastructure. But private ownership is dominant and the market provides the system's dynamic. For these reasons, I classify these countries as "capitalist economies" (type I).

Examples of other economies sometimes called mixed are those of countries with a large state sector, such as Mexico, Brazil, and nineteenth-century Germany and Japan. The state undertakes initial production activities for the long-term benefit of the private sector. The state is in a better position to bear the financial risks associated with early stages of production activities, in particular large-scale ones. But the market remains dominant, and the intention is to stimulate capitalist development. When the risks are lower, the government sells state enterprises to the private sector. This type of economic system is described by Gerschenkron as a road to industrialization for "backward countries." I call it the "late-developing mixed economy," which also is a capitalist economy (type I).

East European countries such as the Soviet Union and the former GDR were on the other side of the spectrum.[5] But some privately owned agriculture always existed there also, and the market played a role as a coordinating mechanism in the distribution of consumer goods and in the allocation of labor, for example. However, I call such systems "socialist countries" (type IV) because state planning fulfills most of the allocative and distributive functions, and the majority of the means of production are state owned.

Contrary to the types of mixed economy described thus far, the Sandinista mixed economy is the kind of economic order adopted by most countries upon the seizure of power by a socialist party or liberation movement. In the 1970s, third world countries such as Tanzania, Mozambique, and Angola chose a mixed economic order. A defining characteristic of this mixed economy is that it is related to a period of "transition," namely a transition to socialism. So it can also be called a "Leninist-mixed economy."

After the seizure of power the new government carries out some nationalizations to achieve state control over the "commanding heights" (Lenin) of the economy: the financial sector, foreign trade, and some "basic" industries.[6] The rest of the economy remains in private hands. Some state planning is introduced, but the market continues to be important. The government aims, in the long run, to socialize the production relations. (The exact nature of this socialization is not clear, as I will show further on.)

This mixed economic order is not equal to Kalecki's "intermediate regime," which he defines as representing the interests of the lower-middle class, including corresponding strata of the peasantry (Kalecki 1972:162). These interests are opposed to, on the one hand, those of the feudal landlords and big business and on the other, those of small landholders and landless peasants. The Kaleckian mixed economy is, politically speaking, an "intermediate" between socialism and capitalism. "My" mixed economy, however, is ultimately based on the interests of the working class or on a coalition of workers and peasants. In this political sense it is not an "intermediate regime" and in fact is closer to a socialist system. But in the short run it may well have some characteristics of the Kaleckian intermediate regime.

Why study the possibilities for industrialization in such a mixed economic order? In fact, the mixed economy of the transition to socialism is usually temporary (at least in the economic if not in the political sense of "my" economy). It lasted from one year to about a decade. In some countries the end of the mixed economy came about when the socialist-oriented party lost power, by causes ranging from a military coup (Chile) to elections (Jamaica). In countries where the socialist government succeeded in maintaining its power, the mixed economy also was a temporary phenomenon. It was replaced in due course by a more centrally planned system with prevailing state ownership of the means of production. This happened in the Soviet Union and in most other current or former socialist countries such as China, Poland, and Vietnam. In Cuba, the general hostility of capitalist countries almost forced the country to establish a Soviet-type economy. In other countries political factors contributed to a centralization of the economy (and the society), and the coercive influence of the USSR often played a role.

Two more general factors led to the substitution of mixed economic orders with socialist orders in the previously mentioned countries. First, the leaders often understood the objective to socialize the production relations to imply a forced collectivization of agricultural production, a nationalization of the rest of the economy, and the establishment of central planning. Second, they assumed that abandoning the mixed economy and establishing state ownership of the means of production and central planning were prerequisites for industrialization. Industrialization was an important objective during the transition period, because, contrary to Marx's expectations,[7] most countries in which a socialist transition took place were underdeveloped agrarian countries.

Both reasons for abandoning the mixed order are now being questioned. With regard to the first, for new socialist regimes in third world countries it is not quite clear anymore what socialist production relations ought to look like. New socialist leaders are less inspired by classic Marxist-Leninist doctrines such as the need for the state to be dominated by the working class, the "dictatorship of the proletariat." These classic ideas have so far always led to the establishment of central planning and to the nationalization of the means of production. Instead, new governments take a more pragmatic view and, more than before, direct their economic policy toward changing the distribution of income and meeting the basic needs of the poor majority. Obviously, new socialist governments are also influenced by the changes going on in almost all "older" socialist countries.

Second, present leaders of countries in transition to socialism question the idea that a centrally planned economic order is necessary to achieve industrialization. In the Soviet Union, where the first socialist revolution occurred, the need to industrialize this agrarian country provoked heated discussions on the growth strategy to be adopted, the so-called industrialization debate of the 1920s. From 1928 onward the Soviet leadership decided to embark upon rapid accumulation and to abandon the mixed economy that had lasted from 1921 onward. Central planning became dominant, and the state took control over the means of production by a forced collectivization of agriculture, among other measures.

Although most people have always rejected the violence that accompanied this economic system, for a long time the dominant opinion was that the Soviet growth model was useful for underdeveloped countries (Dobb 1980; Wilber 1969). In this view the centrally planned economy allowed an effective allocation of resources and avoided resources being used for luxury consumption (Baran 1973:156).

However, more recent research has questioned the value of the Soviet model for achieving high economic growth. These doubts originate from observations of the industrialization process in the Soviet Union itself[8] and from research on the application of the Soviet model in other countries.[9]

The fact that most socialist revolutions took place in countries with a low degree of industrialization and with small commodity production as the dominant mode of production also led to a change in the transition theory (Bettelheim 1975). Bettelheim states that nationalization and the introduction of central planning do not lead to control if they are applied to small commodity production. As long as the forces of productive are not completely "socialized," some kind of "mediation" is necessary. Markets, the "law of value," and private ownership of the means of production must play a role during the transition. When the forces of production have developed sufficiently to be completely socialized, the country can introduce perfect central planning.[10] Bettelheim's theory does have an influence on new socialist governments in third world countries, making them more reluctant to carry out large-scale nationalizations, for example.

It follows from the reduced confidence in the Soviet industrialization model that the mixed economy is likely to become more than a temporary stage. This leads to new interest in the question of whether industrialization in a mixed economy is possible.

## Industrialization

Industrialization is an important objective for most developing countries. It is necessary to achieve high rates of economic growth, provide for the basic needs of the population, create employment opportunities, promote an increasingly diversified economy, and give rise to desirable social, psychological, and institutional changes (Lee 1984:1). Often it is operationally defined as the relative growth of the industrial sector or manufacturing within total GDP. But the process of industrialization implies more. Productivity increases are realized in the whole economy and this is accompanied by changes in social institutions, values, norms, and patterns of behavior. For example, industrialization is "the application of modern knowledge and technology in the whole economy, and not just in the industrial sector." (Myint 1972:51). Be that as it may, in the long run the expansion of manufacturing production proper seems to be necessary to achieve higher levels of productivity and living standards (see also Sutcliffe 1971:103).

An industrialization strategy has three main characteristics: the speed of the industrialization process, the structure of production, and the inward or outward orientation.[11] The speed of the industrialization process depends, among other factors, on the extent to which unused production factors exist and on the rate of accumulation. If no idle production capacity (labor or machines) is available, accumulation is necessary to achieve growth. Accumulation is the use of resources to increase the production capacity of the economy (Chenery 1979:9). Such uses include investment in physical capital, in the quality of human capital (education, health, nutrition), and in the accumulation of knowledge.

Accumulation must be financed, not in the sense that there must be a fund for this purpose but in the sense that total GDP plus the import surplus must equal total accumulation plus total consumption. If a country pursues accumulation, it cannot consume all domestically produced and imported goods. In fact, even to maintain the current production capacity it must assign part of resources to accumulation. The actual process of the replacement and expansion of production capacity is called investment. Gross investment includes the replacement and expansion of existing production capacity, net investment only includes the latter.

The share of accumulation in GDP, the rate of accumulation, is important in determining the economy's rate of growth. In general, the higher the rate of accumulation and the lower the opposite, the rate of consumption, the higher will be the growth rate. But there is no linear relationship between the two. First, a minimum level of consumption and of provisions like education, health, and housing is necessary to maintain the labor force.[12] Second, if the reserve of labor is limited, the economy can grow only by raising labor productivity. But in practice, "a high investment rate based on low wages may not improve labor productivity because work intensity falls at the same time" (FitzGerald 1986:23). Higher wages are necessary; otherwise the potential increase in labor productivity by capital-intensive investment will not materialize. Higher wages reduce the accumulation rate.

The second aspect of the industrialization strategy refers to the sectoral distribution of investment. Together with the third aspect, the inward or outward orientation, this determines the industrialization strategy in a strict sense.

Industrialization strategies differ with regard to the sector they give priority to: production of capital and intermediate goods, production of manufactured consumer goods, or agricultural production. It is also possible to have a balanced development of the three or of two of the three.

Furthermore, in a closed economy, that is, an economy with an inward-oriented strategy, the accumulation rate and the sectoral distribution of investment are interrelated. A fast industrialization process will normally be accompanied by a relative priority on capital goods production. In order to raise the rate of growth of consumer goods output, the share of capital goods production relative to consumer goods production must increase. For a more gradual industrialization, the different sectors can grow at more or less the same rate.

Third, an industrialization strategy can be inward or outward oriented. Large countries have a choice in this respect. Small countries almost inevitably have to choose an outward-oriented industrialization strategy: They must export and import large amounts relative to their GDP. An economy is small if it has relatively few natural resources and a limited population, that is, a limited domestic market.

Within outward-oriented strategies countries may opt for exporting primary products or manufactures. They can use the export income for developing agriculture or the manufacturing industry. But after completing a successful industrialization drive a small country will remain dependent on trade. First, it does not have access to sufficient raw materials. Second, its small size prevents a profitable production of capital goods and requires part of industrial production to be exported.

The natural resource endowment of the country, its population density, and the potential size of the domestic market (determined by the size of the population) are important for a choice between the different industrialization strategies. But the feasibility and effectiveness of a certain strategy also depends on the kind of economic system or economic order.

## Outline for This Book

The existence of a mixed economy in Nicaragua had consequences for the rate of accumulation that was possible and for the sectoral distribution and orientation of the industrialization strategy. With regard to the rate of accumulation, the question is whether Nicaragua could have maintained its mixed economy given that the Sandinistas did pursue state accumulation. More generally, I want to answer the question, Under what conditions is it possible to maintain a mixed economy when a country aims at industrialization? With respect to industrial strategy, I want to find out what more successful industrialization strategies could have been pursued in Nicaragua—or in a small country like Nicaragua with a mixed economy.

Strangely enough, all books on the Sandinista economy to date have concentrated on the country's general economic policy or on the agricultural sector.[13] I believe scholars' lack of interest in the industrial sector is in part because of their frequently repeated false assumptions about the historical performance of Nicaragua's manufacturing industry. For example, it is generally thought that the manufacturing sector constituted only a small part of the country's GDP in 1979, that there were few linkages with agriculture, making the sector merely a foreign-exchange consumer, and that the industrialization model of the Central American Common Market was in crisis already. In reality, manufacturing was an important sector of the pre-Sandinista Nicaraguan economy. It produced 26 percent of the GDP in 1978; the primary sector (agriculture, cattle-breeding, fishing, and forestry) produced 25 percent (see Table 1.2).

This book uses a comparative systems approach. Although titles of other publications on the Sandinista economy include the phrase "mixed economy," they do not focus on Nicaragua's economic system or its implications for development strategy. In this book I attempt to do both, focusing especially on the manufacturing sector.

From the beginning the Sandinista government attempted to apply state planning in industry, although a large private sector remained active. Unlike in other mixed economies in transition to socialism, in Nicaragua the private sector was not confined to small commodity producers but included medium and large producers. This was especially the case within the manufacturing industry. In 1983, 67 percent of gross industrial production originated in private firms (MIND 1984c). The manufacturing sector, therefore, is particularly interesting for investigating the nature and extent of state planning and its effects on both state and private enterprises. In addition, foreign investment is concentrated in this sector. In 1980 foreign-owned enterprises represented 25 percent of manufacturing production.

TABLE 1.2 Sectoral Structure of GDP and Employment (1950–1984 selected years in percent)

| | GDP | | | | | Employment | | | |
|---|---|---|---|---|---|---|---|---|---|
| | *1950* | *1960* | *1970* | *1978* | *1984* | *1950* | *1963* | *1971* | *1977* |
| Primary sector | 46 | 23 | 22 | 25 | 24 | 68 | 60 | 47 | 42 |
| Secondary sector | 15 | 19 | 27 | 32 | 29 | 15 | 16 | 16 | 20 |
| Manufacturing | 10 | 15 | 22 | 26 | 25 | 11 | 12 | 12 | 15 |
| Construction | 2 | 2 | 3 | 3 | 3 | 4 | 4 | 4 | 4 |
| Tertiary sector | 40 | 58 | 51 | 43 | 48 | 17 | 25 | 37 | 45 |
| Commerce | 19 | 21 | 21 | 15 | 19 | 6 | 8 | 10 | 13 |
| Other | 21 | 37 | 31 | 28 | 29 | 11 | 16 | 28 | 32 |

*Sources*: Brundenius, Claes 1984. *Industrial development and strategies in revolutionary Nicaragua*. Lund: Research Policy Institute, University of Lund; for 1984: Ministry of Planning, 1985, Managua. Mimeo.

The fieldwork consisted of conducting interviews with officials of the Ministry of Industry and with directors of manufacturing and agroindustry enterprises, both state and private. This provided me with an inside view of the functioning of the mixed economy. The interviews with directors of private enterprises were fascinating in this respect. For the first time, the opinions and expectations of the private sector in revolutionary Nicaragua were the object of research.

In Chapter 2, I analyze the possibilities for accumulation in a mixed economic order on the basis of the first historical mixed economy, the New Economic Policy (NEP) in the USSR 1921–1928. This leads to five stability conditions for a mixed economy. Chapter 3 gives an overview of Nicaragua's industrialization and economic order before the Sandinistas took power in 1979. The ups and downs of the Central American Common Market in the 1960s and 1970s are an important part of this analysis. Chapters 4–6 describe different aspects of the functioning of the Sandinista mixed economy and analyze whether the stability conditions of Chapter 2 are fulfilled in the Nicaraguan case.

In Chapter 4 I describe the nature and functioning of the Nicaraguan mixed economy, including its changes since 1979. Here I include some results of the interviews with enterprise directors and explain why the Sandinistas opted for a mixed economy after their seizure of power. Chapter 5 focuses on the Sandinista macroeconomic policy and results. Central themes are the accumulation policy and the price policy, which are two important "stability conditions" according to

Chapter 2. In Chapter 6 I analyze Nicaragua's industrialization policy "in a strict sense." In this chapter I also present the opinions and expectations of enterprise directors, leading to a conclusion on the private sector's willingness to maintain production in Sandinista Nicaragua.

Chapter 7 contains a summary and conclusion. Here, I deal more explicitly with the effects of the contra war on Nicaragua's industrialization possibilities. In the Epilogue I give some comments on the impact of the 1990 election result on Nicaragua's economy and industrialization strategy.

## Notes

1. Angola and Mozambique, for instance, suffered from the hostility of South Africa, Vietnam that of the United States.

2. In this book "planning" refers exclusively to "vertical," or state planning. In all economic systems private market parties also carry out a certain amount of planning. I do not include this "horizontal" planning.

3. This classification does not apply to reproductive activities like cooking and child care, which are almost always under private control.

4. The Nazi economy is a good example.

5. By 1990, many of these East European countries are changing toward a capitalist system.

6. Holding the "commanding heights," the state can control the movements in the surrounding fields. See Lenin, *Collected Works*, Vol. IX:165-8; cited in Dobb (1966:145). "Basic industries" are capital goods production and raw materials processing.

7. Marx foresaw a socialist revolution in a developed industrial society. It would originate from the contradiction between development stage of the forces of production and the private ownership of the means of production.

8. For example, at the microeconomic level the USSR industrialization process was not a "planned" process and provoked many unintended consequences. See Zaleski (1980) and Weissenbürger (1983). In addition, the forced collectivization in the USSR does not seem to have provided a net transfer of resources from agriculture to industry, as was supposed for a long time (see Chapter 2).

9. See, for example, P. Gey 1985. "Planwirtschaft und Industrialisierung: Probleme sozialistischer Wirtschaftssysteme in Entwicklungsländer am Beispiel Polens, Jugoslawiens, Chinas und Kubas." In *Sozialismus und Industrialisierung, Die Wirtschaftssysteme Polens, Jugoslawiens, Chinas und Kubas im Vergleich*, eds. P. Gey, J. Kosta, and W. Quaisser. Frankfurt/New York: Methuen, 15-55; and Geske Dijkstra, 1986. "Socialisme en ontwikkeling: De Sovjetunie als voorbeeld?" *Internationale Spectator* 40, no. 12 (December):723-32.

10. Bettelheim's theory is comparable to Lenin's idea of the economy as one big factory. In my opinion, perfect central planning is impossible in any mode of production.

11. I use the term "strategy" to encompass both government policy and resource endowment (see Chenery 1979:27). This does not imply that governments necessarily make deliberate choices among policy alternatives. But in socialist and mixed economies, normally deliberate choices are made.

12. In Marxist terms this is called reproduction of the labor force.

13. Some general books did contain chapters on the industrial sector, however. See Weeks (1985b), Harris (1985b), Brundenius (1987), and Dumas (1988).

# 2

# The New Economic Policy

Historically, mixed economies have recovered rapidly after the turmoil that accompanies a socialist takeover.[1] However, satisfactory growth rates apply to rather short periods, in which quick recovery is the main objective of economic policy. Subsequently, accumulation becomes the chief objective, and governments replace their mixed economies with a more or less centrally planned order. For Nicaragua, the question is whether a mixed system permits a high accumulation rate.

As a comparison, I will analyze the mixed economic order that prevailed in the Soviet Union during the period of the NEP (New Economic Policy). The NEP was a mixed economy initiated in 1921 and abandoned in 1928–1929 in favor of a centrally planned order and collectivization of agriculture. The reason for comparing Nicaragua with the USSR and not with small socialist third world countries such as Cuba, Vietnam, or Mozambique is not obvious. There are, after all, many differences between Nicaragua and the Soviet Union. However, I consider the NEP to provide the best model of a mixed economic order. There are several reasons the NEP serves as a solid comparison:

1. The USSR experimented with a mixed economic order for almost eight years (1921–1928) before abandoning it, which was a much longer trial than practiced by most other socialist countries. Cuba, for example, diluted the mixed system after only two years in 1961 with the introduction of central planning and abandoned it totally in 1963 with the minimization of the private sector in agriculture.

2. During the period of the NEP the objective of accumulation gradually became a greater priority than recovery—thus an analysis of the consequences of accumulation for the economic order is appropriated.

3. While the NEP was in effect, an important debate took place

regarding the industrialization strategy and economic order to be chosen by the developing socialist economy. This "industrialization debate" clarifies most options and dilemmas faced by governments of socialist third world countries with regard to a development strategy.

4. The experience of the NEP has often been used explicitly as a basis for reform discussions in Eastern Europe, for instance in Hungary (Szamuely 1974:9) and in the Soviet Union (Sjmelev 1987).

5. The experience of the NEP is well documented.

## The USSR, 1917–1925

The Bolsheviks' seizure of power in 1917 occurred when Russia was in complete chaos after World War I. In addition, the revolution itself caused a civil war that lasted until the end of 1920. The control of economic resources was critical. The economic order during these first years (1917–1920) was described as "war communism" and was characterized by a centralized control of production and distribution—that was, at least, the intention.

All manufacturing and internal trade was nationalized, trade being called "distribution" (Szamuely 1974:11). The state allocated industrial labor centrally and by force and "purchased" agricultural production by forced requisition. All consumer goods were rationed, but providing for the cities depended to a large extent on illegal commerce, the "second economy." Land reform had taken place in which all land was nationalized and rents were abolished. Peasants received the right to use the land (Nove 1969:48). The result was much more equal land distribution, and only small-scale ownership remained.

During the period of war communism, most Bolsheviks considered this system to be the direct route to socialism.[2] Toward the end of the period, Bukharin and other leading Communists began to have doubts about the value of the system of war communism. They came to see it as a system that had been forced upon them by the war situation.[3]

At the end of 1920 the fighting ended. The country's economy was in ruin. The fall in agricultural production was enormous; peasants had reduced sowing because of compulsory state procurement. No foodstuffs were available in the cities or in the coal mine regions, and about half the urban population fled to the countryside. Industrial production had also declined. Because the Soviet Union did not have access to external credits or imports of foodstuffs, there was a famine in 1921 and 6 percent of the population died (Dobb 1966:152).

When the war was over, the people's discontent mounted. Although the peasants were in favor of the revolution because they had benefited from the land reform, they were no longer willing to cooperate in forced requisition. Several peasant uprisings took place. In February 1921 the insurrection of the Kronstadt sailors, who demanded freedom for the peasants and free elections for the "soviets" (local government councils), brought about a turning point. Although the Kronstadt sailors were shot, their insurrection led to the abolishment of war communism. The New Economic Policy (NEP) was born.

The government abolished forced requisition in agriculture and replaced it with an in-kind tax. It reestablished free trade and allowed peasants to lease land and to hire labor. During 1921 the state also abolished the forced mobilization of labor and the rationing of consumer goods. It denationalized all enterprises of fewer than twenty workers and a minority of the larger enterprises by leasing them to managers. A few enterprises were given back to their former owners. As a result, the private sector regained 88.5 percent of industrial enterprises, but it accounted for only 7.6 percent of production (Carr 1966:302). The government decentralized the management of state enterprises and established "trusts," which were combinations of various enterprises. Private traders, the "NEPmen," handled the relations between the relatively autonomous trusts.

The state maintained its control of the "commanding heights" of the economy (see Chapter 1): the banks, the transport system (the railways), foreign trade, and heavy industry. Trusts in heavy industry were under more central control than trusts in light industry. In all industries, direct control of investment was much tighter than that of current operations. The state was the most important purchaser of agrarian products and had a significant influence on producer prices.

The first objective of the NEP was to reactivate production and productivity. Lenin considered this change in the economic policy to be a necessary "step backward." Abolishing all market relations before the forces of production were more developed had been premature (Dobb 1966:145). A slower advance toward socialism was also necessary because a worldwide socialism was not yet possible. Contrary to expectations, revolutions in other countries had failed or had not come about at all. Lenin considered the economic system of the NEP to be a mixed economy, having elements of capitalism and socialism and a sector of small-commodity production. He also saw it as a "transition economy" that could either develop toward a socialist economy or fall back into capitalism. It was a temporary system, but in his view "temporary" could be up to twenty-five years.[4]

The NEP could have developed into capitalism because the reintroduction of market agriculture could have resulted in economic differentiation in the countryside, which would have threatened socialist objectives. But development toward socialism was probable if the working class dominated the alliance of forces (Dobb 1966:145-6). According to Lenin, the prerequisites for achieving socialism were the progressive extension of collective forms of production in agriculture on a voluntary basis and the industrialization of the country.

The economic situation improved during 1922. The harvest proved good, resulting in a recuperation of 70 percent of the 1916 level. The state fixed agricultural prices at a low level to reduce food prices in the cities. Industrial production however, recovered by only about 35 percent of the prewar (1913) level in 1922–1923 (Dobb 1966:161). The increased purchasing power of the peasants after the harvest led to an upward pressure on prices of manufactures. In addition, the trusts held back a proportion of the limited output from the market by using their monopoly power (Gregory and Stuart 1974:58). As a result, industrial and agricultural prices started to diverge in comparison with the 1913 levels like the two blades of a pair of scissors, creating the "scissors crisis." Industrial prices were about three times the level of agricultural prices compared with the prewar situation.

By early 1923 the share of the harvest sold outside the village was estimated at less than 25 percent; it had been just over 30 percent before the war (Dobb 1966:162). The Soviet government feared a further reduction of marketed grain because of the price divergence between agricultural and industrial goods. It raised agricultural prices and set maximum selling prices for manufactures. It also allowed imports of cheaper industrial commodities and restricted bank credits for the industrial trusts, thereby forcing them to sell their stocks at lower prices.

By October 1924 the relation of industrial and agricultural prices (compared to the prewar level) was reduced to 1.5 to 1. Both agricultural and industrial reactivation continued during 1924 and 1925, and trade relations flourished and expanded each year. These years are called "high NEP."

However, setting maximum selling prices for manufactures in a period of rising wage incomes risked creating excess demand. In spite of the lower official prices, peasants would still be the losers because the commodities would not reach the countryside. In fact, there is some evidence that grain marketings were lower after the price divergence had become smaller (Gregory and Stuart 1974:61). In 1925–1926 grain production reached 80 percent of the 1913 level. However, marketed production of grain was only half that of 1913 (Lorenz 1976:sec. 4.1). Especially in that year there were many problems with the procurement of grain, sometimes referred to as the "grain strike." This reduced exports and so limited imports of capital goods and other inputs, hampering the industrialization process.

TABLE 2.1 USSR: Gross Turnover in Trade per Type of Ownership, 1923/24–1925/26 (in billions of rubles and in percent)

| *Ownership* | *1923/24* | | *1924/25* | | *1925/26* | |
|---|---|---|---|---|---|---|
| State | 3.0 | 28% | 4.9 | 35% | 7.7 | 35% |
| Cooperative | 2.8 | 26% | 5.1 | 38% | 8.9 | 40% |
| Private | 4.8 | 46% | 3.7 | 27% | 5.3 | 24% |
| Total[a] | 10.6 | 100% | 13.7 | 100% | 22.0 | 100% |

[a]Total may not sum to 100% due to rounding.

*Source:* Author's elaboration of Carr, E. H. [1958] 1978. *Socialism in one country: 1924–1926*. London: MacMillan, Vol. 1, 423.

The production of industrial consumer goods had recovered to the 1913 level. But industrial growth in the years 1921-1925 had mainly been based on a reactivation of existing capacity and on a reabsorption of available labor. New investment had not materialized. The state's efforts to set maximum selling prices had caused industrial prices to be sometimes lower than production costs, leading to losses for the enterprises and making it more difficult to expand production. The capital goods industries (mines, melting-furnaces and the machinery industry) had recovered by only 60 percent, and they were already relatively underdeveloped in 1913.

In spite of the recovery of industrial consumer goods production, industrial goods were scarce at the official prices. The price policy gave rise to a phenomenon that from 1925 onward often was referred to as the "goods famine." Consumers' purchasing power exceeded by far the supply of manufactures at the official low prices. Industrial recovery had caused the wage fund to expand by 40 percent. Because almost all products could be sold in the cities, the goods famine was especially severe in the countryside. The shortages made it more difficult to maintain price controls. Private traders could obtain large profits by selling manufactures at higher prices.

NEPmen increasingly came to be seen as black marketeers and enemies of the state (Gregory and Stuart 1974:61), and the state attempted to expand its control of domestic trade. It nationalized part of it and set up trade cooperatives. In spite of private trade's decreasing share of total trade, its volume grew in absolute terms until 1925–1926 (Table 2.1).

The control of private industry and small industry also expanded. These producers depended to a large extent on raw materials and

TABLE 2.2 USSR: Gross Industrial Production per Type of Ownership 1923/24–1925/26 (in percent)

| *Ownership* | *1923/24* | *1924/25* | *1925/26* |
|---|---|---|---|
| Large industry: | | | |
| State | 61.8 | 65.9 | 69.5 |
| Cooperative | 3.8 | 5.2 | 4.9 |
| Private | 3.6 | 3.3 | 2.8 |
| Small industry and rural handicraft | 30.8 | 25.6 | 22.7 |
| Total[a] | 100.0 | 100.0 | 100.0 |

[a]Total may not sum to 100% due to rounding.

*Source:* Author's elaboration of Carr, E. H. [1958] 1978. *Socialism in one country: 1924–1926*. London: MacMillan, Vol. 1, 358.

fuels produced by state enterprises or delivered by state trading organs. The official goal was to stimulate small industry and handicrafts in order to augment the supply of consumer goods and to increase employment in the countryside. This would be done by supplying credits and raw materials at low prices and by stimulating the formation of cooperatives. In practice, the share of small-scale production in total industrial production decreased (Table 2.2). Larger private enterprises also fared badly; if they were propering the state captured them and if not they perished (Carr 1978). Until 1925–1926, however, the private sector in industry was still growing in absolute terms.

## The Industrialization Debate

When the reactivation was more or less completed and problems like the "grain strike" and the "goods famine" became visible, a heated discussion, called the "industrialization debate," began on future economic policy, All participants in the debate agreed upon the need to industrialize the country for theoretical as well as practical reasons. Industrialization was necessary to achieve socialism. It was also necessary to improve living standards and to reach higher productivity levels in industry as well as in agriculture. Industrialization would help the unemployed in the cities, already two million people, and relieve overpopulation—estimated at seven or eight million—in the countryside. Finally, the hostile external environment necessitated a buildup of the nation's defenses and a greater international independence.

However, prospects for manufacturing growth were not very good in 1925. Production costs, for example, were two or three times higher than in Western Europe (Lorenz 1976:129). The main cause was the obsolescence of machinery. A further increase in industrial production would require investment in machinery and equipment on a large scale and the use of new technology. This in turn would require a higher accumulation rate than in the past period. The industrialization debate centered on the *speed* of the industrialization process related to the sectoral distribution of investments and on the *sources* for financing the accumulation.

Theoretically, there were some relatively easy sources for accumulation:

1. Foreign loans from Western European countries. But to obtain those loans, the USSR would be forced to return the land to the former landowners and to recognize the debts of the former government. Both conditions were unacceptable.
2. Foreign direct investment. In practice the amount of concessions given to foreign enterprises was limited.
3. Aid from other socialist countries in Europe. Although there were some attempts at socialist revolutions in Western Europe, all failed. The USSR therefore faced the need to build "socialism in one country."

As a result, the only possibility was an accumulation on the basis of internal sources. State accumulation would be obtained at the expense of private rural producers, tradespeople, or urban workers. The number of urban workers was still small, so they could not provide a substantial contribution. Before the revolution, the agricultural sector provided the surplus for the beginning industrialization; the majority of the peasants were forced to hand over rent in kind to the landowners while they themselves did not have enough to eat. Because the revolutionary government abolished rents and landlords, the problem was how to obtain a surplus from the private agricultural sector.

Three important participants in the debate were Bukharin, Shanin, and Preobazhensky. They represented the diverging views on the industrialization strategy. By 1925, Bukharin agreed with Lenin on the necessity of the NEP as a mixed economy. Developing the forces of production required incentives to producers: prices and profits. So a market economy was necessary. Within such a market economy the agricultural sector had not only a supply function (delivering foodstuffs, raw materials, and exports), but it also functioned as a market for manufactures (Erlich 1960:25-35).

Bukharin believed that the industrialization process should be part of a balanced development involving a transfer of surplus product from agriculture to industry, but not beyond a certain limit. Industrial growth would be maximized on the basis of a rapidly growing agriculture (Bukharin 1964:260). In the same way, growth of light industry would have to equal growth of heavy industry.

Because of the country's underdeveloped industrial structure, the state itself could not yet develop agrarian forces of production, for example, by applying advanced production techniques on large state farms. As a consequence, private accumulation in the countryside should be stimulated. According to Bukharin, private farmers were still afraid to expand production because of what had happened during war communism. The state should give more incentives to stimulate production. Bukharin said to the farmers: "Get rich!" The state should guarantee a socialist development in the countryside, stimulating peasant production and service cooperatives with financial incentives. In that manner, capitalist farmers would be "encircled."

According to Shanin, the "goods famine" in 1925–1926 was caused by an already too high accumulation rate. In particular, capital goods industries had developed too fast. These industries create employment and income, but they do not provide consumer goods (Shanin 1964a). Shanin favored a slower industrialization process. In his view, it was better to start with investment in agriculture. Because of its higher capital productivity, an increase of production and productivity in agriculture was possible at lower costs, permitting a higher overall growth rate. Higher agricultural production would create more exports with which capital goods could be imported. Once the level of agricultural productivity was increased, investment should be directed to consumer goods industries and subsequently to capital goods industries. A growing fund of consumer goods would be created that would permit an increasing accumulation speed without causing inflation or shortages (Shanin 1964b).

But the possibility of carrying out this gradual industrialization scheme would depend on the period the USSR would be allowed to live in peace. If that period lasted ten years, during the first five years all investment should be directed to agriculture.

According to Preobazhensky the principal cause of the goods famine was a too-low accumulation rate in the industrial state-dominated sector (Preobazhensky 1965). The state had permitted capitalist forces to grow faster than socialist forces. Preobazhensky estimated that between one-third and one-half of industrial profits flowed into private hands in January 1924 because of the existence of private trade

(Dobb 1966:183). In addition, the purchasing power of the peasants was too large compared to the period before the NEP. For socialism to survive it was now necessary to strengthen the socialist forces, stimulating vigorously the industrialization process. But the industrial sector itself could hardly provide resources for the necessary investments. Industrial development had been limited and socialism itself set limits on the exploitation of industrial workers.

West European countries had exploited colonies in the third world to finance their early accumulation: "primitive capitalist accumulation." Because the Soviet Union did not have colonies, the country had to consider the agricultural sector as its "internal colony." This sector was to provide the means for industrialization. This primitive socialist accumulation could be achieved in two ways: raising direct taxes on agricultural producers, which might provoke tax evasion and political opposition, and raising indirect taxes by establishing an "unequal exchange": higher industrial prices and lower agricultural prices. The second possibility would be limited only by the state's need of a certain amount of agricultural production, so agricultural prices could not decrease below a certain level.

Bukharin and others criticized Preobazhensky saying he underestimated the possibilities for increasing industrial productivity on the basis of its own resources, for example, labor productivity. More importantly, they argued that implementing a policy of "unequal exchange" with the peasantry would lead to coercion of the peasants (Dobb 1966:186).

At that time, Preobazhensky did not face up to the possibility that the coercion problem could be resolved by expropriating the peasants. In his view the problem was insoluble as long as no other socialist revolutions came about to provide aid. Some years later, however, he would accept Stalin's policy of compulsory collectivization in the sincere belief that this policy constituted, in essence, a vindication of his struggle for a high tempo of industrialization (Erlich 1950:85).

During the following years, the different opinions in the debate approached each other. Bukharin recognized that industry's own resources would not be sufficient for industrialization. Preobazhensky came to agree that there were serious problems in trying to procure grain from the peasants at low prices, particularly because of the actual low level of rural productivity. And all saw that the growth of capital goods industries led to an intensification of the goods famine. However, all became more and more convinced that rapid accumulation was necessary.

The debate during the NEP period concerned the possibilities for industrialization. How could an expansion of the state industrial sector be achieved and financed while agriculture was in private hands and the market dominated the relations between industry and agriculture? In the USSR by that time "industry" coincided with the state sector; "agriculture" was the private sector. However, the debate points to a more general problem in a mixed economy, that is, is it possible to achieve state accumulation in a mixed economy with a large private sector?

Maintaining a mixed economy requires that private producers be stimulated. State accumulation requires that resources be drawn from the private sector. Bukharin and Shanin stressed the first objective, Preobazhensky the second. All three wanted to maintain market relations between the state and the private sector. The question was whether it was possible to put into effect the ideas of Preobazhensky without endangering the stability of the mixed economy.

## The End of the NEP

In 1925 the economic policy of the USSR, led by Stalin and Bukharin after Lenin died in 1924, was in a transition stage. The policy that reacted to the scissors crisis and that stimulated private accumulation of the peasants was at its height, and the orientation toward a more rapid industrialization was also strengthened. In December 1925 the Fourteenth Congress of the Communist Party decided to start an industrialization policy. Officially, the industrialization objective was to be pursued within a dynamic equilibrium that simultaneously achieved a development of the productive forces, an increase in living standards, and an expansion of rural state enterprises and cooperatives (Lorenz 1976:161).

Apparently, the state attempted to implement Preobazhensky's "unequal exchange" policy. It continuously tried to "steer" the market during these years, establishing low official prices for grain and, although to a lesser extent, for manufactures. But the pricing instrument was not used very effectively (Merl 1981). In the harvest years 1925–1926 and 1927–1928, low grain prices were accompanied by low taxes and severe shortages of manufactures, which diminished incentives to sell.

The harvest of 1925–1926 marked a turning point. Until 1925–1926, the state reacted to insufficient procurements by adjusting prices upward. Afterward, private trade was curtailed by administrative measures.[5] In 1926–1927 the state was thus able to enforce low grain prices, but the procured quantity represented a lower proportion of total production than the year before. As a result, the peasants' income and purchasing power decreased, causing a sales crisis for some manufactures like simple agricultural machinery and imple-

some manufactures like simple agricultural machinery and implements.

Because of the restrictions on private trade, market relations in agriculture gradually disappeared after 1925. The administrative measures to impose low producer prices eventually led to the end of private production. By early 1928, local party officials were made responsible for the grain campaign and had the right to punish those who did not cooperate with the grain procurement: traders, rich peasants, and state officials. Many executions took place. Peasants began to react violently to state and party officials.

Although by mid-1928 the state again permitted some private trade, at the end of the year this was replaced by forced state requisition, coercion, and violence. At that time, Stalin considered a compulsory collectivization of the peasants the only way to guarantee that production would be sold to the state. In June 1929 the campaign for a forced collectivization of the peasants began.

During 1925–1928, the country achieved rapid industrial growth (Table 2.3). The amount of industrial investment in 1925–1926 was already greater than the prewar level. In 1926–1927 industrial production in state enterprises increased by 20 percent and in 1927–1928 by 26 percent. In 1928–1929 industrial investment was twice as high as in 1925–1926. In 1925–1926, 64 percent of these investments were directed to the capital goods industries and in 1926–1927, 71 percent (Carr and Davies 1969:313).

The industrial accumulation was a rather unbalanced process. Growth in consumer goods industries was slower and private industry even declined. Between 1926–1927 and 1928–1929 the share of the private sector (private enterprises and cooperatives) in large-scale industry decreased from 9.9 percent to 0.3 percent. Large and small private industries mainly produced consumer goods. From 1926 onward there was a clear priority for state large-scale industry. Official production cooperatives, which were under strict state control as far as prices and marketings were concerned, received more credits and inputs, encouraging private producers to join them. Nevertheless, private small-scale and handicrafts industries survived for some years because of the severe goods famine. But in general, the priority given to the state sector made for an unstable coexistence of state and private industry in the NEP.

The fact that the objective of achieving "balanced growth" was not fulfilled is also demonstrated by the agricultural investment record. The state did not make any direct investment in agriculture. The little private accumulation that did take place in this sector diminished in 1927, when the number of agricultural implements became the basis for determining the income tax and when farmers who paid

TABLE 2.3 USSR: Gross Industrial Production 1913–1933 (selected years, in billions of 1926/27 rubles)

| *Year* | *Large-Scale Industry* | *Small-Scale Industry* | *All Industry* | *Growth All Industry* |
|---|---|---|---|---|
| 1913 | 11.1 | 5.3 | 16.4 | |
| 1917 | 7.0 | 4.6 | 11.6 | -29% |
| 1921 | 2.3 | 2.7 | 5.1 | -56% |
| 1924 | 5.1 | 2.3 | 7.4 | 45% |
| 1925 | 8.3 | 3.6 | 11.9 | 61% |
| 1926 | 12.0 | 4.0 | 16.0 | 34% |
| 1927 | 13.5 | 4.6 | 18.2 | 14% |
| 1928 | 16.9 | 4.7 | 21.6 | 19% |
| 1929 | 21.1 | 4.8 | 25.8 | 19% |
| 1930 | 27.6 | 3.9 | 31.6 | 23% |
| 1931 | 34.1 | 4.1 | 38.1 | 21% |
| 1932 | 39.0 | 4.6 | 43.7 | 15% |
| 1933 | 42.3 | 3.7 | 46.0 | 5% |

*Source:* Kaufman, A. 1962. *Small-Scale industry in the Soviet Union.* Occasional Paper No. 80. New York: National Bureau of Economic Research, 56.

more than a certain amount of taxes lost the right to vote for the local governments (Merl 1981). The only investment that remained in the countryside was in the expansion of livestock.

At the same time, the objective of the NEP to stimulate cooperativization of agriculture on a voluntary basis was almost neglected. Before 1925 cooperatives had been stimulated, especially trade cooperatives. Later on, cooperatives in the countryside sold manufactures at lower prices than did private traders, but their assortment was smaller and of lower quality. Instead of stimulating cooperatives by financial means, the state made them instruments for implementing its price policy. By 1928 hardly any cooperation functioned (Merl 1981).

Given the intensification of the goods famine and the shortage of grain in the cities, the industrialization strategy discussion flared up again by the end of 1927. But at that time Britain broke off its diplomatic relations with the USSR, and many Soviet leaders were convinced of an increasing external threat. In 1929 the "optimal variant" of the First Five-Year Plan (1928-1933) was adopted, which planned for enormous increases in investment and astronomical growth rates.

The adoption of the First Five-Year Plan and the introduction of compulsory collectivization of the peasantry in 1928 are generally considered signals of the end of the NEP. These events marked the end of a market economy and the beginning of a command economy. In fact, the end of the market economy was a gradual process, as described previously.

A review of the literature reveals four approaches to determining why the NEP was abandoned. The first is that Soviet leaders wanted to make a "great leap forward" toward socialism and abandon all remaining capitalist features. The second view stresses wrong policies, in particular the mistaken price policies pursued during the NEP period, and maintains that the NEP could have survived with better management. According to the third view, abandonment of the NEP was necessary given the desired high industrialization rate. Finally, some authors ascribe the end of the NEP to external factors, in particular the increasing external threat—real or perceived.

The first reason is subjective: For political and ideological reasons, the leaders found a market economy no longer suitable. They came to look upon the NEP as an "unwelcome compromise with class enemies" (Gregory and Stuart 1974:57). The existence of private peasants and private tradespeople had temporarily been useful, but the state had now become stronger and the compromise was no longer necessary. A socialist economic system could be built up. Nove writes that there was a "desire...to eliminate the individual peasantry" and speaks of "the political atmosphere, the prejudices against the market and NEPmen generally" (Nove 1969:158-9).

However, this subjective argument might have an objective dimension. It is possible that private producers fight against a socialist government no matter what economic incentives and guarantees they receive. According to Mandelbaum and Meyer this is the natural role of large private owners of the means of production. Nor can the socialist state trust the behavior of small peasants and handicraft producers, in particular in the case of an external threat (Mandelbaum and Meyer 1934). If it is true that private producers are not willing to cooperate in production and investment irrespective of the economic policy, a mixed economy is always unstable. Abolishing private ownership and market relations is then a rational decision.

With respect to external factors, they certainly played a role in abandoning the NEP. The hostile external environment, as it was perceived, strengthened the leaders' opposition to real or supposed internal enemies. The perceived danger of external attacks also made defense a higher priority. This required capturing a larger grain surplus in order to feed the army and made the development of heavy industry and, in particular, military industry, more important.

Was the high speed of the industrialization process in itself a sufficient reason for abandoning the mixed economic order? In this respect the second view (mistaken price policies) and the third view (too high an accumulation rate) oppose each other. The third position, that abandoning the NEP was rational because of the desired high industrialization rate, appears to be dominant in the literature (see Harrison 1980). Compulsory collectivization of agriculture and the introduction of a highly centrally controlled economy were necessary to achieve high industrial growth.

However, research has demonstrated that the contribution of agriculture to industry did not increase during the collectivization period. According to Merl's calculations, in financial terms the agricultural sector contributed most to industrialization during 1926–1927, not only in comparison with other NEP years but also in comparison with the years 1929–1932, the time of compulsory collectivization. In fact, agriculture did provide the resources for investment in heavy industry during 1926–1928. Industrial growth rates were very high during 1925–1928 and hardly lower than during the First Five-Year Plan (Table 2.3).

Ellman also concludes that the net surplus from agriculture to industry decreased during the First Five-Year Plan of 1928-1933 (Ellman 1975). He explains this first by the fact that marketed output of the agricultural sector remained more or less constant during the period. Although marketings of grain, potatoes, and vegetables increased, those of meat, milk, and eggs decreased sharply. Second, the volume of industrial goods delivered to the agricultural sector was larger than that of agricultural goods delivered to industry: Industry supplied agriculture with more tractors (necessary after private farmers had massively slaughtered their cattle in protest at the beginning of the collectivization process and later because a lack of fodder resulted from the state's increased grain purchases). Third, the overall terms of trade for agriculture improved during the period. The low official procurement prices for agricultural products were more than counterbalanced by farmers' prices for products sold in a free market (Ellman 1975:849). The free market was supplied by peasants who had not yet been collectivized and by collective farmers who had marketable surpluses on their "private plots." The state soon had to permit these private plots to prevent starvation in the cities as a result of the fall of production on the collective farms. The improvement of the terms of trade for agriculture brought about an enormous fall in real wages in the cities.

The enormous increase in investment during the First Five-Year Plan was possible because of the increase in the urban labor force, the fall in urban real wages, and the increase in the grain volume marketed by agriculture. As a result, forced collectivization performed several functions for the industrialization process. It did "increase procurements of grain, potatoes and vegetables, thus facilitating an increase in urban employment and exports, swing the terms of trade between agriculture and the state in favor of the state, and facilitate the rapid increase in the urban labor force (by depressing rural living conditions)" (Ellman 1975:859). In addition, collectivization turned agriculture into a residual sector that could absorb the risks of a bad harvest: Although the grain harvest was significantly lower in 1931 and 1932 than in preceding years, net marketed output was not, thus reducing rural living standards.

Apparently, in the Soviet case, collectivized agriculture did not have to provide a net *financial* surplus in order to further industrialization. Instead, it had to expand its volume of production in order to feed the urban labor force. The quantity of industrial goods the state had to deliver to agriculture in exchange for that volume did not matter very much (see Wagener 1979). Industrialization in the period of the First Five-Year Plan was a *labor-intensive* strategy.

According to the second view, the end of the NEP came about because wrong policies had been pursued. The price policies implemented from 1926 onward "could of themselves have destroyed NEP, even if no other complications had ensued" (Nove 1969:159). Nove does not go so far as to contend that with better price policies the market economy could have been prolonged: he also argues that the desired high speed of industrialization was a reason for abandoning the NEP.

Others, like Gey and Merl, are more outspoken on this matter (Gey 1982, Merl 1981). Merl argues that the state utilized all instruments necessary for influencing the quantity and the value of agricultural marketings but did not utilize them well. The state pursued industrial accumulation, but at the same time an ideological desire to maintain low prices prevailed. For that reason, the price policy conflicted with the aim of achieving as large an agricultural surplus as possible. The state could have implemented Preobazhensky's "unequal exchange" policy in a better way.

According to Merl, the events during the procurement campaigns of 1925–1928 show that peasants will always sell part of their production. Poorer peasants sell because they have to pay taxes, and richer peasants sell because they want to buy manufactures. The problem is not to establish prices at such a level that peasants keep selling. Instead, the state should have established prices and taxes at levels that created a balance between the total amount of purchasing power and the total supply of industrial goods.[6]

This is, however, not as simple as it may look. To avoid excess demand, the state must have an adequate understanding of what is going on in the economy. As described previously, this condition was not completely fulfilled during the NEP period, as is evident in the lack of reliable data and the conflicting interpretations of reality. This knowledge is not only important for avoiding macro excess demand while carrying out a price policy but also for preventing shortages and overproduction at the microlevel.

But apart from that, there seem to be more problems that have to be resolved. First, even Merl himself admits that by 1926 agricultural prices were so low that they would lead to the end of the NEP, as did the policy of withholding voting rights to richer peasants one year later (Merl 1981:sec.4.2). Apparently, it is important that private producers be stimulated to produce. Maintaining the market economy of the NEP required that some minimum level of private accumulation be allowed. If not, private production would decrease and the state would ultimately be forced to take over.

Second, it seems doubtful whether the state actually had all the necessary instruments to influence market relations. For the "unequal exchange" policy to be effective, the state must control all trade either in manufactures or in agricultural products. Complete control of trade in manufactures was not achieved during 1926–1928. By 1926, control of trade in agricultural products was fairly large, and this was the reason for that year's relatively successful procurement campaign.[7] Merl's argument also rests upon the assumption that direct taxes can be imposed. In a situation of "unequal exchange," the implementation of a direct tax policy might require the use of force.

In sum, provided that the state in a mixed economy has sufficient knowledge of what is going on in the economy, it seems possible to transfer a certain maximum surplus from the private sector by means of a price policy, but only under the conditions that total purchasing power equals total supply, that is, macroeconomic stability is maintained, that a minimum amount of private accumulation or at least maintenance of private production is allowed, and that the state has access to the necessary complementary instruments with respect to direct taxes and trade.

There is a relation between these conditions and the desired accumulation rate in the state sector, however. As Nuti put it, "Economic decentralization...can only be successful if introduced in the absence of excess demand, i.e., in the absence of the economic strain generated by intensive and accelerated accumulation" (Nuti 1979:257).

### Conclusion and Comparison

From the foregoing discussion it is possible to determine five factors that influenced the abandonment of the NEP. They probably have an impact on the stability of other mixed economies as well, and can therefore be called *stability conditions.*

1. The ideological objectives of the leaders with respect to the economic order. Is the mixed economy only a tactical maneuver or a more lasting objective?
2. The accumulation policy. Is rapid state accumulation pursued and what are the contributions needed from the private sector?
3. The price policy. The price policy can be used to finance state accumulation under the conditions that the state has the instruments to make the price policy effective, in particular with respect to domestic trade and taxes, that the state allows a minimum level of private accumulation or at least the maintenance of private production, and that the government maintains macroeconomic stability.
4. The reaction of private producers to the economic policy. Are they willing to maintain production?
5. External factors.

In the next chapters, these factors are analyzed in the case of the Sandinista mixed economy. Obviously, there are many differences between Nicaragua's mixed economy in the 1980s and that of the USSR in the 1920s. Three striking points must be made at the outset:

1. Differences in the external situation. The USSR adopted the mixed economy after a war and after the experience of a centralized system of "war communism." During this period of recovery the country was left in peace, although the external environment was somewhat hostile. Nicaragua also started its mixed economy after a war but experienced peace for only about two years. Then the economy confronted a new war, which intensified in 1983.
2. Differences in scale. Nicaragua, a very small country, required a different industrialization strategy than the USSR. It was impossible to achieve self-sufficiency, and stimulation of exports had to be an important component of the strategy.

3. Another difference in the external situation is the availability of foreign aid. Contrary to the USSR in the 1920s, Nicaragua had access to foreign loans from many different sources. And because of its small size, external funds could be an important source for financing accumulation. It follows from both the need to maintain foreign trade and from the potential advantages of foreign loans that international relations were far more important for Nicaragua than they were for the USSR.

## Notes

1. For example in China (1949–1953), Czechoslovakia (1945–1948), and Poland (1944–1950) (see J. Kosta, 1978. *Abriss der sozialökonomischer Entwicklung der Tsjechslowakei 1945–1977*. Frankfurt a/M: Suhrkamp; also see J. Kosta and W. Quaisser 1985. "Sozialistische Entwicklungswege: Strategien und Ergebnisse der wirtschaftlichen Entwicklung Polens, Jugoslawiens, Chinas und Kubas im Vergleich." In *Sozialismus und Industrialisierung, Die Wirtschaftssysteme Polens, Jugoslawiens, Chinas und Kubas im Vergleich*, eds. P. Gey, J. Kosta, and W. Quaisser. Frankfurt/New York: Methuen, 56-96.

2. See S. F. Cohen, 1975. *Bukharin and the Bolshevik Revolution: A political bibliography, 1888–1938*. New York: Vintage Books, 87. Bukharin delivered the theoretical foundation for this position in his book *The economics of the transition period*, which appeared in 1920 (Szamuely 1974:39).

3. Lenin later described this system as "dictated not by economic, but by military needs, considerations, and conditions" (Carr 1966:274).

4. This would be a "pessimistic" view according to Lenin. Cited in Dobb (1966:120).

5. This was achieved, for example, by prohibiting peasants from engaging in commercial activities and denying the use of the railway system to private traders (Merl 1981).

6. This conclusion is in line with other literature on the possibility of maintaining a market economy. It amounts to saying that one of the conditions for maintaining a decentralized market economy is that excess demand be avoided (see Nuti 1979:257) or that appropriate financial policies are necessary to avoid financial disequilibria, as Griffith-Jones concludes. (S. Griffith-Jones, 1981. *The role of finance in the transition to socialism*. London: Frances Pinter, 8.)

7. The procurement campaign was successful, at least, in terms of price control—not in quantity of purchases.

# 3

# Industrialization Before 1979

## The Central American Industrialization Model

During the 1950s, 1960s, and 1970s the Central American countries experienced high rates of economic growth. Their average annual real GDP growth rate was 5.3 percent between 1950 and 1978 (ECLAC 1986:116). These countries laid the basis for this growth in the 1950s, when agricultural diversification took place and the economies could benefit from high world-market prices for their agricultural export products—coffee, bananas, cotton, sugar, and beef.

An incipient industrialization process also began. The growers of cotton and other agricultural export crops looked for investment possibilities for their profits. Labor was available because of high population growth and because the expansion of the land area dedicated to export crops and productivity improvements in export agriculture had left many former peasants without means of subsistence. The general income rise expanded the market for manufactures. Export production itself created the possibilities for processing plants: coffee *beneficios* (where the coffee beans are extracted from the raw beans), sugar refineries, beef slaughterhouses, and cotton gins. Factories were also set up in consumer goods areas such as clothing, food, leather and shoes, and wood products, in which formerly only small handicraft production had existed.

Although the domestic markets for manufactures increased, they were still small because of the limited size of the population, the low wage levels, and the uneven distribution of income. Consequently, the bourgeoisie in the different countries began to consider the idea of a regional economic integration. This would allow an expansion of the market without having to change the distribution of income, which would have necessitated radical land reform.

This idea was, for other reasons, warmly supported by the United Nations Economic Commission for Latin America, ECLA.[1] The ECLA, headed at the time by Raúl Prebisch, expressed the opinion that industrialization was necessary to achieve economic development given the fact that agricultural prices had a long-run downward trend compared to industrial prices. Developments in the rest of Latin America during the economic recession of the 1930s and during World War II provided the example for an industrialization strategy: The lack of import possibilities had stimulated an industrialization process substituting domestic production for former imports.

ECLA saw the small size of the markets of the individual Central American countries as an obstacle. For this reason, it proposed establishing a regional common market. In the ECLA proposal regional cooperation was to be based on four principles: Economic integration should be a gradual process so as not to disturb the national economies; integration should lead to a balanced industrial development of the region, that is, the different countries should benefit more or less evenly from the integration process; there should be an emphasis on locally owned industries, with controls on foreign investment; and industrial investment should be based on common regional planning (Brahim and Correia 1983:269-70; Barry and Preusch 1986:164).

In 1958 the five countries signed a treaty on regional cooperation based on these principles. Trade in some products would be liberalized, and gradually this liberalization was to be extended to more products. In addition, the countries signed the Integration Industries Convention (Régimen de Industrias de Integración). This action implied that the countries would define some new large-scale industries, each set up in only one country to avoid duplications.

This ECLA project for Central American integration was not carried out because of U.S. government intervention in the process. The United States feared that a planned integration and industrialization process would hamper North American investments in the economically promising region. Also, after the Cuban revolution in January 1959 it was also considered politically important to expand U.S. interests in the region as one means to prevent "another Cuba." The U.S. project for economic integration was directed first at establishing free trade among the countries and second at promoting foreign, and especially U.S, investment. The U.S. administration promised a $100 million loan to finance industrial development along these lines.

In 1960 El Salvador, Guatemala, Nicaragua, and Honduras signed the Central American Common Market (CACM) General Treaty. Costa Rica followed in 1962 (Delgado 1978:30). As a result, between 1960 and 1963 all trade in industrial products between the Central American countries was liberalized. This was a much less gradual process than ECLA had proposed. The countries also made rapid progress in establishing common external tariffs. By the end of 1966, a uniform external tariff applied to 98 percent of the items listed in the common tariff schedule (Joel 1971:229). In fact, the CACM had by then become a customs union. In addition, the CACM constituted, in effect, a monetary union. All currencies of the region were freely convertible and had a fixed value relative to the U.S. dollar.

U.S. influence prevented controls from being imposed on foreign investment. Threatening to cut off economic aid to the region, the United States also succeeded in postponing the start of the Integration Industries Convention until 1965 (Elenbaas and Silva 1983). The problems with the implementation of the Integration Industries Convention must also be ascribed to intercountry rivalries over the location of plants (Bulmer-Thomas 1987:179). Nonetheless, after 1965 the five countries established some coordination of industrial investment. With the exception of Honduras, all countries succeeded in attracting one or more "integration industries." Nicaragua "obtained," in this sense, the Penwallt plant that produces caustic soda for the whole region and a factory producing nails (INCA: Industria Centroamericana; Central American Industry).

It also took a long time for fiscal policies to be effectively coordinated. Each country tried to attract as much foreign industrial investment as possible by granting exemptions from income taxes and import duties (ECLAC 1982). In 1962 the Agreement on Fiscal Incentives for Industrial Development was drafted. But it could not be put into practice until 1969: Honduras postponed the ratification, demanding and finally receiving the right to establish more incentives (Joel 1971). In general, the implementation of this agreement did not reduce the exemptions but rather harmonized them.

Within the CACM, nine Central American planning, research, and finance agencies were set up. The United States provided the bulk of the financing for these agencies, 54 percent, which guaranteed a dominant influence on their activities. The newly established Central American Bank for Economic Integration (CABEI), for example, promoted U.S. and other foreign investment by financing projects in infrastructure and communications. Sometimes the CABEI even gave loans to U.S. firms directly. The U.S. government could also specify the condition that goods for these projects be purchased in the United States (Barry and Preusch 1986:165).

After the establishment of the Central American Common Market, intraregional trade increased enormously. In 1960 only 7.5 percent of total CACM exports were directed to other countries of the region; in 1968 this proportion was 26.0 percent. Most intraregional trade consisted of manufactures. Relative to total imports of manufactures intraregional imports rose from 5 percent in 1960 to 37 percent in 1970 (ECLAC 1982).

TABLE 3.1 Growth Rates of Manufacturing in Central America 1960-1979 (five-year annual averages)

| | *1960 -1965* | *1965 -1970* | *1970 -1975* | *1975 -1979* | *1960 -1970* | *1970 -1979* |
|---|---|---|---|---|---|---|
| Costa Rica | 8.3 | 8.9 | 7.3 | 8.4[a] | 8.6 | 7.9 |
| El Salvador | 10.0 | 3.3 | 5.6 | 6.9[b] | 6.7 | 6.0[b] |
| Guatemala | 6.8 | 7.9 | 4.6 | 8.0 | 7.4 | 6.1 |
| Honduras | 4.9 | 6.7 | 2.8 | 9.9 | 5.8 | 6.0 |
| Nicaragua | 15.0 | 8.9 | 5.7 | 5.9[b] | 12.0 | 5.8[b] |
| Central America | 8.7 | 7.1 | 5.6 | 7.0[a] | 7.9 | 6.1[b] |

[a]To 1978.
[b]To 1977.

*Source:* Weeks, J. 1985. *The economies of Central America.* New York: Holmes and Meyer Publishers, Inc., 64. Copyright © 1985 by John Weeks. Reprinted by permission.

The region experienced an impressive growth of industrial production. Between 1960 and 1970 an average annual growth rate of 7.9 percent was achieved (Table 3.1). In Nicaragua industrial growth in this period was even higher. The share of the industrial product within the regional GDP rose from 12 percent in 1960 to 16 percent in 1970. In Nicaragua the relative share of industry rose even more: from 15 percent to 22 percent (see Table 1.2). Data on industrial production indicate that traditional branches such as textiles, food production, leather and shoes as well as the sectors of "intermediate goods" and "capital goods and durable consumer goods" experienced growth. For Nicaragua this is shown in Table 3.2.

At the end of the 1960s the CACM experienced its first crisis. The Honduran government had felt for some years that Honduras had benefited much less from the Common Market than the other countries. After a conflict with El Salvador that resulted in a brief war, Honduras withdrew from the CACM in 1969. Intraregional trade diminished during the 1970s, although the other countries continued trade relations with Honduras on the basis of bilateral contracts. In 1978 the proportion of intraregional exports within total exports of the region declined from 26.0 percent in 1968 to 22.4 percent. In the first half of the 1970s regional growth rates of manufacturing production slowed down a little, but they recovered later in the decade (Table 3.1).

At the end of the 1970s and continuing in the 1980s, the region experienced an economic crisis. The terms of trade deteriorated sharply,

TABLE 3.2 Growth Rates of Manufacturing Industry in Nicaragua per Branch 1960–1977 (annual averages)

| | *1960-65* | *1965-70* | *1970-77* |
|---|---|---|---|
| Nondurable consumer goods: | | | |
| Food | 11.8 | 6.1 | 4.9 |
| Beverages | 15.9 | 5.3 | 8.8 |
| Tobacco | 3.7 | 5.7 | 7.6 |
| Textiles | 23.0 | -4.5 | 5.9 |
| Shoes and clothing | 8.4 | 11.8 | -1.9 |
| Wood and cork | -1.1 | 15.5 | 8.8 |
| Furniture and accessories | 15.7 | 11.2 | 1.1 |
| Printing and publishing | 15.5 | 8.5 | 3.2 |
| Leather and leather products | 6.9 | 9.7 | -3.1 |
| Other manufacturing | 42.0 | 17.8 | -0.6 |
| Subtotal | 12.3 | 6.1 | 4.7 |
| Intermediate goods: | | | |
| Paper and paper products | 38.0 | 12.3 | 14.4 |
| Rubber products | 9.0 | 22.0 | 2.5 |
| Chemicals | 22.0 | 16.7 | 8.9 |
| Oil products | 32.0 | 9.1 | |
| Non metallic minerals | 15.8 | 15.6 | 10.4 |
| Subtotal | 23.0 | 18.1 | 9.6 |
| Durable consumer goods and capital goods: | | | |
| Metallic products | 40.0 | 5.8 | 4.0 |
| Machinery and equipment | 23.0 | 60.0 | 8.0 |
| Transport equipment | 30.0 | 21.0 | 11.2 |
| Subtotal | 38.0 | 10.8 | 5.7 |
| Total | 14.2 | 8.1 | 5.7 |

*Source:* Central Bank of Nicaragua 1978. *Estadísticas básicas del sector industrial 1960–1977*. Managua.

large deficits appeared in the balance-of-payments current accounts, capital flight increased, international interest rates soared, and foreign debts mounted. From 1980 onward regional GDP growth rates were negative in real terms for most years. In this situation each country gave priority to addressing its own balance-of-payments problems. The governments took protective measures that also affected the CACM partners, and intraregional trade declined. Manufacturing production was in serious trouble.

Most countries also experienced a political crisis. Guerrilla movements were active in El Salvador and Guatemala, and a civil war was raging in Nicaragua, which led to the overthrow of the Somoza government and the start of Sandinista rule in 1979.

## Interpretations of the Central American Model

There is no one generally accepted interpretation of the industrialization process and of economic developments in Central America, particularly during the 1970s. Most authors maintain that the economic model followed by the Central American countries could not lead to sustained economic growth. Already during the 1970s the inherent failures and contradictions of that model were apparent and brought about an economic crisis. Some authors see this economic crisis as an important cause of the successful insurrection in Nicaragua.

Among those who criticize the Central American economic model there are different interpretations of the nature of the crisis, which follow from different views of the nature of the development model itself. Following Irvin (1987), I broadly distinguish three views of Central American economic development. The first is that of the Latin American "structuralists," reflected, for example, in ECLAC publications. The second view is often associated with neo-Marxism and is strongly influenced by dependency theory. Third, there is the neoclassical position, reflected in publications of the World Bank and the IMF.

Because of the broad acceptance of the "crisis hypothesis," I present and analyze these three views; aim is, however, to show that the economic model of the Central American countries in the 1960s and 1970s was *successful in principle*. As some other authors also argue, it was not the economic model but the anachronistic, oligarchical political systems in most countries of Central America that caused the political crisis (see, for example, Weeks 1986). The enormous economic problems from 1978 onward in Nicaragua were mainly the result of the insurrection against the Somoza dictatorship, which brought about destruction and capital flight, among other difficulties (Vilas 1986).

### *The Structuralist View*

The structuralist interpretation is dominant in the literature. With differences in accent, this view is shared by authors such as Torres-Rivas (1980) and Pérez Brignoli and Baires Martínez (1983). In their view, the inherent failure of the industrialization model pursued within the CACM became apparent in the 1970s through

1. The uneven development between the countries of the region and the lack of planning instruments at the regional level (ECLAC 1982). The continuation of industrial growth required the CACM to continue—but to continue more in keeping with the original ECLA ideas. A more equal distribution of benefits was necessary to assure the participation of all countries. In addition, a more effective implementation of the Integration Industries Convention could bring about more backward linkages and make the region less dependent on imports of industrial raw materials and capital goods.

2. A deterioration of the terms of trade. Because the industrial sector was heavily dependent on imports of capital goods, raw materials, and intermediate goods, industrial growth was very sensitive to the terms-of-trade deterioration of the 1970s.

3. A saturation of the market. This constitutes the core of structuralist theory. An inherent failure of the CACM development model was that it was "exclusive" (ECLAC 1986). The unequal distribution of income had continued and in some countries had even increased. As a result, the markets for manufactures remained small and had become "saturated." The continued dominance of the agricultural export sector hampered industrialization because agricultural exporters were interested in maintaining low wages. Manufacturing production mainly consisted of the production of luxury goods. For this reason, structuralists argue that wages were only a "cost" factor and did not have a "demand" component (Torres-Rivas 1980:28; Catalán Aravena 1981:323).

4. The lack of strong modernizing states that behaved in the interest of a modern manufacturing sector. The development that followed from the industrialization process was only "additive" (Cohen and Rosenthal 1983:21; ECLAC 1986). The agricultural export sector remained the most important, and no substantial land reforms had come about. Government revenues were limited by low tax levels. As a result, state policies had continued to be dominated by the interests of the traditional agricultural bourgeoisie, and no strong modernizing states had developed (Bulmer-Thomas 1983).

### *The Neo-Marxist View*

The neo-Marxist view on Central American development also stresses the uneven distribution of income and the "uneven" development (Biderman 1983; De Janvry 1981). But, contrary to structuralists, neo-Marxists maintain that the skewed distribution of income was the result of *too much* capitalist development.

In the view of the neo-Marxists, the main problem of the model was that it created *dependent* development (Barry and Preusch 1986;

Brahim and Correia 1983). This dependency led to a growing crisis in the 1970s. The dependent state of the economy can be summarized in four characteristics:

1. In spite of some industrialization, the region continued to be dependent on the exports of primary goods and on the imports of intermediate and capital goods and therefore still suffered from falling terms of trade. It was a "peripheral capitalist development," which is always characterized by external "unequal exchange."

2. As a result, the commercial balance and the current account balance were always negative; foreign investment capital had to compensate for the deficits.

3. This foreign investment only worsened the current account of the balance of payments by increasing the profit remittances.

4. Foreign enterprises dominated the most dynamic sectors of the economy and they replaced and weakened the domestic state and the domestic entrepreneurial classes. Local entrepreneurs functioned as a "comprador bourgeoisie" in the interests of foreign capital.[2]

Many writers in this tradition point to the increasing socioeconomic contradictions resulting from the development model as the cause for the political crisis at the end of the 1970s and, in particular, for Somoza's fall in Nicaragua (Black 1981; van Toor 1986; Brahim and Correia 1983). With respect to industry, neo-Marxists agree with structuralists that industrial growth was hampered by the small market (Biderman 1983).

### *The Neoclassical View*

The neoclassical position holds that customs unions like the CACM bring about high-cost industrialization behind the tariff walls. The domestic exchange rates normally are overvalued. Protection prevents internationally competitive industries from coming into being. Growth can only be temporary and cannot be sustained.

Such a customs union also leads to an inefficient state bureaucracy. There is too much state regulation of the economy and too many state enterprises. Budget deficits contribute to inflation and to the "crowding out" of private investment. The extended role of the state hampers the development of an entrepreneurial bourgeoisie. An IMF-like adjustment strategy that reestablishes free trade, stimulates exports, and reduces the influence of the state on the economy is necessary. State enterprises must be subjected to privatization, among other measures (Balassa et al. 1986).

As Irvin observes, neoclassicals have in common with structuralists

TABLE 3.3 Structure of Imports by Economic Use (selected years)

| | *1960* | *1965* | *1970* | *1975* | *1977* | *1980* | *1983* | *1985* | *1987* |
|---|---|---|---|---|---|---|---|---|---|
| Consumer goods: | | | | | | | | | |
| Non-durable | 29 | 23 | 19 | 23 | 14 | 24 | 16 | 15 | 13 |
| Durable | 9 | 9 | 10 | 9 | 9 | 5 | 5 | 6 | 6 |
| Subtotal | 38 | 32 | 29 | 32 | 24 | 29 | 21 | 21 | 20 |
| Raw materials and intermediate goods: | | | | | | | | | |
| Petroleum and fuels | 5 | 4 | 6 | 4 | 3 | 3 | 4 | 6 | 16 |
| For agriculture | 3 | 4 | 4 | 4 | 5 | 7 | 7 | 8 | 9 |
| For manufacturing | 25 | 27 | 31 | 27 | 38 | 45 | 39 | 37 | 26 |
| For construction | 7 | 7 | 7 | 7 | 4 | 3 | 3 | 3 | 4 |
| Subtotal | 40 | 41 | 48 | 41 | 51 | 58 | 53 | 54 | 56 |
| Capital goods: | | | | | | | | | |
| For agriculture | 2 | 5 | 2 | 5 | 3 | 3 | 2 | 3 | 3 |
| For manufacturing | 14 | 18 | 17 | 18 | 15 | 7 | 18 | 17 | 17 |
| For transport | 2 | 2 | 4 | 2 | 7 | 3 | 5 | 6 | 5 |
| Subtotal | 18 | 26 | 23 | 26 | 25 | 12 | 25 | 25 | 25 |
| Other | 4 | 1 | 0 | 1 | 0 | 1 | 0 | 0 | 1 |
| Total | 100 | 100 | 100 | 100 | 100 | 100 | 100 | 100 | 100 |

*Sources:* Central Bank of Nicaragua 1979. *Indicadores económicos 1960–1979*. Managua for 1960–1975; INEC 1983. *Comercio Exterior 1982*. Managua for 1980; INEC for 1985; ECLAC 1989. *Economic survey of Latin America and the Caribbean 1988* for 1987.

the opinion that capitalist development has been hampered (Irvin 1987). The latter stress the insufficient protection for industries producing intermediate and capital goods and the lack of modernizing states; according to the former there is too much state bureaucracy and too much protection.

## Perspectives on the Central American Model

### *The Character of Industrialization*

All three interpretations appear to agree on the character of the region's industrialization process. They assume that it was the first stage of a "classic" import-substitution process that occurred in many third world countries since the 1930s but that in this case was implemented at a regional level. Such an import-substitution process, as described by Little, Scitovsky, and Scott (1970), for example, is based on a high degree of protection for consumer goods industries, which results in industries with a high imports and low employment content. Protection also guarantees high profit margins in spite of low rates of capacity utilization. Hardly any linkages with existing agricultural production or within industrial production come about, and industrial production is concentrated on luxury consumer goods for the national elite. Usually, heavy protection not only results from high import tariffs for final manufactures but also from an overvalued exchange rate, which makes imports of capital goods cheap and discourages exports. Balance-of-payments problems appear.

Is this view of the Central American industrialization process correct? Most authors in all three traditions recognize that Central America's industrialization in the 1960s and 1970s was not accompanied by an overvalued exchange rate or by serious balance-of-payments problems.

The industrialization process did bring about an increase in the imports of capital goods, industrial raw materials, and intermediate goods. The share of industrial consumer goods relative to total imports declined, that of intermediate and capital goods increased (see Table 3.3 for Nicaragua). But this rise in imports did not lead to large deficits in the balance of trade because exports also increased (see Table 3.4 for Nicaragua). These were still mainly agricultural exports, although manufacturing exports also increased (Table 3.5).

Agricultural exports continued to grow during the 1960s and 1970s. The success of this sector was important in fostering industrialization by contributing to a relatively high import capacity (Bulmer-Thomas 1983). This made the Central American industrialization model very different from that of, for example, South America, where import-substituting industrialization began as a response to falling export income, which implies that the industrial sector was dependent on the agricultural export sector.

But authors who rightly stress Central America's imports dependency often overlook that many manufacturing industries do use domestic raw materials and intermediate goods, particularly in food industries (vegetable oil based on the oil from cotton seed, powdered milk, meat packing, sugar refineries) but also in textiles, leather and shoes, furniture and other wood products, and so on. In the early 1970s the rise in world market agricultural prices stimulated the growing of "nontraditional" export crops such as fruits, vegetables, and tobacco.[3] These crops were also processed within Central America. So the growth of the agricultural sector stimulated industrial

TABLE 3.4 Nicaragua's Balance of Payments 1960–1979 (five-year annual averages, in millions of $)

| | *1960-64* | *1965-69* | *1970-74* | *1975-79*[a] |
|---|---|---|---|---|
| Exports fob (free on board) | 90.7 | 152.8 | 254.8 | 553.3 |
| Imports cif (cost, insurance, freight) | 98.4 | 181.6 | 303.3 | 553.0 |
| Trade balance (imp. cif) | -7.8 | -28.8 | -48.4 | 0.3 |
| Trade balance (imp. fob)[b] | | 11.5 | -4.5 | -33.7 |
| 33.9 | | | | |
| Balance of services | -23.3 | -44.9 | -60.7 | -118.8 |
| Net transfers & other factor services | 3.8 | 6.4 | 18.2 | 23.5 |
| Current account balance | -8.0 | -42.9 | -76.2 | -61.4 |
| | | | | |
| Net private capital movements | 7.5 | 17.3 | 20.9 | -57.0 |
| Net official capital movements | 5.7 | 18.6[c] | 71.2 | 104.3 |
| Net total capital movements | 13.2 | 36.0 | 92.0 | 2.9 |
| | | | | |
| Errors and omissions | -1.9 | 0.4 | -5.2 | -8.0 |
| Balance of payments | 3.2 | -6.5 | 10.6 | -64.8 |
| Change in international reserves[d] | -3.2 | 6.5 | -10.6 | 64.8 |

[a]For 1979 preliminary figures.
[b]Adjusted by the Central Bank of Nicaragua for balance-of-payments objectives.
[c]Includes SDR assignments in 1970, 1971, and 1972.
[d]A negative sign (-) means increase.

*Source:* Elaboration of Central Bank of Nicaragua 1980. *Indicadores económicos 1960–1979*. Managua. For the first three rows, Table 5.2; for the other rows, Table 5.1.

production by providing new processing possibilities (forward linkages).

In Nicaragua, imports for the industrial sector were just a little higher than industrial exports. The excess of imports over exports in 1974 was $1 million and, excluding agroindustry, $16 million (Weeks 1985b:287); total industrial exports mounted to almost $170 million in 1974. Agroindustry in itself had a positive foreign-exchange balance.

Regarding the other aspects of the supposed "classic" import-substitution model, it is not true that as a result of the Common Market Agreement tariffs increased. In fact, some tariffs even decreased after the establishment of the CACM (Delgado 1978:28). According to a study by the Inter-American Development Bank and the Institute for Latin American Integration, the differences between intra-CACM prices and world market prices were relatively modest (cited in Weeks 1986:43). The fact that the currencies were freely convertible also points to a relatively modest protection. However, import duties for industrial capital goods and some raw materials

TABLE 3.5 Exports of Nicaragua and Structure of Exports 1960–1979

| | Agriculture | Industry | Mining | Total[a] | Agriculture | Industry | Mining | Total[a] |
|---|---|---|---|---|---|---|---|---|
| | (in millions of $) | | | | (proportion in %) | | | |
| 1960 | 42 | 11 | 9 | 63 | 67 | 18 | 14 | 100 |
| 1961 | 44 | 14 | 11 | 68 | 64 | 20 | 16 | 100 |
| 1962 | 58 | 21 | 12 | 90 | 64 | 23 | 13 | 100 |
| 1963 | 70 | 26 | 11 | 107 | 65 | 24 | 11 | 100 |
| 1964 | 87 | 26 | 12 | 125 | 70 | 21 | 9 | 100 |
| 1965 | 109 | 28 | 12 | 149 | 73 | 19 | 8 | 100 |
| 1966 | 95 | 34 | 13 | 142 | 67 | 24 | 9 | 100 |
| 1967 | 93 | 45 | 13 | 152 | 61 | 30 | 9 | 100 |
| 1968 | 96 | 61 | 6 | 162 | 59 | 37 | 4 | 100 |
| 1969 | 78 | 75 | 6 | 159 | 49 | 47 | 4 | 100 |
| 1970 | 81 | 93 | 5 | 179 | 45 | 52 | 3 | 100 |
| 1971 | 85 | 98 | 3 | 187 | 46 | 53 | 2 | 100 |
| 1972 | 118 | 127 | 4 | 249 | 47 | 51 | 1 | 100 |
| 1973 | 129 | 147 | 1 | 278 | 46 | 53 | 1 | 100 |
| 1974 | 211 | 169 | 1 | 381 | 55 | 44 | 0 | 100 |
| 1975 | 167 | 199 | 9 | 375 | 44 | 53 | 2 | 100 |
| 1976 | 278 | 255 | 8 | 542 | 51 | 47 | 2 | 100 |
| 1977 | 380 | 247 | 9 | 637 | 60 | 39 | 1 | 100 |
| 1978 | 361 | 274 | 11 | 646 | 56 | 42 | 2 | 100 |
| 1979 | 314 | 245 | 8 | 567 | 55 | 43 | 1 | 100 |

[a]Total may be not equal sum of three categories due to rounding and the exclusion of the category "Other activities" (which does not exceed 0.5 million in each year).

*Source:* Central Bank of Nicaragua 1979. *Indicadores económicos 1960–1979*. Managua.

were much lower than for manufactures, which generally made the "effective rate of protection" positive. These lower import duties for some commodities were not stipulated by the CACM but resulted from import tax exemptions that each of the countries granted to industrial enterprises.

According to a survey of managers of foreign enterprises in the region, the effective rates of protection seem to have played a role in attracting industrial investment. These managers said that tax exemptions were the most important factor encouraging then to set up an enterprise in the region (ECLAC 1982). Another study showed that, among tax exemptions, those from import duties on intermediate and capital goods were far more important than profit tax exemptions (Joel 1971).

In a study of comparative advantage and effective protection of manufacturing industry in the region, Cline and Rapoport came to the conclusion that "there is some tendency to provide excessive incentive to traditional sectors and insufficient incentive to capital goods sectors, because effective protection is high for the former and low for the latter." (Cline and Rapoport 1978:307) This supports the ECLA view that a lack of incentives prevented backward linkages (production of intermediate goods and capital goods for manufacturing) from coming into being. In sum, although average protection levels for manufacturing were lower than in South America, effective protection was probably fairly high for consumer goods industries.

If we look at the sectoral structure of manufacturing, the production of nondurable consumer goods such as food, beverages, textiles, and clothing remained the most important share of manufacturing production (see Table 3.6 for Nicaragua). But, especially in Nicaragua, the manufacturing of intermediate goods such as agricultural and industrial inputs and construction materials also expanded. So some backward linkages have come about, both with manufacturing itself and with other sectors. However, further backward linkages in the form of production of capital goods appear to have been limited.

Weeks has shown that for the Central American countries the share of capital goods production is low relative to the combined gross income of the region in comparison with South American countries. The share of consumer durables is even more limited (Weeks 1985a:1-39). In Central America the production of formerly imported luxury consumer goods for an elite has much less accent within total industrial production than in South America. This leads Weeks to the conclusion that the Central American industrialization policy did not foster high-cost industries for a small market and that levels of protection were lower than in most South American countries.

The relative lack of domestic luxury consumer goods industries in the region can probably also be explained by the geographical and cultural closeness of the North American market for the Central American elite (the main purchaser of consumer durables).

The importance of Central America as an export market for manufacturing production appears to be limited. Most manufactures are sold in the domestic market, as Table 3.7 shows for Nicaragua. Given the high growth of manufacturing production, domestic markets must have *expanded* enormously. Many new consumer goods such as cola, beer, and cooking oil were produced—not as substitutes for former imports but probably substituting for more traditional domestically produced commodities. The growing agricultural sector also provided a market for industrial production. Many fertilizer and pesticides factories came into being, especially in Nicaragua.

However, as Table 3.7 also indicates, for some branches the exports to other CACM countries constitute about one-third of total sales. For

TABLE 3.6 Structure of Value Added per Branch of Manufacturing 1960–1983 (selected years)[a]

| | *1960* | *1965* | *1970* | *1975* | *1980* | *1983* |
|---|---|---|---|---|---|---|
| Nondurable consumer goods: | | | | | | |
| Food | 49 | 44 | 40 | 38 | 37 | 41 |
| Beverages | 8 | 9 | 8 | 8 | 15 | 12 |
| Tobacco | 9 | 5 | 5 | 5 | 7 | 5 |
| Textiles | 7 | 11 | 6 | 6 | 5 | 8 |
| Shoes and clothing | 5 | 4 | 5 | 3 | 4 | 4 |
| Wood and cork | 5 | 3 | 4 | 5 | 3 | 2 |
| Furniture | 1 | 1 | 1 | 1 | 1 | 1 |
| Printing and publishing | 2 | 3 | 3 | 2 | 2 | 2 |
| Leather and leather products | 1 | 1 | 1 | 1 | 1 | 1 |
| Other manufacturing | 1 | 2 | 3 | 2 | 1 | 1 |
| Subtotal | 90 | 82 | 75 | 70 | 75 | 77 |
| Intermediate goods: | | | | | | |
| Paper and paper products | 0 | 1 | 1 | 2 | 1 | 2 |
| Rubber products | 0 | 0 | 0 | 0 | 1 | 1 |
| Chemicals | 4 | 5 | 8 | 10 | 8 | 7 |
| Oil products | 0 | 1 | 3 | 4 | 4 | 4 |
| Construction materials | 3 | 4 | 5 | 6 | 5 | 5 |
| Subtotal | 8 | 11 | 18 | 22 | 20 | 18 |
| Capital goods and durable consumer goods: | | | | | | |
| Metal products | 2 | 6 | 5 | 6 | 4 | 4 |
| Elect. & non-electr. machinery | 0 | 0 | 2 | 2 | 1 | 1 |
| Transport materials | 0 | 0 | 0 | 0 | 0 | 0 |
| Subtotal | 2 | 6 | 7 | 8 | 5 | 5 |
| Total | 100 | 100 | 100 | 100 | 100 | 100 |

[a]On the basis of real value added figures, cordobas of 1958.

*Source:* Ministry of Planning 1985. Mimeo.

some particular industries in Nicaragua, mainly basic chemicals and construction materials, the majority of production was sold in other Central American countries. Exports to the rest of the world were important for some Central American agroindustrial products such as vegetable oil, refined sugar, and frozen meat. The hypothesis that Central American industry supplied only a protected regional market is therefore not confirmed.

The question then becomes to what extent import substitution has

TABLE 3.7 Destination of the Industrial Product per Branch (selected years, in percent)

| | *1960* | | | *1970* | | | *1977* | | |
|---|---|---|---|---|---|---|---|---|---|
| | *Domest. Market* | *CACM* | *Rest* | *Domest. Market* | *CACM* | *Rest* | *Domest. Market* | *CACM* | *Rest* |
| Food | 89 | 0 | 11 | 70 | 6 | 25 | 72 | 6 | 22 |
| Beverages | 100 | 0 | 0 | 100 | 0 | 0 | 100 | 0 | 0 |
| Tobacco | 100 | 0 | 0 | 95 | 2 | 2 | 89 | 0 | 11 |
| Textiles | 100 | 0 | 0 | 70 | 23 | 7 | 66 | 26 | 8 |
| Shoes and clothing | 100 | 0 | 0 | 85 | 15 | 0 | 80 | 11 | 9 |
| Wood and cork | 33 | 4 | 63 | 61 | 18 | 21 | 62 | 18 | 20 |
| Furniture and access. | 100 | 0 | 0 | 74 | 24 | 2 | 100 | 0 | 0 |
| Printing & publishing | 100 | 0 | 0 | 99 | 1 | 0 | 80 | 19 | 1 |
| Paper and paper prod. | 100 | 0 | 0 | 91 | 9 | 0 | 80 | 16 | 4 |
| Leather & leather pr. | 97 | 0 | 3 | 76 | 19 | 5 | 93 | 6 | 0 |
| Rubber & rubber prod. | 96 | 4 | 0 | 58 | 42 | 0 | 69 | 31 | 0 |
| Chemicals | 98 | 2 | 0 | 70 | 25 | 5 | 60 | 35 | 5 |
| Oil products | | | | 98 | 2 | 0 | 99 | 1 | 0 |
| Nonmetallic minerals | 100 | 0 | 0 | 84 | 16 | 0 | 84 | 16 | 0 |
| Metal products | 99 | 1 | 0 | 50 | 23 | 27 | 59 | 40 | 1 |
| Machinery & equipment | 100 | 0 | 0 | 88 | 11 | 0 | 69 | 31 | 0 |
| Transport equipment | 100 | 0 | 0 | 100 | 0 | 0 | 99 | 1 | 0 |
| Other manufacturing | 100 | 0 | 0 | 93 | 7 | 0 | 82 | 17 | 1 |
| Total | 91 | 1 | 9 | 75 | 10 | 14 | 76 | 13 | 12 |

*Source:* Central Bank of Nicaragua 1978. *Estadísticas básicas del sector industrial 1960–1977*. Managua.

taken place. This can be estimated by calculating the share of imports in the total "apparent consumption" (the sum of imports and domestic production minus the exports). An over-time declining share of imports in a certain branch points to import substitution. The Central Bank of Nicaragua (1978) calculated to what extent import substitution took place in Nicaragua between 1960 and 1970. It showed import substitution to be important for branches such as oil products (from 100 percent imports to 27 percent), other manufacturing (from 80 to 41 percent), leather and leather products (from 22 to 8 percent), and paper and paper products (from 76 to 59 percent).

However, it seems more accurate to calculate the extent of import substitution at a regional level. "Apparent consumption" must then include intraregional exports and "imports" must only consist of extraregional imports. It follows that the extent of import substitution in the previously mentioned branches was greater (Table 3.8). In

TABLE 3.8 Nicaragua: Import substitution at the Regional Level per Branch 1960–1980 (quotients, in percent)[a]

| | *1960* | *1965* | *1970* | *1977* | *1980* |
|---|---|---|---|---|---|
| Non-durable consumer goods: | | | | | |
| Food | 7.0 | 5.3 | 2.0 | 3.7 | 16.0 |
| Beverages | 4.2 | 3.9 | 4.1 | 4.1 | 4.1 |
| Tobacco | 8.0 | 1.5 | 1.3 | 0.0 | 0.1 |
| Textiles | 53.5 | 35.7 | 18.7 | 12.3 | 8.2 |
| Shoes and clothing | 14.8 | 7.4 | 4.5 | 4.9 | 4.3 |
| Wood and cork | 7.4 | 4.7 | 3.4 | 2.6 | 3.5 |
| Furniture | 9.4 | 40.6 | 9.9 | 7.0 | 8.7 |
| Printing and publishing | 14.3 | 14.8 | 11.8 | 15.0 | 11.6 |
| Leather & leather products | 22.0 | 15.4 | 2.7 | 2.4 | 1.6 |
| Other manufacturing | 76.3 | 47.5 | 27.3 | 32.4 | 16.4 |
| Subtotal | 16.3 | 13.4 | 6.5 | 6.7 | 10.8 |
| Intermediate goods: | | | | | |
| Paper and paper products | 74.0 | 55.1 | 38.6 | 33.9 | 21.2 |
| Rubber products | 79.9 | 78.7 | 47.8 | 43.7 | 38.7 |
| Chemicals | 58.2 | 49.3 | 38.6 | 43.2 | 48.2 |
| Oil products | 98.1 | 34.1 | 25.3 | 21.9 | 14.2 |
| Non-metalic minerals | 36.1 | 36.9 | 20.1 | 15.7 | 10.7 |
| Subtotal | 65.2 | 48.1 | 35.3 | 34.9 | 32.6 |
| Durable consumer goods and capital goods: | | | | | |
| Metal products | 78.0 | 58.4 | 57.8 | 46.8 | 39.3 |
| Elect. & non elect. machinery | 96.6 | 94.5 | 80.5 | 83.8 | 77.4 |
| Transport equipment | 95.5 | 96.9 | 93.3 | 97.0 | 92.8 |
| Subtotal | 89.7 | 82.6 | 74.1 | 77.3 | 64.7 |
| Total | 38.1 | 36.1 | 26.8 | 32.0 | 30.0 |

[a]Imports from the rest of the world divided by production plus total imports minus exports to the rest of the world. A downward trend indicates import substitution.

*Sources:* Elaboration of Central Bank of Nicaragua 1978. *Estadísticas básicas del sector industrial 1960–1977*. Managua; and for 1980, Instituto Nacional de Estadísticas y Census (INEC) 1983. *Comercio Exterior 1982*. Managua; and INEC 1982, *Encuesta anual industria manufacturera 1980*. Managua.

addition, import substitution at a regional level also was important in branches such as textiles and metal products.

In many other branches of consumer goods production such as food, beverages and tobacco and clothing the degree of import substitution was limited. This again points to an expanding domestic market for these goods.

Another characteristic of import-substituting industrialization does hold. The employment content of the manufacturing industry was low. In Nicaragua, for example, the share of manufacturing in total production was 22 percent and in total employment only 15 percent in 1977 (Table 1.2). Many structuralists and neo-Marxists argue that the inability to absorb the labor force was one of the structural weaknesses of the Central American industrialization model (Torres-Rivas 1980:34).

But the lagging behind of employment is a normal feature of an incipient industrialization process. A growing manufacturing sector does not lead to a commensurate employment growth in manufacturing but to a rise in incomes that, in turn, permits employment growth in the economy as a whole.[4] The structuralist criticism is valid in so far as it points to a need for more appropriate technology. Fiscal incentives for imports of capital goods brought about a more capital-intensive and less labor-intensive industrialization process than justified by the relative domestic availability of production factors.

Central American industries are also characterized by low rates of capacity utilization. According to a study of the Secretary of the Central American Economic Integration (Secretaría de la Integración Económica Centroamericana; SIECA), utilized capacity was on average less than 50 percent in 1972 (Weeks 1985a:138). In addition, for many of the fifty-five products in the survey, installed capacity was 50 percent higher than total regional demand.

The most important explanation for the low rates of capacity utilization was fiscal incentives for investment, which raised the demand for capital goods in excess of what was needed for current production (Bulmer-Thomas 1987:193). But another factor probably was the large scale of most new industrial equipment in comparison with the small market; therefore each investment meant a big jump in capacity. Some excess capacity could therefore be explained from the high industrial growth. In addition, the uncertain deliveries of raw materials and other inputs, many of which were of an agricultural origin, might have played a role, as well as infrastructural problems like interruptions in electricity.

The Central American industrialization process was not just a simple import substitution process in which only luxury consumer goods were produced behind high tariff walls. Most industrial production was directed to the domestic markets, which apparently expanded enormously. Furthermore, industry was not such a "terrible foreign-exchange consumer" as is often supposed. Forward and backward linkages, especially with agriculture, developed on a fairly large scale.

The comparison with other Latin American countries indicates that levels of protection for capital goods and durable consumer goods industries were lower in Central America. Higher tariffs for intermediate and capital goods could probably have lowered regional dependence on imports. This could also have increased industrial employment and the rate of capacity utilization.

### *Crisis in the 1970s?*

All three views of Central American development, structuralism, neoclassicism, and neo-Marxism, maintain that the CACM growth model entered a crisis in the 1970s. But they differ on the causes of that crisis. The neoclassicists point to high tariffs. In fact, as shown previously, traditional industries did enjoy high effective protection rates. But it seems unwarranted to ascribe declining growth rates to high tariffs. It can be argued more reasonably that protection for sectors producing intermediate and capital goods was too low, as structuralists maintain.

The structuralists are also correct in stating that the benefits from integration were not equally distributed among the five countries. Honduras, which already had the lowest national income per capita at the start of integration, showed the lowest rate of manufacturing growth during the 1960s. It also had continuous deficits in its intraregional trade balance from 1965 onward.

Nicaragua and Costa Rica also had intraregional trade deficits for most of the 1960s and 1970s. Over these twenty years, Nicaragua had the largest share of the regional trade deficit (40 percent), followed by Honduras (33 percent) and Costa Rica (27 percent) (Torres-Rivas 1980:38). But Nicaragua and Costa Rica were "compensated," in a sense, by high manufacturing growth rates. According to a detailed empirical study, Honduras indeed benefited least from the economic integration during the 1960s (Cline 1978). Still, that country experienced net gains from the integration process and probably suffered from its eventual separation from the Common Market. The benefits of integration were more or less equally distributed over the other four countries.

The argument of the structuralists that if the CACM had had more planning instruments, a more balanced development would have resulted is probably well founded. Nonetheless, the actual integration process was favorable for all five countries. It does not seem justified to consider the uneven development as a cause for the region's economic crisis. In addition, it is not certain that the region would

TABLE 3.9 Static Terms-of-Trade Effect on Central America 1960–1979 (in millions of $)[a]

| | *1960-64* | *1965-69* | *1970-74* | *1975-79* | *Total* |
|---|---|---|---|---|---|
| Costa Rica | 48 | 41 | -302 | -544 | -757 |
| El Salvador | -104 | -158 | -95 | 556 | 199 |
| Guatemala | 10 | -108 | -257 | -804 | -1,159 |
| Honduras | 51 | 88 | -23 | 161 | 277 |
| Nicaragua | 49 | 41 | -85 | 110 | 115 |
| Central America | 54 | -96 | -762 | -521 | -1,325 |

[a]Actual imports and exports were compared with hypothetical imports and exports, had prices remained at 1970 levels. Figures are crude estimations, because quantity changes that have resulted from price changes are not included in the hypothetical values. It is likely that the price elasticity of the demand for exports is almost negligible and that the price elasticity of the demand for imports, though a little higher, is also low. For this reason, some volume changes will have occurred in imports, and almost none in exports. Because over the whole region and over the whole period relative price increases for imports occurred more often than relative price reductions, the overall terms-of-trade loss is probably somewhat underestimated.

*Source:* Weeks, J. 1985. *The Economies of Central America.* New York: Holmes and Meyer Publishers, Inc., 84. Copyright © 1985 by John Weeks. Reprinted by permission.

have had the same high growth rates if more regional planning had occurred.[5]

With respect to the terms of trade, it is true that in the early 1970s the prices of oil and many other inputs such as fertilizers, industrial raw materials, machinery, and equipment rose sharply. But the prices of the export products of the region also increased. So the terms-of-trade loss to the region as a whole was less than rising import prices would suggest. However, on the basis of 1970 prices the loss between 1970 and 1974 was considerable: $762 million (Table 3.9), about 10 percent of the total value of the region's exports during these years. For Nicaragua the loss was $85 million over five years—7 percent of the value of its exports. As Table 3.9 shows, during 1975–1979 Nicaragua and two other countries experienced improvements in their terms of trade that more than compensated for the losses in the earlier years.

The price increases of oil, industrial raw materials, intermediate goods, and machinery and equipment did affect industrial growth in the early 1970s. They raised production costs in the manufacturing industry, which could only partially be compensated for by higher prices.[6]

In Nicaragua the change in prices had occurred by 1967 (Weeks

1982). After 1967, the prices of capital goods rose by 100 percent and those of intermediates by 150 percent. Domestic prices for manufactures increased by lower rates. As a result profits in the manufacturing industry declined. Industrial firms restricted output growth and undertook fewer new investments. In fact, from 1960 to 1967 the annual average growth rate in Nicaragua's manufacturing industry was as high as 12.5 percent; from 1968 to 1977 it declined to 5.6 percent. The rate of capacity utilization also was much higher during 1960–1967 than during 1968–1977.

The "saturation thesis" of structuralists and neo-Marxists is based on the assumption that manufacturing production consisted mainly of luxury consumer goods and only satisfied a small regional market. However, a large share of production consisted of nondurable consumer goods such as food and clothing and of intermediate goods for agriculture, industry, and construction (Table 3.6). I showed previously that, at least in Nicaragua, the market for all these goods expanded tremendously. This makes a saturation of the market rather improbable.

It is true that the distribution of income throughout the region remained extremely uneven during the 1960s and 1970s. In Nicaragua, 50 percent of the population received only 15 percent of the national income in 1977 (FIDA 1980). But it is not justified to conclude that a saturation occurred, because the same processes that maintained and worsened this distribution of income expanded market relations in the five economies.

The growth in agricultural export production was accompanied by a further concentration of land ownership. By the end of the 1970s, 40 percent of the rural labor force in El Salvador and Nicaragua did not have access to land. In Guatemala and Costa Rica the inequality of the land distribution also increased during the 1970s (Bulmer-Thomas 1987:207).

The poorer peasants who still cultivated some land had less access to agricultural inputs, bank credits, and marketing facilities. They were dependent on intermediaries for credits, purchases of inputs, and marketing of their production. Many were permanently in debt. Consequently, they were forced to sell the crop in advance at very low prices. A large proportion of the small-landholder peasants and their families were forced to work during part of the year in the harvests of coffee, cotton, and sugarcane. Many peasant families went to the cities where they lived in very poor conditions. They worked in low-paid, insecure jobs in handicrafts, trade, or services. There were not enough full-time jobs in the cities, and many urban workers participated in the harvests too.

In sum, the ongoing capitalist development in the countryside was accompanied by proletarianization and semiproletarianization, by an expansion of the commercialization of small-peasant production, and by rural-urban migration. It seems justified to assume that these processes brought about an expansion of the market for manufactures.

Although the Central American market for consumer goods expanded enormously, it was still small compared to that of countries with a more equal distribution of income. In this sense the market was "saturated," but this saturation probably did not hamper industrial growth in the 1970s. Most likely, other factors were more important. This is also confirmed by the fact that annual growth rates of manufacturing production returned in some countries to high levels during 1975–1979. In Costa Rica, for example, growth rates rose to 8.4 percent and in Guatemala to 8.0 percent (Table 3.1).

Given the importance of the expansion of the domestic market for nondurable consumer goods industries, wage-earners in the manufacturing sector must have purchased its products. So wages did not constitute only a "cost" factor, as structuralists maintain. Wage rises and increases in industrial employment seem to have been in the interest of industrialists because they would expand the market for manufactures. In fact, the industrial wage level was low and employment possibilities were limited. As argued previously, the employment level in the industrial sector was probably first and foremost determined by the profitability of capital investment. And because of the small relative size of the industrial proletariat, its wage level was much more determined by conditions in the agricultural sector. Low food prices and the predominance of semiproletarianization in the countryside were sufficient to maintain wages at low levels. To attract labor, industrial wages had to be just a little higher than agricultural wages.

Neo-Marxists hold that the dependent nature of the development model led to a crisis in the 1970s. As indicated in Table 3.9, the terms of trade only deteriorated moderately during the whole decade of the 1970s. During the 1960s the terms-of-trade loss for the region was even smaller. Over the whole period 1960–1979, three of the five countries even experienced favorable price developments. The conclusion must be that although primary products constituted most of the region's exports during the 1960s and 1970s, this did not lead to falling terms of trade.

Furthermore, there is not such a tight relationship between the terms of trade, the commercial balance, and the current account of the balance of payments. Guatemala, for example, had the worst terms of trade during the whole period but managed to maintain a surplus in its commercial balance for all years except 1960. El Salvador had a negative commercial balVce from 1975 to 1979 while experiencing the most favorable terms of trade in the region (Weeks 1985a:88). In Nicaragua, the commercial balance more or less followed the terms of trade, with an average surplus during 1960–1964 and 1975–1979 and an average deficit during 1970–1974 (Table 3.4). The years 1965–1969 are an exception; a small commercial deficit existed along with an improvement in the terms of trade.

On the whole, commercial deficits were limited for all countries and for all years between 1960 and 1979. The situation for current accounts was less favorable. Especially during the 1970s the current account's deficits increased rapidly. This is explained by the deficits in the balances for "invisibles": services and profit transfers (Weeks 1985a:91).

With respect to the services, none of the CACM countries possess a sufficient domestic fleet and they have to contract with foreign enterprises to handle the commercial, financial, and insurance services connected with international trade. In this particular sense, these countries are "dependent" on industrialized countries, affecting negatively their balance of payments. The deficit in the balance of services increased more or less in a fixed proportion to commercial exports, as Table 3.4 indicates for Nicaragua.

Net profit remittances dramatically increased during the 1970s. Net direct foreign investment was indeed important to maintain the balance of payments in the 1960s. From 1960 to 1965, more than a quarter of total U.S. investment took place (Brahim and Correia 1983:271). Sometimes the foreign corporations established joint ventures with local firms or bought the local enterprises out. Of total industrial investment between 1962 and 1969, 28 percent was of foreign origin.[7] Local financing was still dominant but less so than in South American countries, where local financing represented 90 percent (Cable 1976).

During the 1970s, the growth of net direct foreign investment decreased. During the 1960s new capital investment more or less compensated for profit remittances; during the 1970s profit transfers by far exceeded net investment in the region (Cable 1976; Weeks 1985a:91-5).

But there is not necessarily a relationship between foreign capital investment and profit remittances abroad (Weeks 1985a:95). Foreign corporations may reinvest their profits in the host country and local capitalists might prefer to send their profits abroad. Costa Rica, for example, had the highest proportion of foreign investment of the region during 1960–1978 (15 percent), but its profit transfers barely exceeded net capital inflow. The annual excess capital movement abroad constituted only about 1 percent of exports from that country.

Nicaragua had a relatively low level of foreign investment. Most profits transferred abroad after 1970 probably came from Nicaraguans themselves—also in 1978 and 1979 when capital flight reached dramatic proportions (Table 3.4). In this country, the net capital movement abroad during the 1970s represented more than 10 percent of the export value. Its causes were probably the same for foreign and local investors: the rise in the prices of capital goods in the early 1970s, the 1972 earthquake in Managua, which caused a profit squeeze, and, later in the 1970s, political insecurity.

According to the neo-Marxist view, foreign investment is damaging to the national economy for another reason as well. Foreign enterprises dominate the most dynamic sectors and their presence leads to a weakening of the state and of domestic entrepreneurs. I will analyze the extent and impact of foreign capital in Nicaragua later in this chapter. But because Nicaragua is an underdeveloped country, it is likely that foreign capital provided financing, know-how, machinery, and marketing facilities that otherwise would not have been available. The prohibition of foreign investment at a low development level probably leads to lower growth rates. The higher the development level of a country, the more restrictions it can impose on foreign investment. Although the results of foreign investment are not always beneficial for the majority of the population in the host country (the same applies to domestically owned enterprises), the presence of foreign capital cannot be the cause of the alleged "crisis of the development model" in the 1970s.[8] This is reinforced by the fact that the high foreign investment levels in Central America apparently did not affect growth rates during the 1960s.

The last question to be addressed is whether the economic model, by bringing forth such tremendous socioeconomic contradictions, caused the political crisis in Nicaragua, as some neo-Marxists maintain. Average real wages fell during the 1970s; by 14 percent from 1972 to 1978 (Vilas 1986:129). It is likely that the deteriorating situation of many people stimulated them to join the armed resistance against the dictatorship. But it is too much to assume that socioeconomic factors provoked the insurrection.

### *Conclusion*

The growth and industrialization model of the CACM countries was not in crisis during the 1970s. Terms of trade fell in the early 1970s but recovered in the second half of the decade for most countries. The small decline in manufacturing growth rates in the early 1970s must be explained by rising production costs. In those countries not affected by serious political crises, manufacturing growth rates recovered in the later 1970s. In Nicaragua it was the political crisis

TABLE 3.10 Nicaragua's Trade Cycles 1963–1979: Some Indicators (five-year annual averages and selected years, in millions of cordobas and in percent)

| | *1963-67* | *1968-72* | *1973-77* | *1978* | *1979* |
|---|---|---|---|---|---|
| GDP in 1958 prices | 3,766 | 4,708 | 6,129 | 6,337 | 4,790.7 |
| Growth rate of GDP | 9% | 3% | 6% | -7% | -24% |
| GDP in current prices | 3,896 | 5,499 | 11,810 | 14,995 | 13,409 |
| Investment | 803 | 937 | 2,766 | 1,850 | -188 |
| Public investment | 185 | 237 | 937 | 867 | 530 |
| Private investment | 535 | 636 | 1,599 | 1,265 | 581 |
| Inventory variations | 83 | 64 | 231 | -282 | -1,300 |
| Relations: | | | | | |
| Investment/GDP | 20% | 17% | 24% | 12% | -1% |
| Public inv./GDP | 5% | 4% | 8% | 6% | 4% |
| Private inv./GDP | 14% | 12% | 14% | 8% | 4% |

*Source:* Central Bank of Nicaragua 1980. *Indicadores económicos 1960–1979*. Managua.

that brought about the economic problems of 1978 and 1979—not the reverse.

Table 3.10 shows the trade cycles of 1960–1979 for Nicaragua's economy. From 1973 to 1977 the growth rate of the economy was even higher than during 1968–1972.[9] In 1978 and 1979 growth rates were negative and an enormous capital flight occurred. During these years the political crisis was at its height.

Although the development model of the region was beneficial for economic growth and industrialization, some characteristics of this model proved to cause problems after 1979, when the Sandinista government seized power in Nicaragua. First, there was the dependence on the agricultural export sector. In 1979 the second "oil crisis" occurred. This time the rise in industrial prices was not accompanied by a rise in the prices for primary goods. Consequently, the favorable price developments of the region's export crops came to an end. This hampered the possibilities for industrialization. Within the region the deterioration of external terms of trade for each of the countries brought about protective measures vis à vis the other countries, which seriously affected intraregional trade. As most intraregional trade consisted of manufactures, this was especially harmful for the industrial sector.

Second, the model was based on a very skewed distribution of land and of income. Tax pressure (the share of tax revenues in GDP) was low and most government revenues came from indirect taxes (see Table 3.11 for Nicaragua). In addition, the level of social services was

TABLE 3.11 Government Revenue and Expenditure 1960–1979: Some Indicators (five-year annual averages, in millions of cordobas and in percent)

| | *1960-64* | *1965-69* | *1970-74* | *1975-79* |
|---|---|---|---|---|
| Government revenue | 300 | 475 | 837 | 1,611 |
| Structure of revenue: | | | | |
| Direct taxes | 14% | 21% | 17% | 21% |
| Indirect taxes | 77% | 68% | 70% | 67% |
| On foreign trade | 52% | 34% | 32% | 25% |
| Other indirect taxes | 26% | 34% | 37% | 41% |
| Other government income | 9% | 11% | 13% | 13% |
| Government expenditure | 284 | 526 | 1,083 | 2,413 |
| Structure of expenditure: | | | | |
| Current expenditure | 74% | 74% | 59% | 61% |
| Capital expenditure | 27% | 26% | 41% | 40% |
| Surplus (+) or deficit (-) | 16 | -51 | -246 | -837 |
| Relations: | | | | |
| Revenue/GDP | 11% | 10% | 12% | 12% |
| Expenditure/GDP | 10% | 12% | 15% | 17% |
| Deficit (+)/GDP | 0% | 1% | 3% | 6% |
| Deficit/Expenditure | -6% | 10% | 23% | 35% |

*Source:* Central Bank of Nicaragua 1980. *Indicadores económicos 1960–1979*. Managua. Tables 2.4, 4.1, and 4.3.

very low. One of the objectives for the revolutionary government obviously would be to improve the distribution of income, for example, by carrying out a land reform, and to expand social services. This would lead to problems for the government budget. Increasing taxes or reducing government expenditures could prove difficult for political reasons. The same applies to a substantial land reform. In addition, a redistribution policy with respect to land and income could affect the basis of the economic model, thus reducing growth possibilities.

The civil war waged in the country in 1978 and 1979 complicated these problems. Decapitalization and other forms of capital flight exhausted the country's foreign-exchange reserves and reduced the available amount of working capital. This was to have serious consequences for the reactivation of the manufacturing industry, as this sector used a relatively high proportion of raw materials in production.

The war itself brought about enormous losses to production and damage to the infrastructure. This would also have long-term consequences. The reduction in the number of cattle and the fall in cotton production, to mention only two, increased the import dependence of the manufacturing industry. After 1979, the excess of imports over exports of the manufacturing sector was estimated at $80 million; the excess was $16 million in 1974 at the same level of production (Weeks 1985b:287).

## Economic Control in Nicaragua

The three views differ regarding the distribution of economic power in the society. The structuralists speak of weak states dominated by a traditional agrarian bourgeoisie. The neoclassical opinion apparently is that the political influence of the industrial bourgeoisie on the state has been too strong. Neo-Marxists maintain that most of domestic economic power is in the hands of foreign corporations. With regard to these issues I limit the discussion to Nicaragua.

### *Foreign Capital*

Until 1960 the presence of foreign capital in the Nicaraguan economy was limited. Foreign capital was active in trading and financing Nicaragua's export crops but not in direct production. During the 1960s foreign investment in Nicaragua expanded enormously, benefiting from high profit margins in the manufacturing industry. Most of the foreign enterprises were from the United States, but gradually more European, Canadian, and Japanese firms began investing in the country. But Nicaragua still had the lowest share of total direct foreign investment in the CACM countries, 12.2 percent at the end of 1967 and 9.4 percent at the end of 1975 (Castillo Rivas 1980a:185, based on figures from DAC/OECD). Unlike the other countries of the region, most of this investment was in the manufacturing industry.

The influence of foreign capital on agriculture was greater than the mere control of direct production indicates. Foreign commercial enterprises bought most export crops (coffee, cotton, sesame, and part of the tobacco crop) in almost raw form to be processed in the industrialized countries. Foreign capital was also involved in local agricultural export production through financing that often used local banks. In addition, large foreign corporations dominated the production and trade of agricultural inputs such as seeds, pesticides, and machinery (Barry and Preusch 1986:144-61). They supplied the local market either through local business houses (which were locally owned or were joint ventures with a foreign supplier) or through establishing manufacturing firms in the country.

In the manufacturing industry, foreign investment represented 25 percent of total fixed assets in Nicaragua in 1980 (CIERA/UNRISD 1984:64). According to ECLAC, foreign corporations in the Central American region dominated the most dynamic branches within industry, such as food, beverages and tobacco, and chemicals and also played an important role in intraregional exports (ECLAC 1982). According to CIERA/UNRISD (1984), the industrial branches with the highest foreign presence in Nicaragua were metal products, chemicals and oil products, food, beverages and tobacco and textiles. As Table 3.2 shows, these branches had fairly high growth rates during the 1960s and 1970s, but not the highest. The highest growth rates were experienced in machinery and equipment, paper and paper products and transport equipment. In these sectors foreign presence was much lower. But the branches with the most outstanding foreign presence were the largest in Nicaraguan manufacturing industry, as Table 3.6 indicates. For Nicaragua it seems that foreign corporations were relatively most active in the most important industrial branches, albeit not the most dynamic ones.

The industrial sectors that had the highest presence of foreign capital in Nicaragua were found to have the highest labor productivity and the highest import content. No relationship existed between sectors with high foreign presence and a high level of exports to Central America (CIERA/UNRISD 1984:64-7). However, these findings at the branch level are not very representative. The foreign oil refinery, which produced only for the domestic market, for example, belonged to chemicals and oil products and had a downward impact on the export level of this branch. And the food, beverages, and tobacco branch contained such diverse industries as (locally grown) tobacco processing for domestic and foreign markets, refining of locally grown sugar for export, and milling of imported grain for the domestic market. To assess the exact influence of foreign capital in manufacturing industry, a more detailed analysis is necessary.

Direct foreign investment in the processing of agricultural export crops was still rare. The initial processing of sugar, cotton, and coffee was in local hands, as were the beef slaughterhouses. All tobacco processing for cigarette production, however, was in foreign hands; only a small cigar factory was local. There was one foreign dairy processing plant along with five domestic plants, but the foreign plant was the only supplier of export-quality dried milk. Foreign investment was important in some second-stage processing industries such as instant coffee manufacturing and vegetable oil production from cotton seed. There was also substantial foreign investment in industries producing food and beverages for the domestic market, for example, the milling of imported grain and soft drink production. Foreign enterprises dominated the production of metal products and were important in the production of pesticides for agricultural production. These types of industries had a high import content and exported a large share of production to the regional market.

The facts that foreign investment was particularly found in industry and that there seemed to be a relationship between foreign domination and labor productivity confirm the earlier hypothesis that foreign investment is important in helping a country obtain modern production technology. From the available information, however, it cannot be concluded that foreign companies had replaced domestic entrepreneurship in Nicaragua.

### *The State*

The role of the Nicaraguan state cannot be described separately from the activities of the Somoza family—almost uninterruptedly in power from 1936 to 1979. Unlike other dictators, father and sons Somoza stimulated capitalist development of the country enormously. Their policies included extensive road building which facilitated access to land; greater credits to export producers; a favorable exchange-rate policy for investors; tariff and pricing policies that stimulated investment in labor-saving machinery and the use of yield-increasing inputs; and publicly subsidized provision of irrigation and research as well as storage, processing, and marketing facilities (Biderman 1983:14-9). With foreign loans and subsidized prices, cotton production, for example, was increasingly mechanized after 1950, particularly the preharvest activities.

Somoza founded the state bank Banco Nacional de Nicaragua and later also established the Instituto de Fomento Nacional (National Development Institute; INFONAC) to provide loans, technical assistance, and subsidized irrigation. These financial institutions also promoted industrial investment by providing cheap credits.

At the same time, the Somoza family used the state machinery to enrich its members. The family often was one of the main beneficiaries of state policies. Half the subsidies for irrigated and mechanized rice production went to Somoza and his direct associates. In the manufacturing industry, Somoza was especially active in industries that enjoyed preferential fiscal conditions. He owned the largest textile factories in the country, a paper mill, and the fisheries industries. Somoza was the largest landowner and also specialized in processing and marketing activities. The Somoza clan owned most of the export beef slaughterhouses and controlled half of sugar production, owning five of the six sugar refineries.

Foreign investors always had to give Somoza a share in the enterprise to be founded in exchange for tax exemptions. After the earthquake of 1972, Somoza established a private bank, the Banco Centroamericano, and a finance company. The family also expanded its interests in land development and construction companies, thus absorbing a large proportion of foreign aid.

As a result of the policies of the Somoza government, a large share of government expenditure consisted of capital spending, as Table 3.11 shows. Current expenditure was limited not only relative to capital expenditure but also in absolute terms. The army was small and social services such as health, public education, and drinking water were scarce (de Groot and Ruben 1982:72; Jung 1980:67-8). Only 20 to 30 percent of the Nicaraguan population could use health services. According to official data, illiteracy among the adult population was as high as 43 percent, and it was probably higher. In the countryside only 6 percent of the population was connected with the drinking water system. Life expectancy in Nicaragua was the lowest of the whole region: 53-55 years (Biderman 1983:21).

In the 1970s, Somoza attracted foreign speculative capital to develop tourism, hotels, and casinos (Black 1981:41). In addition, he expanded public investment (see Tables 3.9 and 3.10). The share of capital expenditure in total government expenditure even increased in the 1970s. Expanded capital spending probably caused the fiscal deficits that started to appear. During the 1960s, the government had more or less maintained a balanced budget.

With respect to revenues, it is clear from Table 3.11 that establishment of the CACM led to a sharp reduction of taxes on foreign trade. Still, indirect taxes remained the most important source of government income. The share of direct taxes in GDP was low. Nicaragua's income tax had the lowest rates and most generous personal deductions among Central American countries. Even with these low rates there was widespread evasion. Profit margins in the Nicaraguan manufacturing industry were the highest in the region (Biderman 1983:25).

With such low current expenditure levels and tax rates, the government bureaucracy was limited. This implies that the Nicaraguan state was "efficient" and not "bureaucratic," as neoclassicists maintain. But the state was not very active in fostering education and health services, in providing housing, and in constructing infrastructure in regions that were not directly productive. Government policy did not stimulate long-term economic and social development.

From the viewpoint of the bourgeoisie, however, the state appears to have had a modernizing effect. Capitalist development was heavily promoted, and the high growth rates of the economy in the 1950s, 1960s, and 1970s can be ascribed partly to state policies. Large producers in both agriculture and industry benefited from these state policies. They enjoyed income tax and import duty reductions, could finance current production and investment with cheap credits, which were available in large amounts, and there were no restrictions on profit remittances abroad. Small producers did not have access to credits and other facilities. The government maintained low food prices, which permitted a low wage level. Furthermore, the National Guard was always present to suppress labor conflicts. Labor unions hardly existed, and official minimum wages were evaded on a large scale. The Somoza family itself was the main beneficiary of these state policies.

After the Sandinista victory, when the properties of Somoza and his direct associates were nationalized, his group proved to have economic assets worth about 25 percent of GDP (19 percent of agricultural production, 25 percent of industrial production, 30 percent of construction, and 24 percent of commerce and other services) (Black 1981:202).

### *The Local Bourgeoisie*

Apparently, the bourgeoisie did not dominate direct agricultural production. Large producers accounted for the largest share of production only in rice and sugar (Table 3.12). Most other agricultural production came from small and medium producers. Small peasants were important producers of corn and beans and were the most important cattle raisers and milk producers. However, the small group of large producers owned almost all processing plants. Smaller producers depended on these large producers and on intermediaries for credit, marketing, and inputs.

As for the manufacturing industry, the figures indicate that direct production was much more concentrated. In 1979, the enterprises employing more than fifty workers, which constituted 12 percent of the total number of factories, produced 87 percent of manufacturing value added. The enterprises employing more than thirty workers produced more than 90 percent of total value added (INEC 1982). Seventy-five percent of total industrial workers worked in enterprises of the latter size. However, manufacturing enterprises of less than five workers are not included in these figures. In 1971, 60 percent of the labor force worked in these small enterprises (Central Bank of Nicaragua, Informe Anual 1971, cited in PREALC 1973). But the squeeze in

TABLE 3.12 Nicaragua: Weight in Production of Major Strata of Producers Before 1979 (in percent)[a]

| | *Small* | *Medium* | *Large* | *Total* |
|---|---|---|---|---|
| Cotton | 6 | 52 | 42 | 100 |
| Coffee | 22 | 58 | 20 | 100 |
| Bovine cattle | 52 | 29 | 19 | 100 |
| Sugarcane | 4 | 18 | 78 | 100 |
| Rice | 9 | 18 | 73 | 100 |
| Sorghum | 34 | 28 | 38 | 100 |
| Corn | 32 | 57 | 11 | 100 |
| Beans | 59 | 38 | 3 | 100 |
| Total | 25 | 45 | 30 | 100 |

[a]Percentages are approximate and must be interpreted as "images" of reality rather than statistical data. "Small" producers are here defined as having farms up to 35 hectares, "medium" producers, from 35 to 350 hectares, and "large" producers, more than 350 hectares. In the case of cattle-raising "small" is up to 140 hectares, "medium," from 140 to 700 hectares, and "large," more than 700 hectares.

*Source:* Baumeister, E. 1985. "The Structure of Nicaraguan Agriculture and the Sandinista Agrarian Reform." In *Nicaragua, a Revolution under Siege*, ed. R. L. Harris and C. M. Vilas. London: Zed Books, 17. Reprinted by permission.

industrial profit margins during the 1970s brought about an enormous concentration in manufacturing (Bulmer-Thomas 1987:209). In 1980 the Ministry of Industry did a survey of manufacturing establishments employing fewer than thirty workers. Only 37 percent of total industrial workers were found to work in these small plants, and they produced 18 percent of total gross industrial production (Vilas 1986:96). This implies that the larger enterprises employing thirty or more workers accounted for 82 percent of total gross industrial production.

On the basis of these figures, the bourgeoisie can be located in finance, the manufacturing industry and, with respect to agriculture, mainly in marketing and processing activities. The question now becomes whether there was a division of economic power between different groups of capitalists and along what lines the division occurred.

According to several studies, apart from the Somoza clan two big business groups dominated the Nicaraguan bourgeoisie, along with some smaller groups (Strachan 1976; Wheelock Román 1980). These business groups were conglomerates of families that worked together closely and owned, or had interests in enterprises in several economic sectors. One of the two big groups consisted of large cotton growers, who established the Banco Nicaragüense in 1953. This group was connected with the liberal faction of the bourgeoisie, originally based in the city of León. The group invested in cotton gins, in business houses that imported foreign machinery and other inputs for production, and in cotton seed processing plants. They also grew coffee and had coffee processing plants, started a savings and loan association and an insurance company, and had interests in construction activities. In manufacturing they owned the largest brewery of the country, among other factories.

The other large group was formed around the Banco de América, which was also established in 1953. This group originally represented the sugar and cattle interests, as well as the big business houses that historically were located in the conservative city of Granada. Apart from agricultural and commercial interests they owned construction industries and land development companies, as well as a number of industrial factories.

On the basis of research work carried out by Strachan in the early 1970s, the two main groups were relatively most active in finance and construction (of these sectors they controlled respectively 68 percent and 71 percent of value added). In industry, agriculture, and trade they controlled respectively 25 percent, 22 percent, and 35 percent. In absolute terms however, trade, agriculture, and industry absorbed larger portions of their activities (Strachan 1976:50). Of total GDP they directly controlled 20 percent. Adding the firms over which they had a potential indirect control (e.g., by means of outstanding debts with the finance institutions of the group), they controlled almost 40 percent of GDP.

Both groups also had links with foreign capital. In 1966 the Wells Fargo Bank bought a minority interest in the Banco de América and founded, together with members of the group, a holding company with shares in finance companies, an insurance company, and several construction material businesses (Strachan 1976:10). In the early 1970s the First National Bank of Boston also established links with the Banco de América. The Chase Manhattan Bank and the Morgan Guarantee Trust, among others, had interests in the Banco Nicaragüense. Members of both groups established many other finance, construction, and industrial enterprises as joint ventures with North American multinationals (Wheelock Román 1980:154-6,162-3).

The Somoza clan also operated more and more as a business group. Contrary to the other groups, Somoza was able to use the state machinery for his private businesses. He also specialized in illegal activities. He used his fisheries fleet for drug traffic, for example, and his family owned a blood plasma factory for which they drew blood from prisoners, draining them to death.

Strachan showed business groups to be a normal phenomenon in many countries in the process of industrialization (Japan, India, Chile, Mexico, for example). He found from interviews with thirty managers from the two main groups that of many potential services group members can provide each other, the financial intermediary service was the most important in Nicaragua. Group members reduced the risks of new undertakings by financing through a commonly owned bank or finance company. It is likely that the existence of these groups fostered domestic savings and contributed to the development of a financial sector in Nicaragua.

Marín (1971) came to the same conclusions regarding financing practices in Nicaragua. He noted a big difference between the 1950s and 1960s with respect to the financing of industrial investment. In the 1950s, bank credits were mainly used for agriculture and trade; industrial investments were financed out of savings. In the 1960s and 1970s, financial intermediaries began to play an important role in industry. The big business groups established a number of finance companies. Two-thirds of new industrial investment was then financed by loans from these intermediaries. Agriculture and commercial activities were still financed by commercial credits.

Probably the easy access to cheap credits was an important reason for the low rates of reinvestment in Nicaragua (Biderman 1983:25-6). Marín, for example, showed that 67 percent of industrial profits gained between 1965 and 1968 was paid in dividends. In his opinion, dividends were used to satisfy consumer demands.

From the 1960s onward, all large producers in agriculture, trade, and manufacturing were dependent on the services of finance institutions. Apparently, the risks in undertaking industrial activities were considered greater than those in agriculture. Agricultural producers could easily get loans from the banks; industrial investment depended on the financial cooperation of various capitalists who made their "hard money" in agriculture.

### *Conclusion*

Before 1979, economic power in Nicaragua was divided among the Somoza clan, a few big business groups, and foreign capital. All had relatively weak interests in direct agricultural production. The only crops in which local capitalists and Somoza had an important share were irrigated rice and sugar. Somoza and the rest of the local bourgeoisie were heavily involved in activities closely related to agriculturalral production: finance and processing. Foreign corporations were important in the deliveries of inputs for agriculture, in marketing, and partly in finance. The control of these activities related to agricultural production was highly concentrated.

In the manufacturing industry, the degree of concentration in direct production was much higher. Economic power was divided among foreign corporations (which represented about 25 percent of production), Somoza (also 25 percent of production), and other local capitalists. In the early 1970s, the two big business groups also controlled 25 percent of manufacturing production. In construction, Somoza and the other local business groups were in competition with each other.

There did not seem to be a fundamental conflict of interest between the industrial and the agricultural entrepreneurs. Both could benefit from favorable state policies with respect to taxes and credits. The business groups were active in all sectors of the national economy. However, agricultural producers could easily get commercial loans; industrial investors depended on loans from finance companies in which various capitalists worked together. This difference proved to be important for the attitude of the different large producers after the victory of the Sandinistas, when the financial system was nationalized.

There was a clear contradiction, though, between large producers on the one hand and small and medium producers and wage workers on the other. The latter did not benefit from state policies, and the effect of the high growth rates of GDP on their incomes was minimal.

In the course of the decade, an intrabourgeoisie conflict appeared. After the earthquake in 1972, Somoza benefited much more than the other groups from the construction boom, using foreign-aid funds to enrich himself. The possibilities for profit making for the other groups were reduced, and they were more and more dissatisfied with the situation. This was one of the causes for the increasing capital flight at the end of the 1970s and also contributed to the possibility of a change in power.

The division of economic power in the Nicaraguan economy before 1979 was an important determinant for the possibility of the Sandinista government's controlling the economy. First, the fact that a large share of the economy was in the hands of the Somoza family would seem to have provided the new government with a profitable state sector. In practice, the quality of Somoza's possessions was disappointing, as he had decapitalized many of them and even ordered the bombing of his own factories when he perceived his situation as hopeless.

More important for the possibility of controlling the economy was the fact that all large producers proved to be dependent on loans and credits from finance institutions. Therefore, nationalization of the banking system in 1979 was to be an important instrument. The great dependence on imports in the manufacturing industry and in the agricultural export sector would further enhance control possibilities.

A large part of the economy would not be easily controlled. These were the small producers in agriculture, trade, and handicrafts, who were not dependent on imports or on credits. The fact that foreign—mainly U.S.—companies played an important role in the economy, in particular in manufacturing, would force the new leaders to pursue a cautious policy toward them and toward the U.S. government. The alternative would be to accept heavy losses in industrial production.

## Notes

1. Later on, this commission was called Economic Commission for Latin America and the Caribbean, ECLAC. For that reason, this book uses both ECLA and ECLAC.

2. For Nicaragua this is described in Wheelock Román (1980:chap. 6).

3. Traditional export products are coffee, cotton, sugar, bananas, and beef.

4. See, for example, D. Seers 1963. "The role of industry in development: Some fallacies." *Journal of Modern African Studies* 1, no. 4:461-5.

5. An empirical study on economic integration in developing countries shows that, to a certain extent, there are trade-offs between the objectives of growth and balanced development. See Robert N. Gwynne 1985. *Industrialization and urbanization in Latin America*. London: Croom Helm.

6. Local prices could not increase in the same proportion as imported input prices because several countries imposed price controls after the rise in oil prices in 1974 and because the region's products had to remain competitive with extraregional imports (Bulmer-Thomas 1987:209).

7. See ECLAC 1982. This included direct foreign investment (36 percent), reinvested earnings (27 percent), and external loans (37 percent). See Bulmer-Thomas 1987:191.

8. As Weeks also stated, the presence of foreign capital in underdeveloped countries should be considered to be a consequence of underdevelopment, not its cause. See J. Weeks 1977. "Backwardness, foreign capital, and accumulation in the manufacturing sector of Peru, 1954–1975." *Latin American Perspectives* 4, no. 3 (Summer):124-45.

9. Some adjustment must be made for the years 1973 and 1974 with exceptionally high growth rates after the earthquake in Managua of December 1972.

# 4

# The Mixed Economy

The Nicaraguan mixed economy was remarkably stable from 1979 to 1989. In 1989 the private sector still accounted for more than 50 percent of the GDP, and the market played an important role. The question is, however, whether destabilizing tendencies were at work. In Chapter 2, I deduced five factors that may influence the stability of a mixed economic order. In this chapter I show that the first factor—the ideology of the leaders and the reasons they opt for a mixed economy—did not affect the stability of the Nicaraguan mixed economy. With respect to the third factor—the price policy—my field work of 1984–1985 and 1988 shows that the state had access to sufficient instruments to influence a large share of private production and seemed to leave room for private accumulation.

Many participants in the public and academic debate about the feasibility and stability of the Sandinista mixed economy have doubted this stability. They pointed to one or the other factor as likely to have caused the end of the mixed order. I begin this chapter by presenting some different opinions in the debate.

1. The ideology of the leaders and the reasons they opt for a mixed economy. Some critics from the right argued that the Sandinistas would not maintain the mixed economy and that they only employed it as a tactical maneuver. According to these critics, speeches of the Sandinistas clearly pointed to the desirability of ending private ownership (see Cruz Sequeira 1983:150). This was also the opinion of the Nicaraguan employers' organization COSEP (Consejo Superior de la Empresa Privada; Superior Council of Private Enterprise). Others put it more mildly: "[although the government is giving incentives to the private sector] at the ideological level the possibility of a completely nationalized model has not been excluded" (Medal 1985:29). Often it was also said that the system could not be stable because there were no clearly defined "rules of the game" (see, for example, World Bank 1982:13).

2. The accumulation policy. From 1984 onward, many authors pointed to the high level of state accumulation in Nicaragua as one of the causes of the country's economic problems (see, for example, Díaz 1984; Pizarro 1987). The Nicaraguan government also recognized as early as 1983 that a lower accumulation rate was necessary (JGRN 1983) but maintained a high state accumulation rate in practice. Most of these publications considered the effect of the high accumulation rate on the macroeconomic balance (see further on). Irvin (1986) criticized the automatic "crowding out" of new private investment and the replacement of existing production capacity that resulted from the foreign-exchange assignment system.

3. The price policy. For a long time, participants in the Nicaraguan debate paid more attention to the effects of the foreign-exchange policy and much less to the price policy in general. The overvaluation of the cordoba was often seen as a cause for the macroeconomic disequilibrium because it stimulated imports and discouraged exports (Pizarro 1987). The linkage between domestic prices and international prices had also been broken because of the system of multiple exchange rates (see also Medal 1985:32 and Medal 1988:77-78).

Some authors did refer to the price policy, arguing, for example, that state price policies lacked "coherence" (Coraggio 1985:17) or "coordination" (FitzGerald 1985b:8). But they seemed to refer more to the implementation of the price policy and did not touch upon more fundamental issues. Other authors pointed to the negative effects on private production of the alleged deterioration of the terms of trade for the agricultural sector (Cruz Sequeira 1983:147; Medal 1985:40; Utting 1987:133).

In later years critics began to point to errors in the pricing of, for example, basic grains, which had also caused the macroeconomic disequilibrium and had led to less, instead of more, economic planning (Kaimowitz 1989). The economic reform measures of February and June 1988 reflected the official recognition that the state was not able to control all prices, that wrong prices had often caused serious economic distortions, and that the price policy had had negative consequences for the possibilities of private acumulation for small and medium peasants in particular.

4. The attitude and behavior of large private producers. Many authors pointed to the lack of political willingness of large private producers to continue producing in Nicaragua's mixed economy. This affected the stability of the mixed economy, as the government would be forced to nationalize those producers. Coraggio (1986), for example, maintained that the problem was the bourgeoisie's lack of

acceptance of its loss of political power. Many authors argued that the incentives given to private producers had merely been losses for the state, as private producers had not used these incentives productively.[1]

Later on, some other opinions were raised on this issue. According to IHCA (1987), some large private producers were either positive about the revolution or made their cooperation dependent on the incentives given. Other authors argued that large producers in manufacturing were willing to maintain production; Castillo (1987) maintained this in general and Austin and Ickis (1986) for managers of foreign enterprises in particular.

5. External factors. It is clear that for Nicaragua, the war waged by the contras and financed by the U.S. government affected the possibilities of maintaining a mixed economy. Foreign aid and credits from capitalist and socialist countries were also affected. In the Nicaraguan debate, FitzGerald in particular (for instance in 1987) emphasized the effects of the war on the functioning of the Nicaraguan mixed economy.

## Ideology

### *The FSLN in Power*

The struggle against the dictatorship of the Somoza family started in an organized manner in 1961 with the founding of the FSLN (Frente Sandinista para la Liberación Nacional; Sandinista Front for National Liberation). For a long time, the FSLN was only a small guerrilla movement. Whenever it achieved some success, it was smashed by severe repression. After the Somoza-inspired murder of opposition newspaper director Chamorro in January 1978, the resistance against Somoza grew. In June 1978 the FSLN formed the MPU (Movimiento Popular Unido; United People's Movement) to direct spontaneous popular insurrections (Black 1981:120). The power of the bourgeois opposition parties weakened. The previously formed FAO (Frente Amplio de Oposición; Broad Opposition Front), which included those parties, split in January 1979 when the leftist political parties and the Group of Twelve[2] joined the FSLN and the MPU to create the FPN (Frente Patriotico Nacional; National Patriotic Front).

Despite their limited strength, the rightist political parties and the representatives of the business class continued to attempt a *Somocismo* without Somoza, perpetuating Somoza's National Guard and excluding the FSLN in a new Nicaraguan government. On June 2, 1979, when the FSLN victory was near, the U.S. ambassador, in cooperation with what was left of the FAO, proposed a seven-member junta dominated by the rightist sectors to replace Somoza. The junta included a representative of the National Guard and allowed only one representative of the FSLN/FPN.

In reaction, the FSLN proposed its own junta with participation of the different sectors of the Nicaraguan society that had cooperated in the struggle against Somoza. Of the five members, one was a member of the traditional Conservative party, one was the widow of Chamorro (the former director of the opposition newspaper *La Prensa*) and one was Alfonso Robelo, leader of the rightist political party MDN (Movimiento Democrático Nacional; National Democratic Movement) and representative of the bourgeoisie. The other two members were Sandinistas: Sergio Ramírez of the Group of Twelve and Daniel Ortega of the FSLN. This National Reconstruction Government was proclaimed in Costa Rica on June 16. On July 19 it started its operations after being symbolically installed by Tomás Borge of the FSLN. The FSLN had exclusive power over the army and police. It was clear that, at that moment, the FSLN held real power in Nicaragua, the junta being its executive authority (Black 1981:171).

The FSLN remained the most important political power in the country until February 1990. To maintain the political support of the masses, the FSLN had to carry out ideological and organizational work (Castillo Rivas 1980b). In the organizational work the FSLN consolidated its power rapidly. It used the support of the people to set up FSLN-inspired mass organizations (women's and youth organizations, neighborhood committees, and labor unions). After one year, 600,000 people had become members of mass organizations. Apparently, the ideological work also was successful during the first years. In the November 1984 elections the FSLN obtained the support of a large majority of the population. Daniel Ortega, one of the *comandantes* of the front, became the legally elected president of the country.

### *The FSLN's Ideology*

The leading ideology of the FSLN is *Sandinismo*. It is based on the ideas of the popular leader of the 1930s, Sandino,[3] and was later elaborated upon by one of the founders of the FSLN, Carlos Fonseca. Among the core themes of Sandino's ideas, agreed upon by Fonseca and by the historian and vice president from 1984 to 1990 Sergio Ramírez, are the following (NACLA 1985:19, italics mine): *anti-imperialism*, which implies an end to all political and economic dependency on the United States and to all treaties that injure Nicaragua's interests; an independent government that meets the needs of the *peasantry and the working class*; a preference for *non-capitalist forms of economic organization*, with an emphasis on *cooperatives*.

In the footsteps of Sandino, the ideology of the FSLN has a strong nationalistic, anti-imperialistic component. The anti-imperialism is directed against the domination of the U.S. government rather than against the presence of U.S. firms in the country. Although some FSLN leaders are Marxists, Sandinismo is not the same as Marxism or Leninism (Harris 1985a:6). The Sandinista idea of *popular hegemony* does not mean that it strives after the dictatorship of the proletariat (see Chapter 2). Instead, it seeks to exert state power in the interests of workers *and* peasants. The Sandinista leaders are influenced much more by Latin American structuralist thought than by Marxism (see also Chapter 3). Like other structuralists, they advocate land reform and cooperativization and are convinced of the necessity and feasibility of planned industrialization.

However, many FSLN leaders' speeches during the first years were full of classist rhetoric (Vilas 1986). The intention appeared to be to impose class consciousness on workers and peasants; they had to see the FSLN as their vanguard and the large producers as their natural adversaries—guilty of exploitation. The real power, the Sandinista leaders used to say, belongs to workers and peasants. "Now, the workers and peasants are the ones who grant concessions to the classes which have been expelled from the power of this country" (Borge 1981). "Here other sectors that are not Sandinista subsist, but only in so far as this power [the Sandinismo] allows them to, and in so far as they really do not affect the revolutionary project" (H. Ortega in FSLN 1981:90).

During the struggle against Somoza, the mixed economy as a characterization of the "new society" already appeared as an objective, for example, in the fifteen-point program of the MPU. The program called for nationalization of the possessions of Somoza, the banking system, and natural resources. At the same time, it stressed the need to provide "guarantees" encouraging the private sector to produce and invest. The program of the national reconstruction government was based on the keywords "political pluralism," "international nonalignment," and "mixed economy."

The essence of the plan for a mixed economy was the idea that workers, peasants, and employers had to cooperate in the reactivation of the economy. The FSLN leaders' speeches stressed "national unity" based on nationalism (Carrión 1981). They generally distinguished a *patriotic* bourgeoisie (cooperating in the new structure) from a bourgeoisie *vendepatria* (not producing and thereby robbing their country). Employers who accepted the "logic of the majority" (Gorostiaga

1982:195) as the guiding principle of state economic policy and continued to produce were praised. The term "mixed economy" reflected in this respect the "philosophy that the riches produced are redistributed in favor of the large mass of workers of our country" (D. Ortega in FSLN 1981).

Contradictions appeared in FSLN ideology regarding the desired economic order. Many speeches of FSLN leaders, especially during the first years, stressed the leading role of workers and peasants and condemned capitalist exploitation. But many leaders also advocated national unity in which workers, peasants, and the bourgeoisie would cooperate to increase production. It proved difficult to reconcile the two FSLN objectives—consolidating its power and maintaining a mixed economy—for the short term. Maintaining a mixed economy required private producers to have some confidence in their long-term position in Nicaragua. The class rhetoric of the FSLN speeches was likely to frighten parts of the bourgeoisie, causing them to conclude that the mixed economy was only a tactical maneuver and would be set aside in due course.

### *Why a Mixed Economy?*

Given that, according to the Sandinistas, the real power was in the hands of workers and peasants, why did they allow a large sector of private producers to continue? This private sector consisting of large and small producers accounted for about one-third of the GDP.

About 50 percent of the economically active population of Nicaragua were small peasants, artisans, or traders, and there was not much discussion about the maintenance of these private small producers. The Nicaraguan leaders adhered to the theoretical argument put forward by Bettelheim: An effective socialization of small and dispersed units of production is not possible; the division of labor must be more advanced (Bettelheim 1975; see also Chapter 1). Wheelock, one of the comandantes, stated: "According to the theory of scientific socialism, for one mode of production to prosper in mathematic form into another, it requires at least the full ripeness of the mode of production to be substituted." (Wheelock Román 1985:23) Fidel Castro also used this underdevelopment argument when he warned the Sandinistas not to nationalize the small production and service sector.[4]

The maintenance of large private producers was less obvious, but several reasons made a mixed economy in this respect desirable. First of all, there was a practical argument. The nationalization of Somoza's possessions had passed on a production potential for about one quarter of GDP into state hands. From one day to the next, the government had to administer a large number of agricultural, industrial, and service enterprises. The task to develop a management and administration system for the confiscated enterprises was hard enough (Irvin 1983:27-8). With more nationalizations, an effective administration of state firms would have been almost impossible.

Secondly, there were political reasons—both domestic and international. The new government leaned on the support of a broad coalition of almost all former anti-Somoza opposition. Although the FSLN had proved to be the strongest in the military struggle, it was not capable of organizing the society and the economy on its own. More nationalizations would have strangled large groups of the middle class and the bourgeoisie, whose cooperation was necessary to build up and reactivate the economy.

In the international scene it was important to receive support from as many countries and organizations as possible. The economy was nearly bankrupt and the country needed immediate imports of foodstuffs, medicines, etc. Attempts at more nationalizations would have minimized aid from the international community, now conceded in large amounts during the first months after Somoza's overthrow.

The third argument to maintain a mixed economy was of a geopolitical nature. As Tomás Borge pointed out in an interview with *Pensamiento Propio*: "The geopolitical factor has forced us, independently from our will, to develop political pluralism and a mixed economy" (INIES 1985:8). Nicaragua is not an island; it has borders with Costa Rica and Honduras and is a member of the Central American Common Market. The intensive trade and other relations with the neighboring countries impeded the establishment of an economic system completely different from that of those countries.

Nicaragua's location on the Central American isthmus so close to the United States further inhibited great alterations from a capitalist system. Even a moderate mixed economy proved to be untolerable for the U.S. administration, and has led to open hostility and indirect warfare. Maintaining a mixed economy helped in continuing the support of other Western and Latin American countries, and also in preventing a direct U.S. military intervention against Nicaragua.

An alternative for this survival "balance" based on maintaining a mixed economy and political pluralism was hardly feasible. The Soviet Union did not seem willing to go as far in supporting Nicaragua as it has gone with Cuba. The costs of another economically dependent nation appeared to be too high. Furthermore, the geographical position of Nicaragua precluded any military or strategic advantages for the Soviet Union. However, the advantage for the USSR in supporting Sandinista Nicaragua was that it confronted the U.S. government. As long as the U.S. administration pursued the overthrow of the Sandinista government and was willing to spend significant resources to obtain this objective, it was in the interest of the Soviet Union to guarantee the military and economic survival of Nicaragua.

Nicaragua, for its part, did not want to be completely dependent of the Soviet Union for political and economic reasons. The goods the Soviet Union can provide not always suited Nicaragua's tropical, agrarian economy. Trade relations with, and the support of, Western countries continued to be necessary and were also important in maintaining positive influences on public opinion in the United States.

Some of the arguments for choosing a mixed economy appear to be of a short-term nature, in particular, the practical and the political arguments. Once the FSLN cadre would have been more numerous and would have been trained in management and other skills, a mixed economy would no longer be necessary. The internal political argument might lose its ground, when the FSLN would have consolidated its power to a larger extent.

The underdevelopment argument only applied to small-scale production. In theory, this argument also is of a short-term nature: once productive forces are more developed, large-scale nationalization is possible. In practice however, small-scale production would be a long-term characteristic of the Nicaraguan economy.

The geopolitical reason does play a role for large-scale production, and this argument appeared to be a lasting factor. As Borge put it: "The development of this tactic has converted itself into a strategy" (INIES 1985:8). The continuing military threat from the United States and the exhaustion strategy it pursued, made it all the more necessary that the Nicaraguan government received aid from as many countries as possible. In conclusion, the Sandinista leaders would in the short and medium term continue to adhere to a mixed economy, whatever economic system they might have liked to opt for in the future.

## The Mixed Economy in Practice

### *Ownership and Land Reform*

In July 1979 the new government announced Decree No. 3, which nationalized all property of Somoza. Decree No. 38 extended the nationalizations to producers that had had "close links" to Somoza. Since in the time of the dictatorship all producers had to collaborate with Somoza in order to survive, this last decree caused some confusion and the government had to cancel it (Vilas 1986:219). In practice,

TABLE 4.1 Nicaragua: Balance of Public and Private Ownership, 1978 and 1980 (share of GDP in percent)

| | *1978* | | *1980* | |
|---|---|---|---|---|
| | *Public* | *Private* | *Public* | *Private* |
| Agriculture | 0 | 100 | 19 | 81 |
| Industry | 0 | 100 | 25 | 75 |
| Construction | 40 | 60 | 70 | 30 |
| Mining | 0 | 100 | 99 | 1 |
| Services | 31 | 69 | 55 | 45 |
| Total GDP | 15 | 84 | 41 | 59 |

*Source:* Black, G. 1981. *Triumph of the people: The Sandinista Revolution in Nicaragua.* London: Zed Press, 202. Reprinted by permission.

nationalization was limited to owners who had fled the country. About 20 percent of arable land, and productive capacities for almost 25 percent of total material production came under state control. The government could do this without provoking opposition from the national non-Somocista bourgeoisie.

Other nationalizations involved the small and decapitalized foreign gold and silver mining companies. The government also nationalized the banks and other financial institutions. Foreign trade was effectively controlled by centralizing the most important exports and paying all export producers in local currency. Table 4.1 shows the result of this first wave of nationalizations. After 1980, the ownership structure changed slightly in favor of the APP (Area of People's Property) as a result of a somewhat higher growth rate in the state sector and some additional nationalizations of private enterprises.

Most nationalizations after 1980 took place on the basis of so-called decapitalization by the owner. Government Decree No. 330 of March 1980 forbade all types of decapitalization by private producers. It allowed for state intervention in the enterprise and announced fines and imprisonment for persons found guilty of decapitalization (Ramírez Suárez 1980). Decapitalization included activities such as not reporting to the Central Bank foreign exchange received, personal use of company accounts abroad, overbilling imports and underbilling exports, and other actions leading to capital flight. According to this decree, decapitalization had to be confirmed by the court. Sanctions, including nationalization of the enterprise involved, were also subject to a court decision to which appeal was possible.

On July 19, 1981, the government confiscated fifteen industrial, agricultural, and service enterprises by decree, on the basis of presumed decapitalization detected by the workers (Ministry of Justice 1982:33-4). In the industrial sector, the amount of confiscations after 1981 was limited (see Table 6.1 for the development of the ownership structure in manufacturing). In agriculture, however, the "battle" for juridical ownership rights continued.

An exception in the industrial sector was the June 1988 intervention in Nicaragua Sugar Estates Ltd., which included a large but decapitalized sugar mill and a highly profitable rum factory. The decapitalization of the sugar mill was at least partly due to the state policy of not assigning sufficient dollars for reinvestment purposes. Political motives probably also played a role in the intervention, as the family who owned Nicaragua Sugar Estates also possessed a bank in the United States which transferred funds to the contras.

In the Sandinista land reform policy some stages can be distinguished (Baumeister 1985a:53; Ruben, de Groot, and Wattel 1988). In the first stage, the policy gave most attention to establishing and consolidating state farms on the land confiscated from Somoza. Some state farms came to replace the CAS (Cooperativa Agraria Sandinista; Sandinista Agrarian Cooperative) formed on land captured from Somoza during the liberation war, because most of this land had produced export crops in a rather capitalistic way. Leaving these farms to the peasants implied the risk of a loss of export production, either by a switch to basic grains production or by a reduction in productivity. The government was also afraid that giving land to peasants would reduce the supply of labor to the coffee and cotton harvests. Moreover, it assumed that the establishing of state farms would allow the wage-earning (proletarianized) labor force to grow, implying historical progress (Collins 1985:80).

The government stimulated the forming of cooperatives. It saw cooperatives as a superior form of work organization because they enhance the spirit of solidarity and cooperation between human beings and overcome relations of competition and exploitation (MIDINRA 1983:26). In addition, peasants participating in cooperatives would have a better access to bank credits, social services, equipment, and technical assistance. Learning from other experiences, the government carried out this policy in a voluntary manner, mainly by giving financial incentives such as a lower interest rate. Most cooperatives had one of the following forms: CASs, in which the land was collectively owned, and CCSs (Cooperativas de Crédito y Servicios; Credit and Service Cooperatives), in which the land was individually owned but the peasants worked together in obtaining credits, inputs, or machinery, or in commercialization.

By June 1980 some 1,185 CCS had been organized among small and medium property owners and about 1,300 CAS had been formed (Deere 1981:197). Hardly any of the CAS' members were former peasants who had owned their own land; most were former renters or landless peasants who had received land in the land reform (Collins 1985:102).

The second phase of the agrarian reform started on July 19, 1981, when the Agrarian Reform Law was proclaimed. This law guaranteed the ownership of the land to all who "productively and efficiently" used it. Since the law did not clearly define this concept of productivity and efficiency, the state obtained a considerable amount of decision-making power (FitzGerald 1985c). Confiscation was apt to affect owners of land of more than 500 manzanas[5] in the Pacific region and 1000 manzanas in the Atlantic region, who left the land idle, deficiently exploited it or rented it in whatever form; of land of more than 50 manzanas in the Pacific region and 100 manzanas in the Atlantic region that was not directly worked by the owner but was rented for cash or labor or sharecropped; and of abandoned land of whatever size (Ministry of Justice 1982:58-68).

Compared to land reform laws proclaimed in other Latin American countries (Peru, Chile), these limits were fairly high, in particular in the Atlantic region. The reason is that Nicaragua, in comparison, is not densely populated. In fact, the Sandinista government did not set limits on private landownership. Large landowners who continued to produce were not affected. All owners, except those who abandoned their land, received a small indemnity. The affected owners could appeal to special Agrarian Tribunes, but its members were named by the government. No appeal was possible against the verdict of these tribunes (Ministry of Justice 1982:155-7).

Cooperatives had to register themselves with MIDINRA (Ministerio de Desarrollo Agropecuario y Reforma Agraria; Ministry of Agricultural and Livestock Development and Agrarian Reform) to get preferential treatment from the government institutions that supply the countryside, for example, with technical assistance and bank credits (Ministry of Justice 1982:139-49). The interest rate was lowest for production cooperatives and was also lower for service cooperatives than for individual peasants.

In 1981 and 1982 the number of confiscations on the basis of the Agrarian Reform Law was limited; only 4 percent of arable land was involved (see Table 4.2). One percent of the land passed into the hands of peasants and the rest went to the state sector (IHCA 1985a). In general, confiscations were carried out in keeping with the law, but there were some exceptions (Collins 1985).

This first and second stage of the land reform policy hardly

TABLE 4.2 Land Tenure in Nicaragua 1978–1988 (in percent)

| | *1978* | *1981* | *1982* | *1983* | *1984* | *1985* | *1986* | *1987* | *1988*[a] |
|---|---|---|---|---|---|---|---|---|---|
| Individual sector | 100 | 77 | 74 | 65 | 64 | 62 | 61 | 60 | 60 |
| Large producers (140 ha and more) | 52 | 30 | 28 | 26 | 26 | 24 | 22 | 22 | 21 |
| 350 ha and more | 36 | 15 | 13 | 13 | 13 | 11 | 10 | 10 | 9 |
| 140 to 350 | 16 | 15 | 15 | 13 | 13 | 13 | 12 | 12 | 12 |
| Medium producers (35 to 140 ha) | 30 | 30 | 30 | 30 | 30 | 30 | 30 | 30 | 30 |
| Small producers (less than 35 ha) | 18 | 17 | 17 | 9 | 9 | 9 | 9 | 9 | 9 |
| 7 to 35 ha | 16 | 15 | 15 | 7 | 7 | 7 | 7 | 7 | 7 |
| Less than 7 ha | 2 | 2 | 2 | 2 | 2 | 2 | 2 | 2 | 2 |
| Cooperative sector | 0 | 5 | 15 | 15 | 18 | 19 | 21 | 23 | 23 |
| CAS | 0 | 1 | 2 | 5 | 8 | 9 | 11 | 13 | 13 |
| CCS | 0 | 4 | 4 | 10 | 10 | 10 | 10 | 10 | 10 |
| State sector | 0 | 18 | 20 | 21 | 19 | 19 | 13 | 13 | 12 |
| Abandoned land[b] | 0 | 0 | 0 | 0 | 0 | 0 | 5 | 3 | 4 |
| Total[c] | 100 | 100 | 100 | 100 | 100 | 100 | 100 | 100 | 100 |

[a]Until May.
[b]From state farms; is apt to be redistributed.
[c]Total does not always sum up to 100%, due to rounding.

*Source:* MIDINRA, General Direction of Agrarian Reform (DGRA), 1988. Mimeo.

implied redistribution of land to small or landless peasants. The accent was on the preservation of large-scale production, in order not to affect the possibilities for accumulation. The government was careful not to annoy large private producers.

By mid-1983, the third stage of the land redistribution policy began. mainly under the pressure of the war: Disappointed peasants went over to the ranks of the U.S.-supported contras who fought a devastating war in large parts of the countryside. In the third stage, the government confiscated more land from large private landholders. Often this land redistribution meant a legalization of an existing situation: The peasants already used the land but now obtained more security.[6] The government also handed over some state farms to cooperatives of private peasants because the state farms proved to be inefficient. This was the first retreat from the policy of giving priority to large-scale production units.

In 1982 and 1983 private cooperatives received most of the land confiscated, but in 1984 more individual peasants benefited. Some peasants received legal ownership rights instead of user titles, which meant that they were allowed to sell their land. According to the minister of agriculture, Jaime Wheelock Román, the technological and cultural conditions necessary for successful production cooperatives did not yet exist.[7]

In the meantime, the pressure from landless peasants increased. In the densely populated region of Masaya in June 1985 there were peasant demonstrations and land occupations. In response, the government confiscated the land in Masaya, offering the landowners other land in a less densely populated region or, if they chose, an amount of money. All affected landowners except one accepted the deal (IHCA 1985a). This inaugurated a new phase in the land redistribution policy. More demonstrations occurred and more large private owners had to cede their land to small peasants. In addition, more state land went to small individual producers.

In January 1986 this fourth phase of the land redistribution policy was established formally with the announcement of the new Agrarian Reform Law. The government justified it by saying that the amount of land available for redistribution on the basis of the old law was not sufficient to meet with the land hunger of both landless peasants and peasant families displaced by the war. According to this new law, the following categories of land could be confiscated: all land of any size that was left idle, rented, or deficiently exploited; and land considered necessary to expropriate for reasons of "public utility" or "social interest," to be judged by MIDINRA.[8]

All absentee landownership could now be "punished" by confiscation—not only the land rented in precapitalistic forms. In addition, the state was no longer obliged to pay indemnities in case the land had been left idle. And the land could be given to individual peasants who guaranteed its efficient use. The law maintained the land was not tradable and could only be handed over by inheritance and in undivided parcels.

In the fourth phase, the share of large private owners declined a little further, from 24 percent in 1985 to 21 percent in 1988. But in fact, most redistributed land came from the state sector (Table 4.2). Apparently, most beneficiaries formed cooperatives. Especially during 1987 and 1988, the government does not seem to have expropiated large amounts of private land. In 1988 the government publicly stated it would no longer apply the land reform law. This policy was related to the signing of the Esquipulas II peace accords in August 1987, which made it again important to maintain good relations with the private sector. The gradual reduction of fighting during these years also diminished the pressure for land.

Overall, the Nicaraguan land reform was moderate. The share of the large landowners declined, but most of this reduction was due to the nationalization of the former lands of Somoza. The share of the medium producers (35 to 140) remained constant from 1978 to 1988. The share of small peasants diminished as many formed service cooperatives. Overall, the beneficiaries of the land reform shifted from state farms to mainly cooperatives and then to cooperatives and small private producers.

What the Sandinistas saw as the appropriate final distribution of land is not clear. Internal projections of MIDINRA of 1981/82 stipulated that, in due course, the share of state enterprises in total production would be about 25 percent and that of cooperatives 40 percent; 30 percent of total production would come from private medium and large farmers and 5 percent from small farmers (Collins et al. 1985:89). According to FitzGerald (1985c:213) the apparent intention was to have only state enterprises and cooperatives.

The practice from 1984 onward of giving land to private small producers conflicted with this long-term objective, however. By May 1988, individual producers cultivated 60 percent of the land. Land reform was not only the result of policy but also of changing circumstances. Once-stated objectives were substituted for others for the short and medium term.

In 1988 a debate began on whether it was possible to base agrarian development on the production of small peasants and cooperatives and whether it was a risk for the socialist state to stimulate profit-minded individual farmers.[9] An ownership structure of only collective forms (state farms and cooperatives), as seemed to be the long-term objective, would lead to another problem experienced by many other socialist countries; that of motivating the labor force. This problem could be partly solved if autonomous cooperatives dominated the socialized sector.

### *Administrating the State Sector*

Most former Somoza enterprises did not have good financial administration because the dictator shifted funds from the government budget to his firms and vice versa to evade taxes and to mislead external lenders. The government had to set up from scratch an administrative system for state enterprises in agriculture, industry, and the service sector.

***Agriculture and agroindustry.*** The INRA (Instituto de Reforma Agraria; Agrarian Reform Institute) began to administer the state farms in 1979 (FIDA 1980:90-1). It consolidated the 2,000 confiscated fincas (farms) in 827 UPEs (Unidades de Producción Estatal; State Production Units) under the direction of a state manager. The UPEs were grouped together in 170 complexes, according to production lines, and the complexes in 27 agrarian reform enterprises. INRA administered the enterprises from its eight regional offices. In 1980 INRA fused with the Ministry of Agricultural Development to form MIDINRA.

In 1981 the regional offices of MIDINRA received more autonomy, which meant some decentralization in administering the state farms. But the enterprises still had a ministerial delegate in their directive councils who represented MIDINRA. The intention of the decentralization was to improve the administrative efficiency of the enterprises. MIDINRA remained responsible for the allocation of the surplus.

The MIDINRA director of AGROINRA began to administer the agroindustrial enterprises in a rather centralized manner (FIDA 1980:87). The forty confiscated enterprises were reduced to twenty-two and grouped according to thirteen different production lines, including coffee, tobacco, sugar, and cotton. The MIDINRA director of a production line directly supervised the managers of the enterprises. In 1981 some decentralization also occurred in agroindustry.

To provide the central MIDINRA level with the necessary information to evaluate and supervise the operations of the decentralized enterprises, MIDINRA introduced from Cuba the SUCA (Sistema Uniforme de Control Administrativo; Uniform Administrative Control System). Researchers estimated that by 1983, 75 percent of the enterprises worked with this system to some extent. The implementation was hampered by "the lack of trained accounting personnel, the relative sophistication of the system, and uneven levels of commitment to the implementation process" (Austin, Fox, and Kruger 1985:22). Implementation proved to be difficult on small farms in particular.

The establishment of an indirect control mechanism is a difficult undertaking. There will always be distortion in the information, and the setting of success indicators tends to bring about undesired consequences. As a result, the degree of central control over officially decentralized enterprises is limited. In Nicaragua in response to this problem, the government used centralized decision-making for day-to-day operations of state enterprises in agriculture and agroindustry.

The economic reform measures of February 1988 included an institutional reform called the Compactación. It was intended to streamline the government bureacracy, economizing 10 percent on its costs (IHCA 1988a). For the state agricultural and agroindustrial enterprises, the Compactación implied the end of the regional structure. The enterprises came under the direct supervision of eight

MIDINRA corporations vertically organized according to production line.

***Manufacturing.*** The confiscated manufacturing enterprises were grouped together in COIP (Corporación Industrial del Pueblo; Industrial Corporation of the People) under the Ministry of Industry. COIP consisted of six complexes, in which about 120 manufacturing enterprises were organized in branches in a vertical structure.[10]

Until January 1983 the Ministry of Industry had a separate department for the private sector whose main function was the assignment of foreign exchange. To achieve better coordination in the foreign-exchange policy toward state and private enterprises, the Ministry of Industry integrated the private enterprises in the complexes, now called branches. The ministry was organized in nine branches (MIND 1984c:4-5).

The directors of the state enterprises in manufacturing were accountable to the general director of their branch. In practice there was more decentralization in day-to-day operations than in agriculture and agroindustry. Although legally the Ministry of Industry decided on the allocation of after-tax profits of state enterprises, this was not so in practice.[11] Some branches collected funds for their own investment projects. In 1985 the Ministry of Industry began establishing norms for the firms' contribution to COIP. According to the vice-minister of industry, the implementation of these norms would be relatively easy because of an improved accounting system within the enterprises and the high inflation rate, which made directors more willing to hand over their financial resources.

With the Compactación of February 1988 the Ministry of Industry fused with the Ministries of Internal and External Commerce to form the Ministry of Economy, Industry and Commerce. Within the Vice-Ministry of Industry, the number of branches was reduced to four. Their principle function became the assignment of foreign exchange to state and private enterprises. In other administrative matters of the state enterprises, COIP obtained more autonomy.[12]

***Labor participation.*** In state agricultural enterprises, worker representation was in the form of consultative councils at the complex level. However, the complexes proved to be too big and the UPEs often too dispersed to make effective worker participation possible (Ortega 1985:43). In addition, the annual economic plans for the enterprise (the most important decision the council had to make) were not broken down by UPE, so it was difficult for workers to understand the meaning of the plan for tens of UPEs.

In 1981 consultative councils came to function at the UPE level, in which workers' representatives participated. They discussed the tasks of the UPE along with production goals, the hiring of workers, and the organization of the labor process (Ortega 1985:44). To expand the participation to all workers, some UPEs organized production councils, which were open to all workers, prior to the meetings of the consultative councils. By December 1982, 66 percent of the agrarian reform enterprises had established worker participation at UPE and complex levels (Austin, Fox, and Kruger 1985:22).

To stimulate worker participation in state manufacturing enterprises, the Ministry of Industry set up enterprise committees. Larger enterprises also had production councils in their different units, which also functioned on the basis of representation. The objective of worker participation in industry was "to promote the creative participation of workers in the productive and technical transformation, and in the increase of productivity" (MIND 1983b). Decision-making power remained with the director of the enterprise, who was responsible for its operation.[13]

Thirteen of the fourteen state manufacturing enterprises of the sample of enterprises interviewed in 1984–1985 had an enterprise committee. Representatives of workers and management participated in these committees, and most of them met every month. In private enterprises no enterprise committees existed, but two managers said they had something similar to it. Three private enterprises had a general assembly that met one to three times a year. Enterprise committees and assemblies discussed production and labor problems.

In addition to an enterprise committee, some state industrial enterprises were experimenting with other forms of labor participation at different levels. There were big differences in this respect between the enterprises. The functioning of worker participation seemed to depend to a large extent on the attitude of the management. This proved to range from "the management must make the decisions" to "the management explains a problem in the enterprise committee and the latter makes the decision." The attitude and actions of the workers were also important. Apparently, enterprise committees were not functioning well in all enterprises: The MIND (Ministerio de Industria; Ministry of Industry) mentioned as one of its aims for 1985 "reactivating and consolidating" the committees (MIND 1985a:10).

There appeared to be some limits to promoting worker participation in decision-making. One stemmed from the workers' lack of experience and skills, the other from the enterprises' reduced decision-making power. In view of the latter, worker participation would also have to be introduced at higher levels. This, in fact, happened. The CST (Central Sandinista de Trabjadores; Sandinista Labor Union) and the ATC (Associación de Trabajadores del Campo; Agricultural Labor Union) participated in meetings at the ministry level.

### *How Effective Is State Planning?*

***The planning process.*** Although the greater part of production was in private hands, the government set up annual economic plans for the whole economy. They contained figures on production and exports per product, on imports per product and source of financing (cash, credit line, etc.), on wages and the total wage fund, and on the monetary and budgetary policy. In 1984 economic plans included for the first time material balances for fifteen important consumer and producer goods. These balances established the whole production chain, from necessary imports of inputs to consumption and stocks (or additional imports of final goods).

The Ministry of Planning—since January 1985 called SPP (Secretaría de Planificación y Presupuesto; Secretary of Planning and the Budget)—played an important role in the planning process. The sectoral ministries set up a first draft of the plan and sent it to SPP. SPP normally made cuts in the proposed plans and established ceilings of financing and foreign exchange for each ministry. On the basis of the financing and foreign-exchange inputs and the achievements of former years, SPP also estimated the result in terms of production and exports per product (only as far as the ministries of material production were concerned).

In June, SPP would return these drafts of the plans to the ministries, which discussed them extensively. Almost all medium and large private manufacturing enterprises were individually included in the plan. The directors (also of private enterprises) gave their opinion to the ministry's director of the branch.

After having consulted enterprises, complexes, and UPEs, MIDINRA elaborated the drafts from SPP into technical-economic plans for each state enterprise. They established production and export objectives by category of output, defined the supply of inputs, the state institution providing them, and the market (the state organization to receive the output).

The overall agricultural plan, including financing, foreign exchange, production and exports, wages, prices, and availability of inputs, implements, and machinery, was discussed in general terms in the Production Commissions, in which representatives of small and medium farmers and of large farmers participated, in addition to the ATC and state officials.[14]

The plan was broken down by production line, by region, and by category of producers (cooperatives, large farmers, and small and medium farmers) but not by individual private producer. However, most production cooperatives (CASs) were individually included by means of agreements that defined the amount of inputs, credits, and sometimes also machinery and consumer goods the cooperative would receive in exchange for a certain amount of production they committed to deliver to the state. The intention was to expand these agreements to service cooperatives and even to individual producers.

After the discussions within the ministries, the adjusted drafts would go "up" via the ministry to SPP, and the plans were finally established by the government. The planning process was accompanied by many discussions and conflicts within and between ministries. The fact that MIDINRA planned on the basis of production cycles that began and ended in the middle of the year complicated the comparison between agriculture and the other sectors.

The effectiveness of the planning depended on the ability of the state to influence production and distribution decisions. To address this question, I interviewed a sample of thirty-four directors of state enterprises and executives of private enterprises in the industrial sector. The results also reveal whether, and how, the industrial policy discriminated between enterprises, thus allowing an answer to the question whether planning instruments left room for private accumulation. With the interviews I tested the hypothesis (reflecting the official policy, see MIND 1983a and MIND 1984c) that industrial planning did not discriminate between state and private enterprises, only between enterprises representing different priorities in the industrial strategy. With respect to the latter, four categories are distinguished: Basic consumer goods, other consumer goods, intermediate goods, and export goods, respectively. In Appendix 1 I present the research methods, and Appendix 2 contains the list of questions used in the interviews.

***Foreign exchange.*** The nationalization of foreign trade actually meant that the government obtained control over the major share of foreign exchange entering the country. The Central Bank received the foreign exchange earned by exports and the exporters received only cordobas. The Ministry of Foreign Trade began to export the most important export products, such as coffee, cotton, sugar, molasses, meat and cattle, tobacco and sesame, by means of specialized enterprises (ENAL, ENCAFE, etc.). These enterprises dealt with the procurement of these products and functioned as independent export organizations (Girling 1983). The state first expanded its number of exporting organizations (Ministry of Justice 1982:36-7) but carried out a decentralization in this respect later on.[15]

The producers of agricultural export crops received prices in cordobas according to a system of guaranteed prices. The government guaranteed producers a margin of income over costs—independently of the world-market prices for these crops. If world-market prices went up, the extra profits accrued to the state. But the state also bore the risk of falling prices, in which case the producers were subsidized. This system made these private producers functionaries in a bureaucratic organization, and they no longer responded to market forces.

All individuals and enterprises had to apply to the government (the Central Bank) to receive foreign exchange, to import, or to travel abroad. As of 1982, the government applied different exchange rates to different kinds of imports (see Chapter 5). In principle, the yearly economic plan was the guide for the assignment policy. However, because of changing needs and the changing availability of foreign exchange, the decisions about concrete assignments were made every week by the Economic Council, in which the president, the Central Bank, the SPP, and many other ministries participated. From 1985 onward, the Economic Council was replaced by the smaller National Planning Council. Because almost all production in Nicaragua (including many services provided by ministries like that of Health and Education) was dependent on imports, the National Planning Council was the most important economic policy body of the country. Decisions were prepared within the ministries using a cyclical round of meetings every week culminating in the National Planning Council meeting. The decisions of this body were transmitted to the Central Bank, which then made the foreign exchange available.

The larger manufacturing enterprises, once having received approval from the Central Bank, usually imported directly from enterprises abroad. In agriculture and agroindustry MIDINRA imported the inputs centrally by means of its enterprise ENIA (Empresa Nacional de Insumos Agrarios; National Enterprise of Agricultural Inputs). Specialized institutions of MIDINRA, such as PROAGRO (Provisiones para el Agro; Provisions for Agriculture) and AGROMAQ (Agro Maquinaria; Machinery for Agriculture; see further on) distributed the goods. Each agricultural and agroindustrial enterprise had to apply to MIDINRA for each separate spare part. Because there were many more of these enterprises—than manufacturing enterprises, this led to inefficiencies. The system was "a disaster" according to a functionary of MIDINRA in 1985. For this reason, the government again assigned some foreign exchange to private business houses specializing in agricultural machinery and spare parts.

State control of foreign exchange was most strict between 1982, when dollars became very scarce, and 1985. There were only a few exceptions to the state monopoly on foreign exchange. Some direct barter took place between enterprises in Central America, and some international petty commerce was handled by the so-called *buhoneros* (merchants). And of course, a black foreign-exchange market also existed. But the difference between the official and the black-market rate was so big that the prospect of buying dollars in this market for import purposes was very unattractive. In 1985 estimates of the volume of this parallel circuit ranged from 5 to 10 percent of annual export earnings. The supply of dollars on this market came from foreigners or from Nicaraguans with foreign income or wealth abroad. The capital flight of 1977 and 1978 had provided many wealthy Nicaraguans with an important reserve in this respect.

In 1985 the government started to give private export producers part of their income in dollars.[16] The intention was to facilitate purchases of spare parts, but this was not effectively controlled. In June 1985 the government legalized a parallel market in dollars. Soon, however, it faced a big difference between the parallel and the black-market rate. After the monetary reform of February 1988, which included a devaluation of 3,000 percent and the unification of the official exchange rates, the differences between official, parallel, and black market rates diminished. The parallel and black markets again became feasible alternatives for importers.

In manufacturing, the high black-market price of the dollar from 1982 onward forced more and more industrial enterprises to apply to MIND for their imports. As a result, almost all medium and large private enterprises were included in the annual industrial plans by 1983. MIND knew the technical coefficients of imported inputs of these enterprises. As of mid-1984, the enterprises also had to give information on their stocks of imported raw materials and inputs.

As of 1983, enterprises in "small industry"[17] had to unite themselves in service cooperatives in order to receive imported inputs. By 1984 small industries were also included in MIND's annual plans.

The industrial enterprises of the sample proved to be very dependent on imported inputs. They imported between 5 and 100 percent of their total inputs, with an average of 71 percent. Table 4.3 indicates that the majority of both private and state enterprises did not receive enough foreign exchange to maintain current production. Private enterprises were treated no better than state enterprises. The enterprises of category 1 (basic consumer goods with high priority, see Appendix 1) appeared to be better off than the rest of the enterprises, and enterprises of category 4 (exporting enterprises) were worst off.

Some manufacturing enterprises received foreign-exchange assignments from other ministries—ministries they supplied with their products, for example, the Ministry of Construction or MIDINRA. In the case of one private enterprise producing inputs for agriculture, MIND reduced the foreign-exchange assignment for raw materials so much that production fell enormously. As a result, MIDINRA began to import the products from abroad and even supplied foreign exchange to another industrial enterprise in Central America, enabling it to import its raw materials. In other cases, the differential import

TABLE 4.3 Sample of Enterprises: Assignment of Foreign Exchange for Imports of Raw Materials and Inputs[a]

| | *Yes, Sufficient* | *Yes, Not Sufficient* | *No* | *Total* |
|---|---|---|---|---|
| State | 6 (36) | 8 (50) | 2 (13) | 16 (100) |
| Private | 8 (44) | 8 (44) | 2 (11) | 18 (100) |
| Category: | | | | |
| 1 | 6 (75) | 2 (25) | 0 (0) | 8 (100) |
| 2 | 3 (33) | 4 (44) | 2 (22) | 9 (100) |
| 3 | 3 (37) | 3 (37) | 2 (25) | 8 (100) |
| 4 | 2 (22) | 7 (78) | 0 (0) | 9 (100) |
| Total | 14 (41) | 16 (47) | 4 (12) | 34 (100) |

[a]In this and the following tables figures represent absolute numbers of enterprises, with percentages in parenthesis. Total may not sum to 100% due to rounding.

*Source:* Interviews.

exchange rate harmed manufacturing production. The Ministry of Health, for example, imported medicines formerly produced in Nicaragua, because the import exchange rate for that ministry was lower than for the Ministry of Industry. Apparently, coordination between ministries in the foreign-exchange assignment was not very good.

After 1982 MIND pursued an economy in the use of imported inputs and raw materials in the enterprises.[18] According to Solórzano and de los Ríos (1984), this economization policy might have resulted in the substitution of domestic for foreign inputs (with supposedly no impact on the final product or products) or products of a lower quality or a smaller assortment of products, among other consequences.

Table 4.4 shows to what extent the enterprises applied these two kinds of economy. The second kind of economization (lower quality or fewer products) was found a little more often in state enterprises than in private enterprises. But many private enterprises also had to accept one or the other type of economization. Again, enterprises producing basic consumer goods (the first category) were privileged in the sense that they did not have to accept fewer imports. With respect to the other kind of economization, exporting enterprises were relatively better off.

TABLE 4.4 Sample of Enterprises: Application of Economization[a]

| | *Fewer Imports* | | | *Lower Quality or Smaller Assortment* | | |
|---|---|---|---|---|---|---|
| | *Yes* | *No* | *Total* | *Yes* | *No* | *Total* |
| State | 4 (42) | 7 (58) | 11 (100) | 12 (86) | 2 (14) | 14 (100) |
| Private | 7 (47) | 8 (53) | 15 (100) | 7 (47) | 8 (53) | 15 (100) |
| Category: | | | | | | |
| 1 | 0 (0) | 4 (100) | 4 (100) | 5 (71) | 2 (29) | 7 (100) |
| 2 | 5 (83) | 1 (17) | 6 (100) | 6 (86) | 1 (14) | 7 (100) |
| 3 | 3 (33) | 6 (67) | 9 (100) | 5 (71) | 2 (29) | 7 (100) |
| 4 | 3 (50) | 3 (50) | 7 (100) | 3 (37) | 5 (63) | 8 (100) |
| Total | 11 (42) | 15 (58) | 26 (100) | 19 (66) | 10 (34) | 29 (100) |

[a]In this table and in some of the following that represent the results of the interviews, the total number of answers is smaller than the complete sample of thirty-four enterprises. This is because a question was not always asked in all enterprises.

*Source:* Interviews.

Imported raw materials and inputs came from all over the world. The interviewed directors of enterprises mentioned Western Europe (20 times), Latin America (17 times), the United States (10 times), Eastern Europe (9 times), and other countries, for example, Canada or Japan (4 times).[19] State enterprises mentioned Eastern European countries more often than did private enterprises (7 and 2 times, respectively). Almost all enterprises imported more inputs from another country than before the revolution. More inputs came from the United States before the Sandinistas came to power; afterward inputs came from countries with which Nicaragua had established credit lines.

In six cases (three state and two private enterprises) the importation of some inputs was carried out at the branch level. Only in one case did the ministry carry out the importation.

Most industrial enterprises needed imported spare parts for their machinery and equipment. A large proportion of them did not receive foreign exchange for that aim (Table 4.5). Many directors said they had not received foreign exchange for spare parts in the last three years but expected to receive it for the first time in 1985. More private enterprises than state enterprises had not received any dollars for spare parts. But more private enterprise directors who had received some aid said it was enough. Basic goods (category 1) and exporting

TABLE 4.5 Sample Enterprises in Need of Imported Spare Parts: Assignment of Foreign Exchange

| | *Yes, Sufficient* | *Yes, Not Sufficient* | *No* | *Total* |
|---|---|---|---|---|
| State | 2 (15) | 6 (46) | 5 (38) | 13 (100) |
| Private | 4 (24) | 3 (18) | 10 (59) | 17 (100) |
| Category: | | | | |
| 1 | 0 (0) | 5 (71) | 2 (29) | 7 (100) |
| 2 | 2 (25) | 1 (13) | 5 (63) | 8 (100) |
| 3 | 0 (0) | 2 (33) | 4 (67) | 6 (100) |
| 4 | 4 (44) | 1 (11) | 4 (44) | 9 (100) |
| Total | 6 (20) | 9 (30) | 15 (50) | 30 (100) |

*Source:* Interviews.

(category 4) enterprises appeared to enjoy a higher priority in this respect.

Enterprises not receiving sufficient foreign exchange for spare parts applied various solutions. Most had their own repair shop and some succeeded in finding spare parts on the domestic market. Four private directors traveled abroad to find spare parts.

The dependence on imported inputs in small industrial enterprises was considerable (Laenen 1988:155). But many problems remained in controlling the use of state-distributed inputs (Laenen 1988:181,241-2).

Many producers in agriculture and agroindustry were also dependent on imports to a certain extent, for example, of pesticides, fertilizers, and transport equipment. According to the interviews with some private agricultural and agroindustrial producers, the lack of imported spare parts for machinery and transport equipment was a serious bottleneck. Private producers in this sector complained more than their colleagues in industry about preferential treatment of state enterprises. According to functionaries of MIDINRA, it was indeed likely that private enterprises received less imported inputs than state enterprises, because state institutions generally preferred selling to state enterprises. In the case of a private customer they were not sure whether they were dealing with a producer or a merchant.

Apparently, foreign-exchange policy had an important impact in both the state and private sectors in manufacturing. It influenced the quantity of production, the kind of inputs used, the country of origin of imports, and the quality and assortment of the product. Manufacturers were no longer producing for a market but for a plan. One problem was the lack of coordination between different ministries in the assignment policy.

***Financing.*** After confiscating the national banks and forbidding subsidiaries of foreign banks from accepting any payments from the public, thereby effectively nationalizing them, the government established the National Financial System. All financial institutions maintained juridical independence, but their operations became subjected to the decisions of the Superior Council. The different banking institutions specialized in certain sectors, for instance, the BND (Banco Nacional de Desarrollo) was the only bank dealing with the agricultural sector. The regional offices of the BND made decisions on concrete credit assignments on the basis of production costs that varied by region. The central MIDINRA level had lists of average production costs, but the regional offices made their own estimates per producer.

The impact of the financial policy on state and private production could be considerable. Most medium and large producers in agriculture and industry applied for credits to finance current production, and all producers applied for credits to finance investment. In addition, small and medium producers dependent on middlemen before the revolution now received credits from the banking system and so had become dependent on the state.

In the first year after the Sandinista victory—1980—credits were assigned in large amounts to small peasants, without guarantees that the necessary inputs were available and beyond the capacity of the state procurement network. As of 1981, the banks made the money available only in combination with a package of agricultural inputs (Austin, Fox, and Kruger 1985:21), which is likely to have increased the negative impact of the credit policy on production.

The share of state enterprises in the assignment of agricultural credit climbed from 31 percent in 1981 to 40 percent in 1985—much more than their share in production. The proportion conceded to large private producers declined during these years but remained more or less in line with their share in production. Recuperation problems with credits given to small and medium peasants through the Rural Credit Program led to a reduction of this program after 1980. In 1984–1985 about 30 percent of total agricultural credit was extended through this program. Thus, the program serviced roughly half of all small- and medium-sized producers. Most of them were affiliated with cooperatives; in 1983, 78 percent were affiliated (Enríquez and Spalding 1987:114-8).

The interviewed large private agricultural and agroindustrial producers all needed credits for their current production. They complained that the decentralized credit assignment system was humiliating, that bank functionaries always lowered their production costs, and that interest rates were too high.[20]

In manufacturing, only four out of sixteen directors of private enterprises said they needed credits for current production, as did eight of the sixteen directors of state enterprises. All except one director of a state enterprise were satisfied with the amounts received. Only one director of a state enterprise said he would not be able to repay in time.

Only seven enterprises had received long-term credits after 1980: three state and four private enterprises. Two private foreign enterprises had received credits in dollars from their parent company. Because they did not have access to dollars, they paid the money back to the Central Bank in cordobas. But the Central Bank did not reimburse the dollars to the company. For the enterprises, this meant that they would not receive any new credits from abroad.

In ten of the fourteen private enterprises that had carried out investment (see further on) I asked the director whether they had used external financing. Six enterprises had used their own money and one had received financing from its parent company. Only three had used credits from the National Financial System.

I asked eight of the fourteen directors who received credits (seven directors of state enterprises and one of a private enterprise) whether it would be easy to postpone repayment if need be. All answered positively. Most directors also thought it would be easy to obtain credits or to obtain more credits. The answers did not prove to be different in the different ownership sectors.

Thus, the credit policy did not seem to have a strong impact on manufacturing enterprises, either on current production or on investment. Most enterprises had sufficient access to cordobas and if not, they could easily obtain credits. The only real money appeared to be the U.S. dollar, with which imported raw materials and spare parts could be obtained. Also in this respect the manufacturing sector was centrally planned: Producers experienced a "soft budget constraint"—at least in cordobas (this means that enterprise budgets will be supplemented if need be, so the firms never go bankrupt; see Kornai 1979:813). The budget constraint probably hardened after the reform measures of February 1988, when the credit policy became much more restrictive.

In agriculture, the cordoba continued to play an important role, as producers were much more dependent on financing. State enterprises and cooperatives enjoyed a clear priority within the credit policy, and about half of small and medium peasants were still excluded from bank credits. Although large private producers clearly had more troubles in obtaining bank credits than before the Sandinista victory, they still received a share in keeping with their importance in production.

***Means of production.*** State control of imported inputs and machinery was almost complete because of the control of foreign exchange. The state also controlled a great deal of domestically produced raw materials and other means of production for agriculture and industry. It owned, for example, almost all enterprises producing construction materials.

In agriculture, some locally produced pesticides, fertilizers, and fodder were still available in the private domestic market, as well as some spare parts for machinery. However, for most imported inputs, machinery, transport equipment, and construction materials (especially important in cattle-raising), private producers were dependent on the state. Representatives of the producers of different crops negotiated each year in the production commissions with the government on the quantities and prices of inputs to be assigned.

Twenty enterprises confiscated from Somoza provided inputs and services (transport, hiring out of machinery) to the agricultural sector. Those enterprises were used to supply medium and large producers only. Small producers were dependent on intermediaries who also purchased their crops and supplied them with credits and technical assistance. The intermediaries were specialized in one crop. This was an efficient and effective system in the sense that it reached almost all small peasants and led to extensive control of their production. Apart from the Somoza-confiscated enterprises, the state established new institutions to supply the countryside. These institutions involved all kinds of production, which meant a disruption of the old system. They were not very efficient, nor were they effective in reaching the small peasants, often located in the mountains (Grigsby 1988:211). The most important institutions were PROAGRO and AGROMAQ.

PROAGRO produced and distributed imported and locally produced agricultural inputs such as fertilizers, pesticides, fodder, and light agricultural implements. After 1981 the credit policy determined its assignment policy to a large extent. Of PROAGRO sales in 1981, 60 percent was with bank credit, and the bank determined the package of inputs (MIDINRA 1983:76). In the same year, 40 percent of PROAGRO deliveries were to state enterprises, another 40 percent to cooperatives, small producers, and medium producers, and 20 percent to large producers (MIDINRA 1983:70).

AGROMAQ administered and hired out agricultural machinery such as combines and tractors. AGROMAQ hardly worked for small and medium farmers and gave priority to state enterprises. In 1986 the government converted state farms into territorial production organizations, which had to provide services to individual peasants in

TABLE 4.6 Sample of Enterprises: Decisions on Prices

| | *State* | *State and Enterprise*[a] | *Enterprise* | *Total* |
|---|---|---|---|---|
| State | 13 (81) | 2 (13) | 1 (6) | 16 (100) |
| Private | 10 (59) | 1 (6) | 6 (35) | 17 (100) |
| Category: | | | | |
| 1 | 7 (87) | 1 (13) | 0 (0) | 8 (100) |
| 2 | 5 (63) | 0 (0) | 3 (37) | 8 (100) |
| 3 | 6 (75) | 2 (25) | 0 (0) | 8 (100) |
| 4 | 5 (55) | 0 (0) | 4 (44) | 9 (100) |
| Total | 23 (70) | 3 (9) | 7 (21) | 33 (100) |

[a]Enterprises sold more than one product.

*Source:* Interviews.

their neighborhood. The intention was to improve service to the peasants, but state farms gave priority to their own rentability instead of meeting the needs of the peasants (Frenkel 1988). In 1988 the government abolished the territorial production organizations. With the revitalization of the production commissions in that year the government pursued more integration per crop between the different MIDINRA institutions working in the countryside.

Many locally produced inputs for manufacturing were of an agricultural origin, for example, cotton fiber for textile factories, cotton seed for vegetable oil producers, skins for leather processors, and corn for tortilla makers. The state often attempted to control distribution of these inputs. State institutions distributed part of the corn and all cotton fiber. Small industrial producers had to unite themselves in service cooperatives to receive raw materials and inputs from these institutions. Other inputs, such as cotton seed and skins, were privately supplied according to a quota established by the Ministry of Industry. In these cases the number of purchasing factories was small.

Manufacturing enterprises also produced raw materials. Among most enterprises of the third category in the sample (producers of intermediate goods), the state established the prices of the products and made distribution decisions (see Tables 4.6 and 4.7). State regulation of distribution appeared to depend on the priority accorded to the production. A high priority implied a state-determined relatively low price, which in turn made regulation of the distribution necessary—at least when there was more than one purchasing factory. Examples were the distribution of locally produced textiles for the

TABLE 4.7 Sample of Enterprises: Decisions on Domestic Sales

| | State | State and Enterprise[a] | Enterprise | Total |
|---|---|---|---|---|
| State | 5 (31) | 4 (25) | 7 (44) | 16 (100) |
| Private | 4 (24) | 1 (6) | 12 (71) | 17 (100) |
| Category: | | | | |
| 1 | 3 (37) | 2 (25) | 3 (37) | 8 (100) |
| 2 | 1 (13) | 1 (13) | 6 (75) | 8 (100) |
| 3 | 5 (63) | 1 (13) | 2 (25) | 8 (100) |
| 4 | 0 (0) | 1 (11) | 8 (89) | 9 (100) |
| Total | 9 (27) | 5 (15) | 19 (58) | 33 (100) |

[a]Enterprises sold more than one product.

*Source:* Interviews.

clothing industry and leather for shoe production. In other cases with lower priority or with only one or a few buyers, the enterprises could handle their sales themselves.

As of 1983 industrial service or production cooperatives could purchase their inputs at state-guaranteed prices from the ERAIN (Empresas Regionales de Abastecimiento Industrial; Regional Enterprises for Industrial Supply). However, in 1985 the ERAIN did not work very efficiently and the cooperatives complained heavily about their functioning (Laenen 1988:240). Small industrial enterprises seemed to have a lower priority than medium and large enterprises.

With respect to the allocation of means of production the efficiency of the market was reduced—at least for producers with a high priority. They purchased their inputs at below-market prices on the basis of criteria other than market efficiency. Production having a lower priority still operated in a market environment; prices of inputs and consequently of outputs were much higher. In manufacturing, contrary to the situation in agriculture, the state did not seem to discriminate between state and private enterprises in the assignment of raw materials and inputs.

***Prices and sales.*** The state established prices for the export crops before and after processing and established tariffs for the processing itself. This allowed discrimination against private agroindustrial installations in favor of state-owned installations. The interviewed private agroindustrial producers were convinced that this happened, but it was difficult to verify.

Coffee, sesame, sugar, and cotton need some processing before they can be sold or exported. This facilitated procurement control. The government nationalized all domestic trade in sugar in 1982. This was relatively easy because at that time there was only one private sugar refinery (nationalized in 1988). With cattle and meat control was more difficult. In addition to the state export slaughterhouses, private slaughterhouses existed that supplied the domestic meat market. Apparently, farmers got higher prices at the private slaughterhouses. The state lacked control over these private slaughterhouses, so the quantity of exported meat and cattle was often smaller than possible. Especially from 1985 onward, the state also lost procurement control of the other export products. The guaranteed prices for exports were lower than the uncontrolled high domestic prices (Pilarte, Ubau, and Guevara 1988:14).

For basic grains (beans, corn, rice, and sorghum), mainly produced for the domestic market, the government set up a marketing and distribution institution, ENABAS (Empresa Nacional de Abastecimiento; National Procurement Enterprise), under MICOIN (Ministerio de Comercio Interior; Ministry of Internal Trade). ENABAS supplied the "popular shops," the state supermarkets, and the army, among other institutions. At first, the intention was to outbid private merchants by offering higher prices for basic grains (Steenhuis and Teunissen 1982:17). In practice, official prices were often lower than the prices offered by private traders, especially in the case of corn (MICOIN 1983). ENABAS also had transport, storage, and personnel problems, and private traders offered cash instead of checks to the producers and supplied them with goods in exchange for the harvest. State procurement of corn and beans was most difficult, as these crops were mainly produced by small and medium peasants. In 1980 ENABAS only captured 12 percent of the corn and bean crops (Collins et al. 1985:123); in 1984 these figures were 27 percent and 33 percent, respectively (Utting 1987:142).

In August 1984 ENABAS officially obtained a monopoly on basic grain purchases, but official prices increasingly did not reflect the market, and private trade could not be eliminated. From 1986 onward, the government gradually liberated prices for basic grains. ENABAS still attempted to purchase part of the crop but had to offer competing prices.

Milk was produced mainly by small peasants. The state fixed the prices for raw milk delivered at the dairy plants. Both state and private traders were active in the milk procurement. In practice the state price for raw milk was too low (MICOIN 1983), so producers chose to consume the milk themselves or to sell it to small private cheese producers. Very little milk was supplied to the dairy plants; they increasingly depended on imports of powdered milk.

Many interviewed directors in manufacturing said the state established the prices of their products. Table 4.6 shows that this occurred more with products of state enterprises, but not with all. State influence on prices appeared to depend more on the importance placed on the product. State-determined prices existed for most intermediate goods (category 3) and for final consumer goods considered essential for the population (category 1).

Most enterprises were free to decide whom they sold their products to (Table 4.7). Relatively more private enterprises and more enterprises of categories 2 and 4 (enterprises producing nonbasic consumer goods and exporting enterprises, respectively) could make their own decisions about sales.

The directors of nineteen of the thirty-two enterprises said they sold their products to a state institution (MICOIN, the army, or the Commercial Corporation of the People, which supplied the state supermarkets). The enterprises producing basic consumer goods did not sell to private wholesale traders and only two of them sold to private retail traders. Of all enterprises, only two sold to private wholesale traders and nine to retail traders. Thirteen enterprises delivered to other enterprises and six sold directly to the public. In the destiny of products, there was no difference between state and private enterprises.

Tables 4.6 and 4.7 compare state control of prices with state control of sales in manufacturing; the former was more extensive than the latter. Given the increasing scarcities, the state could not maintain consumer prices, and private traders could make large profits.

The price policy's effect on producers was different by sector. Most producers of agricultural export crops purchased their inputs at subsidized prices and sold at state-determined prices, which guaranteed a profit margin. The situation was fairly similar for many medium and large manufacturing enterprises—at least for production with some priority within the industrial strategy. State-determined low output prices did not cause losses because producers also purchased their inputs at below-market prices. All these producers no longer functioned in a market environment.

Procurement control of agricultural export crops was more successfulcessful than in manufacturing, although the state increasingly could not prevent agricultural producers from selling part of the crops on the domestic market where prices were higher. In manufacturing, private traders could make big profits from the difference between official producer prices and the market prices created by high demand.

Producers of corn and beans, mainly small and medium peasants, did lose money due to the state-determined procurement prices, because they had much less access to subsidized inputs. In practice, the state lacked the instruments for implementing the price policy for this sector. The result was a reduced availability of basic grains. The same happened with milk. In beef production and increasingly also in other export production, the state supplied inputs at subsidized prices but did not control procurement sufficiently, leading to high profits for producers and traders and to losses for the state.

From February 1988 onward, the state fixed only the prices of forty-six final products, including basic consumer goods and public services such as water and electricity. This implied low prices for basic grains and reversed the trend toward better terms of trade for its producers. Between February and December 1988, the real incomes of rice, corn, and beans producers suffered a 70 percent drop (IHCA 1989b:41).

After 1988 the state left the prices for intermediate products free and abolished sales control of these products. Because of the monopolistic and oligopolistic structure of the Nicaraguan industry and the lack of competing imports this sometimes resulted in disproportionately high prices. For this reason, the government started to control again the prices of a number of intermediate goods in November 1988.[21]

***Wages and labor conditions.*** In 1980 MITRAB (Ministerio de Trabajo; Ministry of Labor) proclaimed official minimum wages for industry and agriculture, which were successfully enforced. The wage policy was directed at limiting nominal wage increases, and MITRAB decreed annual maximum wage increases. It also had to approve the collective agreements of the enterprises that established nominal wages and secondary labor conditions such as pay in kind, deliveries of medicines, uniforms, and meals.

Although nominal wages were controlled more or less effectively, the control of secondary labor conditions was not very strict, leading to diverging conditions in the enterprises. Moreover, many enterprises of more than thirty workers had commissaries, little outlets selling basic consumer goods to the workers at relatively low prices. The range of goods for sale in the commissaries varied enormously.

In 1984 MITRAB unified the wage system for the state as well as the private sector by introducing the SNOTS (Sistema Nacional de Ordenación de Trabajo y Salarios; National System Ordaining Work and Wages). The first phase of SNOTS applied a twenty-eight-point classification of the different kinds of work and established wages according to that classification. The system allowed retention of "historical wages": any higher wages set before the introduction of SNOTS. By the end of 1984, this first phase of SNOTS was officially implemented in 90 percent of the industrial enterprises and in all of agriculture. The government could now proclaim wage increases for almost all workers. The implementation of SNOTS was accompanied by an increase in the minimum wage; and many more general increases followed during 1985, 1986, and 1987—necessarily, given the then galloping inflation (see Chapter 5).

Of the sixteen state manufacturing enterprises included in the sample, all applied SNOTS. Two directors mentioned that they still paid historical wages.[22] Four private enterprises did not apply SNOTS. Two foreign enterprises and one local enterprise of a branch not yet included in SNOTS all paid much higher wages that were also much higher than historical wages. The fourth director said wages according to SNOTS could be found "in the books" in case functionaries of MITRAB visited the enterprise. But in reality this enterprise's wages were more than double the official ones. He showed me another list of wages that were the ones paid in practice. In one of the foreign enterprises the director had been fined for not applying SNOTS; the workers had paid the fine. Three other directors of private enterprises said they paid historical wages that were much higher than those according to SNOTS.

The vice minister of industry told me later that, in general, there were no sanctions for manufacturing enterprises refusing to introduce SNOTS. He knew that, in particular, many foreign enterprises did not pay official wages. The policy was directed at not provoking conflicts with these enterprises on the wage issue. But in the future, all industrial enterprises would have to implement SNOTS.

In 1985 MITRAB started to implement the second phase of SNOTS, which implied a unified incentive structure for wage laborers. By 1984, each enterprise's incentive system had to be approved by MITRAB. The norm was that hourly wages for extra work could be at most 20 percent higher. Later this norm was revised to 30 percent. The aim of the incentive policy was to increase both production (the supply of goods) and workers' purchasing power.

Before the second phase of SNOTS was introduced, many enterprises of the sample were already working with some kind of incentive policy (Table 4.8). There were many different systems and in many cases the level of incentives was much higher than the official norm. In addition, these policies were not always approved by MITRAB and sometimes they were only partially approved. In this respect there were no differences between state and private enterprises. Apparently, already in 1984–1985 the incentives functioned as an "escape valve" for directors who considered the official wages to be too low. The two directors of private enterprises who said they did not apply incentives gave as the most important reason the enter-

TABLE 4.8 Sample of Enterprises: Application of Incentive System and MITRAB Approval

| | *Incentives* | | | *Approval* | | | |
|---|---|---|---|---|---|---|---|
| | *Yes* | *No* | *Total* | *Yes* | *Partly* | *No* | *Total* |
| State | 13 (87) | 2 (13) | 15 (100) | 7 (78) | 1 (11) | 1 (11) | 9 (100) |
| Private | 9 (82) | 2 (18) | 11 (100) | 4 (50) | 2 (25) | 2 (25) | 8 (100) |
| Total | 22 (85) | 4 (15) | 26 (100) | 11 (65) | 3 (18) | 3 (18) | 17 (101) |

*Source:* Interviews.

prise's lack of raw materials. It was clearly more difficult for the state to control the incentive structure than to control basic wages.

When scarcities intensified, workers could raise their incomes substantially by selling goods acquired in the commissary or received as pay in kind. The commissaries and pay in kind reduced the supply of manufactures at official prices and diminished labor productivity: It was more profitable to sell some of these products on the market than to aim at a small increase in the nominal wage by surpassing the normal work load. In June 1985, the government abolished pay in kind and changed the organization of the commissaries. Instead of keeping many different outlets at the different enterprises, it set up some big commissaries in the state supermarket buildings. All workers could shop there with identity cards and buy fixed quantities depending on the size of their families. But the supply of goods never was sufficient and real wages remained very low. For these reasons, the government could not prevent pay in kind and enterprise outlets from reappearing.

The interviewed directors of agricultural and agroindustrial enterprises all paid wages according to SNOTS. One said "he had no choice." Historically, wages in the countryside have been lower than in the cities. For that reason, agricultural employers did not judge wages according to SNOTS to be too low—at least, at the time of the interviews.

On paper, state control of wages and salaries gradually increased from 1979 to 1988. But in practice there were many ways to evade this control. In addition, there was no rule for extra remuneration (in kind or in dollars) of higher personnel, which made control of these incomes even more difficult. In June 1988 the government gave up wage control. Only the budget sector continued to apply SNOTS. In

TABLE 4.9 Sample of Enterprises: Investment and Assignment of Foreign Exchange Since 1979

| | *Investment* | | | *Received $?* | | | | |
|---|---|---|---|---|---|---|---|---|
| | *Yes* | *No* | *Total* | *Yes* | | | *No* | *Total* |
| | | | | *CBN*[a] | *IDB*[b] | *PC*[c] | | |
| State | 11 (69) | 5 (31) | 16 (100) | 8 (73) | 1 (9) | | 2 (18) | 11 (100) |
| Private | 14 (82) | 3 (18) | 17 (100) | 8 (57) | 1 (7) | 1 (7) | 3 (21) | 13 (100) |
| Total | 25 (76) | 8 (24) | 33 (100) | 16 (67) | 2 (8) | 1 (4) | 5 (21) | 24 (100) |

[a]From Central Bank of Nicaragua.
[b]From Inter-American Development Bank.
[c]From parent company.

*Source:* Interviews.

other enterprises, wages came to depend on negotiations between management and the union, which usually resulted in higher wages than those according to SNOTS. In compensation, workers in the budget sector received a monthly package of rice, beans, and corn at subsidized prices. This was supposed to be a temporary measure—for three months—but SNOTS wages were so low that the measure was continued.

***Investment.*** Most interviewed directors in manufacturing said they had invested in the past five years (Table 4.9). Of the twenty-five enterprises that had invested, just three had not invested in machinery and equipment but only in, for example, construction or in the improvement of labor conditions. Consequently, most enterprises probably had needed foreign exchange. Not all had had access to dollars. Relatively more state than private enterprises had received dollars from the Central Bank. Two enterprises had received foreign exchange from the Inter-American Development Bank (IDB), and one foreign enterprise was given foreign exchange by its parent company. In one enterprise I did not ask this question.

I also asked the directors whether they had had investment plans that could not be carried out because of a lack of foreign exchange. Among directors of private enterprises, 31 percent answered yes; in the state sector only 10 percent did so. These results might indicate that state enterprises enjoyed more priority within the investment policy of the Ministry of Industry.

## *Conclusion*

Before the 1988 reforms, the state determined prices for many medium and large manufacturing enterprises and these prices guaranteed a profit margin. In agriculture, the guaranteed prices for export products, in principle, also included a reasonable profit margin. This meant the policy left room for private accumulation for these, in general, large private producers. However, the practical possibilities for both sectors to make investment or even to replace existing machinery and equipment were limited.

The state distributed the majority of the means of production and seemed to discriminate against large private producers in agriculture and agroindustry. In addition, these producers could not be as sure as manufacturing producers of their juridical ownership and so already were less likely to maintain production and to invest.

In manufacturing, the policy did not discriminate against private producers in the assignment of raw materials, financing, and inputs for current production, but the private sector did seem to have less access to imported machinery. State and private producers had difficulties in maintaining production to some extent because the state did not assign sufficient raw materials, inputs, and spare parts. Production with a higher priority within the industrial strategy was relatively better off.

In general, the state had the instruments to implement a price policy for these large producers in agriculture and industry. In manufacturing, the assignment of foreign exchange almost determined the type of production to be carried out. In agriculture, the banking system played an important role, and control of inputs and machinery also was extensive. All these producers, except those of beef, really sold their products at state-determined prices. In sum, the state distributed the most important means of production and determined most output prices. Large enterprises in manufacturing and agriculture no longer produced for the market but for a plan.

So, Nicaragua was likely to experience the same problems as other centrally planned economies. Examples are wasteful criteria for plan fulfillment, instability of the plans, irrational use of means of production, long gestation periods for investment, and problems with innovation such as risk aversion on the part of managers (Ellman 1980:75-83). These inefficiencies are caused by the impossibility of providing perfect information, the insufficiency of the techniques to administer economic data, and the complexity of the economy, which prevents efficient decision-making at the National level (Ellman 1980:115). In addition, there is the problem of motivating the individual actors to comply with the plan.

Furthermore, production under a plan has a built-in tendency toward shortages (Kornai 1979 and 1980). Production plans are always taut; production is hampered by resource constraints. Planned economies are resource-constrained as opposed to capitalist systems that are demand-constrained. Each enterprise in a planned economy has an insatiable demand for inputs in an attempt to guarantee plan fulfillment. Investment plans are also taut, so all firms wish to get hold of as many investment goods as possible. Shortage in itself creates uncertainty and stimulates hoarding at all levels. Hoarding in turn creates more shortages. "Shortage breeds shortage" (Kornai 1979:813).

The most important cause for shortages, according to Kornai, is that firms experience a "soft budget constraint," which was indeed the case in Nicaragua: profitability did not really matter. Enterprise directors expected, on the basis of prior experience or on the basis of the experiences of other firms, that if need be, credits or budgetary supplements would be granted. According to Kornai, the soft budget constraint leads to both allocative inefficiencies (because input-output combinations do not adjust to price signals) and "X-inefficiencies" (there is no sufficient stimulus for maximum efforts) (Kornai 1986:10). In Nicaragua it was clear that state intervention led to these inefficiencies. Price distortions existed that, among other problems, caused producers with access to official imports to prefer imported inputs or machinery to local products or spare parts.

In other sectors of the economy the problem was the implementation of the price policy, in particular because of a lack of control of domestic trade. State control of manufactures' prices stopped at the factory door. Private traders benefited by selling these goods at much higher prices. In addition, many workers improved their poor salaries by reselling goods acquired in the commissaries or as pay in kind.

State prices for basic grains and for milk, mainly produced by peasants with small and medium landholdings, did not seem to leave room for private accumulation. These producers had much less access to subsidized inputs. In addition, they suffered from deteriorated terms of trade because they had to pay the high private market prices for manufactures, both inputs and consumer goods. The gradual liberation of prices implemented in 1986 and 1987 temporarily reversed this trend in the internal terms of trade, but in 1988 the government again set low prices for basic grains. In practice, until 1986 the state could not implement the price policy for these goods, and their supply at official prices was limited.

In February 1988 the state unified the exchange rate of the cordoba and afterward maintained it much closer to the black-market rate. This implied that many producers could no longer purchase their inputs at subsidized prices. The state also liberalized the prices of almost all manufactures, making an exception for some intermediate goods in November of that year. The credit policy also became more restrictive. As a result, many producers became subjected again to market forces. However, agricultural exporters still benefited from some kind of guaranteed prices, which gave them an implicit exchange rate higher than the official rate.[23]

The liberalization of prices of basic grains and the 1988 economic measures in general reflected the recognition that the state had lacked the instruments to control many domestic prices and that price distortions had reduced the efficiency of the economy. But, given the tendency to maintain some kind of guaranteed prices for export producers, for example, it remained doubtful whether the liberalized policy was sufficient to stimulate efficient production.

## Notes

1. Baumeister (1985b) and Vilas (1985), for example, maintained this for the agricultural sector and Weeks (1985b) for the manufacturing industry.

2. The Group of Twelve was a group of progressive Nicaraguan intellectuals and business people who acted as "ambassadors" for the struggle against the dictatorship—in Nicaragua and abroad.

3. Augusto César Sandino was a general from a peasant background who fought in the Liberal Army against a coup led by a conservative general and supported by US Marines in 1925. Sandino was the only liberal general not accepting the US government proposal to install a liberal as president, because it implied US Marines staying in the country. He continued fighting against US intervention. In 1934, he was killed on the instigation of the father of the in 1979 expulsed Somoza.

4. See his speech addressed to the Nicaraguan people on the first anniversary of the revolution (*Barricada*, July 20, 1980).

5. One manzana is 0.7 hectare.

6. That makes it impossible to detect this type of redistribution in Table 4.2.

7. "The cooperative form of production is more complicated, requires levels of cultural comprehension, technological development, organization, and education; the application of intensive production methods, mechanization, the use of agro-chemicals, infrastructure, and buying centers." (Wheelock Román according to *Barricada*, July 8, 1985)

8. *Barricada Internacional*, January 30, 1986.

9. See E. Baumeister 1988. "Desarrollistas y campesinistas, el debate en la política agropecuaria." *Pensamiento Propio* 52 (July-August):26-31.

10. Producers of leather and shoes, for instance, were integrated in one complex.

11. At least with respect to profits in cordobas. For investment in imported machinery and equipment they were always dependent on decisions at higher levels.

12. According to an interview with a branch director in November 1988.

13. Vice minister of industry Gilberto Guzmán confirmed this in an interview in May 1985.

14. During the years 1986 and 1987, the Production Commissions hardly functioned but they were reestablished in 1988.

15. From 1987 onward, the state would only export the traditional exports coffee, cotton, sugar, and meat. See INIES/SPP (1987:159).

16. For cattle and meat exporters this policy started in September 1984.

17. Officially this sector consisted of enterprises with less than thirty workers, but most of them have only one to five workers.

18. The director of planning of the Ministry of Industry gave some examples of successful rationalizations: the matches factory put fifty instead of forty matches in a box; soap was produced in a square instead of in a round form which also saved on the packing material.

19. The interviews were held before the U.S. government announced, in May 1985, a complete trade embargo.

20. Although at that time real interest rates were negative; see Chapter 5.

21. From then on, the government would have to approve price increases for these intermediate goods (*El Nuevo Diario*, November 10, 1988).

22. I did not ask this question systematically.

23. They also continued to receive part of the price in dollars.

# 5

# Accumulation and Sources for Accumulation

An important objective of the Nicaraguan revolutionary government was to initiate an accumulation process capable of creating a structural change in the economy. State investment was expected to constitute the bulk of total investment. The state was to be "the future pivot of the accumulation process" (MIPLAN 1980:47). The new economy should be less externally dependent. It should foster basic-goods production for the poor majority as well as maintenance of and improvement in real wages. The distribution of income should be improved by government-provided social services such as health and education.

As time passed, the most important objective became the physical defense of the revolution. The Sandinistas had to defend themselves against the attacks of the counterrevolutionaries, or contras, financed by the U.S. government and against the threat of a direct invasion by U.S. forces. The state needed more and more resources to achieve this objective.

The question is, Could state accumulation have been achieved and the redistributive goals fulfilled within a mixed economy? In this chapter, I analyze the impact of two stability conditions for the Sandinista mixed economy: the accumulation policy and the price policy. As deduced in Chapter 2, too high a rate of state accumulation can affect the mixed economy by endangering the macroeconomic balance and by changing the kinds of contributions required from the private sector. The price policy is here analyzed at a more general level, focusing in particular on its effects on macroeconomic stability.[1]

In view of the Sandinista government's objectives, the stability of the Nicaraguan mixed economy was under greater pressure than that of the NEP. The state needed resources from the private sector not only for accumulation but also to provide social services and, increasingly, for defense. At the same time, the maintenance of a private sector required that some private accumulation be allowed; and the objective to maintain real wages meant that wages could not be used as a source for state accumulation. It would be difficult to reach all these objectives and to maintain macroeconomic stability. Unlike the Soviet Union in the 1920s, however, Nicaragua in the 1980s might have access to external sources for accumulation, either in the form of a surplus of exports over imports or in the form of foreign aid.

The Sandinistas had specific ideas about how to achieve their objectives within the mixed economic order. First, they thought the nationalization of the banking system and foreign trade would "encircle" the bourgeoisie, that is, would allow the state to acquire a substantial share of private-sector surplus. This idea was based on an evaluation of the Somoza era, in which a financial bourgeoisie dominated by Somoza himself and by some foreign banking companies controlled most of domestic production (see Chapter 3). In the words of Jaime Wheelock, "We did not need to expropriate the means of production; in fact what we expropriated were the surpluses." (Wheelock Román in FSLN 1981:258).

A second idea determining the Sandinista vision of the mixed economy was the concept of a "mixed planned economy" (Gorostiaga 1981). State intervention in prices, wages, and taxes would support the production and redistribution goals. This idea was also often referred to as controlling the economy by controlling exchange relations but not production relations.

With respect to macroeconomic stabilization, the Nicaraguan government intended to pursue what FitzGerald called a "Kaleckian rather than Keynesian" approach (FitzGerald 1982). The supply of basic-wage goods was expected to increase, and total supply of these goods times its prices would have to equal the total wage bill. The state would control nominal wages and maintain low prices for "necessities." The supply of luxury goods ("nonnecessities") would be reduced, thereby increasing their prices (Kalecki 1972:145). Because the state could only partly determine the income policy, the market for nonnecessities would provide a clearing function (FitzGerald 1984:9).

This policy of aiming to improve the distribution of income by influencing the supply side of the economy could only succeed in combination with financial and monetary equilibrium. In addition, a Kaleckian approach implied the need to control, and necessarily expand, the production and marketed supply of basic wage-goods—activities in which the private sector dominated.

The aim of this chapter is to investigate three aspects of the feasibility of accumulation within the Sandinista mixed economy. First, did the state become the pivot of the accumulation process? That is, what was the investment rate and what share of investment was state investment? Second, what external and internal sources financed state investment and to what extent did the government succeed in acquiring a share of private surpluses? And third, what happened to the distribution of income? To what extent was it possible to maintain planned prices for basic consumer goods?

## Reactivation and Accumulation: An Overview

During the first years, the government gave priority to a reactivation of the economy. In 1980 and 1981 the economy recovered to some extent from the damages of the liberation war. GDP increased by 4.6 and 5.4 percent, respectively (Table 5.1). Still, this growth was not sufficient to compensate for the fall of almost 30 percent in 1979.

Although the banks made credits available on a large scale to facilitate repairs and reactivate production, this policy did not always meet with success. In some cases, destruction proved to be worse than expected; and some large private producers lacked confidence in the new government and preferred decapitalization to reactivation.

The government stimulated demand by expanding employment and by improving the distribution of income, especially in the countryside. Open unemployment diminished from 40 percent in July 1979 to 13 percent one year later (Dijkstra, van Hees, and Krop 1983:5). The proclamation and enforcement of a minimum wage raised incomes of agricultural laborers. Many small peasants received bank credits for the first time and often used them for consumption purposes. The distribution of income also improved in the cities, for example, because of a rent reduction.

Social services such as health, housing, and education improved.[2] Government expenses in this regard increased enormously. Government income was raised by a more effective tax policy, but a large deficit persisted. Imports filled the gap between increased demand and lagging supply, leading to a large balance-of-payments deficit (Table 5.1).

Yet, the financial problems (the fiscal deficit and the balance-of-payments deficit) did not lead to a high inflation rate in 1980. To the contrary, the high rate of 1979 (70 percent) declined to about 25 percent in 1980. Generous foreign aid directly after the victory of the Sandinistas helped finance the government deficit, and the availability of foreign loans made it possible to import goods that were in short

TABLE 5.1 Macroeconomic Indicators for Nicaragua 1979–1988

| | *1979* | *1980* | *1981* | *1982* | *1983* | *1984* | *1985* | *1986* | *1987* | *1988*[a] |
|---|---|---|---|---|---|---|---|---|---|---|
| GDP (index 1980=100) | 96 | 100 | 105 | 105 | 109 | 108 | 103 | 102 | 101 | 93 |
| GDP per capita (1980=100) | 99 | 100 | 102 | 98 | 99 | 94 | 87 | 84 | 80 | 71 |
| Growth GDP (%) | -26.5 | 4.6 | 5.4 | -0.8 | 4.6 | -1.6 | -4.1 | -1.0 | -0.7 | -8.0 |
| Growth GDP per capita (%) | -28.5 | 1.5 | 2.0 | -4.0 | 1.2 | -4.8 | -7.3 | -4.3 | -4.0 | -11.1 |
| Increase cons. prices (%) | 70 | 25 | 23 | 22 | 33 | 50 | 334 | 747 | 1374 | 33603 |
| Increase real wages[b] (%) | -14 | -15 | 1 | -4 | 2 | -7 | -17 | -26 | 12 | -72 |
| External sector: | | | | | | | | | | |
| Exports (millions of $US) | 672 | 495 | 553 | 447 | 471 | 431 | 351 | 294 | 328 | 237 |
| Imports (millions of $US) | 511 | 909 | 1037 | 826 | 901 | 921 | 938 | 857 | 986 | 951 |
| Trade balance | 161 | -414 | -484 | -379 | -430 | -490 | -587 | -563 | -658 | -714 |
| Current account balance | 90 | -491 | -563 | -557 | -635 | -727 | -827 | -799 | -856 | -865 |
| Public ext. debt (billions of $US) | 1.1 | 1.6 | 2.6 | 3.1 | 3.8 | 4.4 | 4.9 | 5.8 | 6.3 | 7.2 |
| Change in terms of trade (%) | | -7 | -10 | -5 | -3 | 26 | -5 | 10 | -9 | 2 |
| Index terms of trade | | 100 | 91 | 86 | 83 | 105 | 98 | 104 | 100 | 99 |

[a]Preliminary figures.
[b]Total average monthly wage received by workers registered with the Nicaraguan Social Security and Welfare Institute.

*Sources:* ECLAC 1989. *Economic survey of Latin America and the Caribbean 1988, Tables 1, 11, 16 for 1982-1988.* For 1981: ECLAC 1988. *Notas preliminares para el estudio económico de América Latina y El Caribe 1987: Nicaragua.* Tables 1, 10, 16. For 1979 and 1980: ECLAC 1986. Ibid. Tables 1, 11, 16.

TABLE 5.2 Accumulation Balance for Nicaragua 1977–1985 (in percent of GDP at 1980 prices)

| | *1977* | *1978* | *1979* | *1980* | *1981* | *1982* | *1983* | *1984* | *1985* |
|---|---|---|---|---|---|---|---|---|---|
| 1. Investment | 23 | 11 | -6 | 15 | 23 | 19 | 20 | 20 | 19 |
| 2. Domestic saving | 19 | 16 | 11 | -3 | 10 | 15 | 14 | 7 | 6 |
| 3. External saving | 4 | -5 | -18 | 18 | 12 | 4 | 7 | 13 | 12 |
| 4. Consumption | 81 | 84 | 89 | 103 | 90 | 85 | 86 | 93 | 94 |
| 5. Int. financ. (2/1) | 81 | 149 | -179 | -18 | 46 | 78 | 74 | 35 | 33 |
| 6. Ext. financ. (3/1) | 19 | -45 | 279 | 118 | 54 | 22 | 36 | 66 | 67 |

*Source:* Argüello and Kleiterp 1985. "Inversiones 1979–1985: Análisis del proceso inversionista Nicaragüense de 1979 a 1985." Managua: Fondo Nicaragüense de Inversiones, 71. Mimeo.

supply. It was clear, however, that a more restrictive policy in several respects would be required in the future.

The economic program of 1981 was called the Program of Austerity and Efficiency (MIPLAN 1981). The intention was to exercise more control over the credit policy, for example, by giving agricultural credits only in combination with the necessary inputs. Government expenses were still far ahead of income, and in September 1981 the government announced the Law of Social and Economic Emergency, which included a 5 percent reduction in the expenses of all ministries. In 1982 a large cut in imports was made.

At the same time, from 1981 onward the government gave more priority to accumulation. In 1980 the investment rate was low and the domestic savings rate was negative (Table 5.2). The next year, the state began some large state investment projects. From 1981 onward, the accumulation rate was fairly high. On average, gross investment absorbed 19 percent of annual GDP between 1980 and 1985 (Table 5.2). Results of the investment were not yet visible in this period because most investments were in long-term projects (see next chapter).

According to Argüello, Kleiterp, and Croes (1988:31), 75 percent of all gross investment from 1980–1985 was state investment.[3] If we compare the share of investment with the share in GDP, an investment rate for the private sector of only 6.9 percent is implied. For the state sector this rate was 31.2 percent, but this figure includes investment in social and economic infrastructure, which constituted about half of all state investment.

In 1981 external conditions also changed. In the United States the new Reagan administration immediately cut all aid to Nicaragua. Under U.S. pressure, multilateral organizations such as the World

TABLE 5.3 Property Damage and Production Losses Due to the Armed Conflict (in millions of $)

| | *1980* | *1981* | *1982* | *1983* | *1984* | *1985* | *1986* | *1987* | *1988*[a] | *1980-1988* |
|---|---|---|---|---|---|---|---|---|---|---|
| Property damage: | | | | | | | | | | |
| Agriculture | 0.0 | 0.1 | 2.3 | 12.2 | 14.0 | 10.4 | 4.0 | 18.6 | 0.5 | 62.1 |
| Logging and forestry | 0.0 | 0.0 | 0.1 | 24.2 | 5.3 | 0.4 | 0.0 | 0.0 | 0.4 | 30.4 |
| Fisheries | 0.6 | 2.2 | 1.6 | 4.8 | 2.6 | 0.6 | 0.5 | 0.1 | 0.4 | 13.4 |
| Mining | 0.0 | 0.0 | 0.0 | 1.7 | 1.0 | 0.0 | 0.0 | 36.7 | 0.0 | 39.4 |
| Construction and transport | 0.0 | 1.7 | 6.9 | 6.0 | 2.0 | 4.4 | 0.9 | 8.0 | 0.5 | 30.4 |
| Other sectors | 0.0 | 1.8 | 0.1 | 9.7 | 1.9 | 4.0 | 8.6 | 24.0 | 0.1 | 50.2 |
| Subtotal | 0.6 | 5.8 | 11.0 | 58.6 | 26.8 | 19.8 | 14.0 | 87.4 | 1.9 | 225.9 |
| Production losses: | | | | | | | | | | |
| Agriculture | 0.1 | 0.0 | 0.2 | 36.9 | 74.3 | 71.1 | 148.4 | 100.1 | 112.7 | 543.8 |
| Logging and forestry | 0.0 | 0.0 | 0.0 | 24.9 | 52.7 | 41.5 | 49.9 | 167.2 | 55.0 | 391.2 |
| Fisheries | 0.9 | 1.2 | 2.8 | 13.2 | 15.8 | 15.7 | 4.7 | 4.9 | 6.2 | 65.4 |
| Mining | 0.0 | 2.2 | 3.1 | 1.3 | 2.0 | 4.5 | 2.5 | 9.3 | 0.0 | 24.9 |
| Construction | 0.0 | 0.0 | 15.0 | 30.0 | 45.0 | 12.4 | 24.1 | 40.0 | 2.3 | 168.8 |
| Subtotal | 1.0 | 3.4 | 21.1 | 106.3 | 189.8 | 145.2 | 229.6 | 321.5 | 176.2 | 1194.1 |
| Total | 1.6 | 9.2 | 32.1 | 164.9 | 216.6 | 165.0 | 243.6 | 408.9 | 178.1 | 1420.0 |

[a]Real figures up to November and estimated figures up to December 15, 1988.

*Source:* ECLAC 1989. *Economic survey of Latin America and the Caribbean 1988.*

Bank and the Inter-American Development Bank became reluctant to grant new loans to Nicaragua. The Reagan administration also began to finance former members of Somoza's National Guard who had fled to Honduras.

As a result, the Sandinistas had to confront the economic consequences of this contra war. Especially from 1983 onward, war damage to infrastructure and production installations and loss of production were considerable (Table 5.3). In addition to the costs of this direct damage, more government funds were needed for defense, in particular for maintaining an army. Annual defense expenditure climbed from 7 percent of the budget in 1980 to about 40 percent in 1985–1987 (ECLAC 1988).

In 1982 GDP fell by 1.2 percent, in part because of floods that destroyed basic-grains crops. In 1983 Nicaragua still had one of the highest growth rates in Latin America. Production had recuperated to prewar levels to a certain extent (see Table 5.4 for agricultural production and Table 5.5 for industrial production). From 1984 to 1986, growth rates were negative and after a slight revival in 1987, GDP dropped by 8 percent in 1988 (Table 5.1). So, GDP per capita fell by 33 percent between 1981 and 1989 (ECLAC 1989b).

Imbalances in the economy were already visible in 1983. The balance of payments and the government account showed large deficits (Table 5.1). The inflation rate was still relatively moderate. It was probably contained in part by a reduction in the circulation velocity of money. FitzGerald (1984:10) estimated that this velocity declined from 5 to 3 between 1980 and 1984, probably because peasants held a larger proportion of the money stock.

Not surprisingly, after 1983 the maintenance of a high state accumulation rate, coupled with less access to foreign aid and increasing damage from the contra war, intensified the imbalances: The balance-of-payments deficit as well as the inflation rate increased (Table 5.1). After 1984 the fiscal deficit diminished, but the global deficit, which included investment financing and exchange losses of the Central Bank, did not (see further on).

## Sources for State Accumulation

Most investment was in machinery and equipment. According to SPP figures, such investment constituted 61 percent of total investment from 1980 to 1985 (Argüello, Kleiterp, and Croes 1988:4). Consequently, the investment required a large amount of imports. The balance of trade does not seem to have provided the planned surplus

TABLE 5.4 Indicators of Agricultural Production

| | *1975* | *1981* | *1982* | *1983* | *1984* | *1985* | *1986* | *1987* | *1988*[a] |
|---|---|---|---|---|---|---|---|---|---|
| Production indexes (1980=100) | | | | | | | | | |
| Primary production | 118 | | 113 | 122 | 121 | 107 | 98 | 95 | 95 |
| Crop-farming | 125 | 122 | 126 | 137 | 123 | 115 | 103 | 104 | 98 |
| Livestock | 110 | 90 | 101 | 101 | 104 | 101 | 94 | 82 | 92 |
| Forestry | | 204 | 137 | 143 | 107 | 85 | 89 | 100 | 104 |
| Fishing | | | | | | 61 | 52 | 63 | 69 |
| Production of main crops[b] | | | | | | | | | |
| For export: | | | | | | | | | |
| Ginned cotton | 118 | 72 | 67 | 81 | 81 | 64 | 50 | 45 | 31 |
| Cotton seed | 189 | 107 | 101 | 121 | 119 | 93 | 77 | 68 | 46 |
| Unroasted coffee | 42 | 58 | 63 | 65 | 46 | 47 | 37 | 41 | 39 |
| Sugar cane | 2304 | 2520 | 2756 | 2795 | 2814 | 2607 | 2487 | 2241 | 2160 |
| Bananas | 170 | 153 | 141 | 128 | 128 | 113 | 101 | 137 | 100 |
| Havana tobacco | 2 | 1 | 1 | 1 | 1 | 1 | 1 | 1 | 1 |
| Blonde tobacco | 2 | 1 | 1 | 2 | 3 | 2 | 2 | 2 | 2 |
| Sesame | 4 | 7 | 5 | 11 | 10 | 3 | 4 | 4 | 3 |
| For internal consumption: | | | | | | | | | |
| Corn | 189 | 197 | 185 | 205 | 215 | 199 | 207 | 257 | 258 |
| Milled rice | 58 | 74 | 91 | 98 | 89 | 82 | 79 | 72 | 89 |
| Beans | 44 | 46 | 53 | 54 | 58 | 52 | 52 | 49 | 54 |
| Sorghum | 60 | 90 | 70 | 70 | 102 | 120 | 147 | 153 | 105 |
| Soya | | | | | | 5 | 8 | 10 | 2 |
| Indicators of livestock production | | | | | | | | | |
| Slaughtering: | | | | | | | | | |
| Beef cattlec | 325 | 273 | 311 | 341 | 341 | 359 | 302 | 230 | 280 |
| Pigs[c] | 168 | 243 | 279 | 270 | 271 | 228 | 242 | 321 | 321 |
| Poultry[b] | 10 | 12 | 14 | 13 | 10 | 10 | 12 | 11 | |
| Other products: | | | | | | | | | |
| Milk[d] | 433 | 306 | 315 | 301 | 318 | 162 | 185 | 176 | 192 |
| Eggs[e] | 32 | 43 | 42 | 41 | 21 | 23 | 23 | 18 | |

[a]Preliminary figures.
[b]Thousands of tons.
[c]Thousands of head.
[d]Millions of liters.
[e]Millions of dozens.

*Sources:* ECLAC 1986. *Notas para el estudio económico de América Latina y el Caribe 1985:* Nicaragua for 1975; ECLAC 1988. *Estudio económico de América Latina y El Caribe 1987:* Nicaragua for 1981–1984; ECLAC 1989. *Economic survey of Latin America and the Caribbean 1988* for 1985–1988.

TABLE 5.5 Indexes of Manufacturing Value Added 1978–1983 (selected years; 1977=100)[a]

| | *1978* | *1979* | *1980* | *1981* | *1982* | *1983* |
|---|---|---|---|---|---|---|
| Nondurable consumer goods: | | | | | | |
| Food | 105 | 89 | 89 | 92 | 104 | 110 |
| Beverages | 105 | 83 | 123 | 119 | 110 | 111 |
| Tobacco | 97 | 76 | 112 | 108 | 93 | 94 |
| Textiles | 97 | 61 | 70 | 97 | 100 | 132 |
| Shoes and clothing | 87 | 49 | 129 | 142 | 131 | 139 |
| Wood and cork | 83 | 50 | 51 | 53 | 46 | 44 |
| Furniture | 98 | 68 | 60 | 63 | 55 | 46 |
| Printing and publishing | 83 | 59 | 98 | 110 | 115 | 117 |
| Leather & leather products | 111 | 106 | 114 | 90 | 97 | 103 |
| Other manufacturing | 105 | 59 | 37 | 41 | 37 | 39 |
| Subtotal | 101 | 79 | 91 | 95 | 98 | 104 |
| Intermediate goods: | | | | | | |
| Paper and paper products | 108 | 71 | 56 | 60 | 74 | 97 |
| Rubber products | 102 | 75 | 190 | 200 | 206 | 233 |
| Chemicals | 101 | 68 | 73 | 70 | 62 | 68 |
| Oil products | 87 | 65 | 95 | 106 | 91 | 95 |
| Construction materials | 89 | 43 | 72 | 68 | 64 | 72 |
| Subtotal | 96 | 61 | 77 | 77 | 71 | 79 |
| Capital goods and durable consumer goods: | | | | | | |
| Metal products | 105 | 50 | 70 | 68 | 76 | 84 |
| Electr. and non-el. machin. | 101 | 54 | 42 | 33 | 26 | 26 |
| Transport materials | 102 | 61 | 66 | 76 | 55 | 52 |
| Subtotal | 104 | 52 | 60 | 57 | 58 | 63 |
| Total | 100 | 73 | 86 | 88 | 89 | 96 |

[a]Based on real value added figures in 1958 cordobas.

*Source*: Ministry of Planning, Manufacturing and Mining Division, 1985. Mimeo.

to make these imports of capital goods possible. Instead, foreign loans filled the gap. Foreign savings were a very important source for accumulation (see Table 5.2). In addition, gross domestic savings were positive in all years except 1980. It remains to be seen whether these were real savings or forced savings (savings that accumulates as a result of low supply).

### *External Sources*

The intention was that a high accumulation rate be sustained by increased export production. As Table 5.1 shows, after 1980 the value of imported goods and services was much higher than the value of exports. Instead of increasing, the volume of exports diminished. Some exports, cattle and beef in particular, could not recuperate quickly from the damage caused by the liberation war. Cattle-holders had driven their "walking capital" over the border during the war, and massive slaughter had taken place. In the first years after the Sandinista victory, capital flight from this sector persisted. The result was a serious fall in dairy and meat production, leading to imports of powdered milk and even causing shortages of hides for leather and shoe production (Weeks 1985b:286).

Cotton production lagged behind because large private producers were reluctant to produce in the new political situation. For the same reason, some coffee producers neglected the maintenance of their plants, thereby diminishing production. The system of guaranteed profits and the accompanying uncoupling of domestic and world-market prices (Chapter 4) may have reduced productivity in private export production.

Export production of sugar, coffee, and cotton suffered from a serious lack of labor in the harvest season. Productivity on state as well as private farms had fallen because of more humane labor conditions: a workday shortened from about eleven to eight hours (and at times in practice only four hours), a free Sunday, and the absence of repression. In addition, laborers from El Salvador and Honduras who formerly came for the harvests did not anymore. Other factors were the improved distribution of income and the high population growth, which resulted in higher consumption levels of exportable goods. This was the case with sugar, meat, vegetable oil, and many other manufactures.

The largest fall in the volume of export production was in industrial exports, as shown in Table 5.6. Manufacturing exports diminished in absolute terms from $170 million to $51 million between 1978 and 1984. They represented 26 percent of total exports in 1978 but only 13 percent in 1984. Reactivation of production in this sector required extensive imports of raw materials, inputs, and machinery and equipment, which did not always come about. Manufacturing enterprises were given a lower priority within the overall economic strategy (see Chapters 4 and 6). Industrial production also suffered from the consequences of the fall in primary production.

In addition, the crisis in the CACM played a role. Some factories had lost their markets in CACM countries because buyers had found

TABLE 5.6 Exports of Goods 1976–1985 (in millions of $)

| | 1976 | 1977 | 1978 | 1979 | 1980 | 1981 | 1982 | 1983 | 1984 | 1985 |
|---|---|---|---|---|---|---|---|---|---|---|
| Agricultural products | 393 | 470 | 465 | 452 | 327 | 393 | 331 | 372 | 334 | 271 |
| Cotton | 131 | 151 | 141 | 136 | 30 | 122 | 87 | 110 | 134 | 91 |
| Coffee | 119 | 199 | 200 | 159 | 166 | 136 | 124 | 154 | 122 | 121 |
| Sugar | 53 | 28 | 20 | 20 | 21 | 49 | 36 | 32 | 21 | 7 |
| Beef | 38 | 37 | 68 | 94 | 59 | 21 | 34 | 31 | 18 | 11 |
| Shrimp, lobster | 20 | 22 | 15 | 22 | 27 | 18 | 22 | 17 | 13 | 13 |
| Bananas | 5 | 5 | 5 | 6 | 8 | 21 | 10 | 15 | 12 | 17 |
| Other | 28 | 29 | 18 | 17 | 16 | 26 | 18 | 14 | 16 | 12 |
| Industrial products | 141 | 157 | 170 | 107 | 84 | 81 | 59 | 57 | 51 | 31 |
| Chemical products | 42 | 51 | 51 | 31 | 33 | 29 | 20 | 17 | 18 | 9 |
| Cotton-byproducts[b] | 16 | 18 | 25 | 18 | 0 | 9 | 6 | 8 | 9 | 5 |
| Wood products | 13 | 11 | 10 | 6 | 3 | 2 | 2 | 1 | | |
| Textiles | 12 | 12 | 12 | 8 | 6 | 3 | 2 | 1 | 1 | 0 |
| Dairy products | 7 | 7 | 7 | 3 | 0 | 2 | 4 | | | |
| Cereal products | 4 | 5 | 5 | 3 | 5 | 4 | 3 | 2 | 2 | 1 |
| Clothing | 3 | 4 | 1 | 0 | 1 | 1 | | 3 | 3 | 3 |
| Soluble coffee | 0 | 2 | 1 | 1 | 4 | 5 | 4 | 5 | 4 | 4 |
| Other | 45 | 47 | 59 | 36 | 32 | 26 | 18 | 19 | 14 | 9 |
| Mining | 8 | 9 | 11 | 8 | 40 | 25 | 15 | 0 | 0 | 0 |
| Total[a] | 542 | 637 | 646 | 567 | 450 | 500 | 406 | 429 | 385 | 302 |

[a]The total refers to the original data, not to the rounded figures.
[b]Includes cotton-tart, linter, and cotton-seed oil.

*Source*: INEC, *Comercio Exterior 1982*. Managua: INEC; and INEC 1987. Mimeo.

other suppliers to compensate for the temporary fall in production during and after the liberation war. Demand in CACM countries also decreased absolutely because of the foreign-exchange crises these countries suffered.

The intensification of the contra war also had consequences for the volume of export production, in particular from 1983 onward. Production was lost due to damage to the infrastructure and to the means of production (fisher boats, wood-cutting capacity, mining) and to the practical impossibility of cultivating the land and getting in the crop (Table 5.3). In May 1985 the U.S. government announced a complete trade embargo, which caused further damage to the value of export production. The share of exports to the United States had already decreased to about 12 percent of the total; however, for this 12 percent new markets had to be found and in all cases this caused higher transport costs. The total loss caused by the embargo in 1985–1988 is estimated at more than $300 million (IHCA 1989a:16).

In contrast to exports, imports increased. Imports of intermediate and capital goods expanded both absolutely and relatively (Table 3.3). The share of consumer goods diminished. The state had used its foreign trade monopoly after 1979 to reduce the share of durable consumer goods (often luxury goods). In addition, the proportion of nondurable consumer goods diminished, from 24 percent in 1980 to 13 percent in 1987. The expansion of imports of intermediate and capital goods can be explained by the high state investment rate and by the fact that many foreign loans were tied to goods, and donor countries often preferred to sell capital goods.[4]

Until 1984 the problems with the balance of payments were exacerbated by deteriorated external terms of trade. After 1984, however, the relation between export and import prices developed rather favorably (Table 5.1). The gap between imports and exports was increasingly caused by the overvalued exchange rate of the cordoba. Imports were cheap for enterprises that enjoyed a high priority in the economic strategy. There was no incentive to reduce import-dependent production. From February 1981 until February 1988 there was a multiple exchange-rate system for imports (Table 5.7), which complicated efficient import allocation decisions and probably further stimulated imports that were not really necessary.

The overvalued exchange rate did not stimulate exports sufficiently. With respect to the traditional export crops (coffee, cotton, sugar), the system of guaranteed prices in cordobas produced implicit exchange rates that were often higher than the official rate, reducing the negative effect on export volumes to some extent. As of February 1982 the government also applied export-stimulating measures for nontraditional exports, for example, it permitted producers to change

TABLE 5.7 Exchange Rates in Nicaragua 1979–1989

| | *Official* | *Imports*[a] | *Exports*[b] | *Parallel* | *Black* |
|---|---|---|---|---|---|
| 1979, February | 7 | 7 | 7 | | 8 |
| 1979, April | 10 | 10 | 10 | | 10 |
| 1980, June | 10 | 10 | 10- | | 21 |
| 1981, March | 10 | 10/15 | 10-14.5 | | 26 |
| 1981, September | 10 | 10/15 | 10-14.5 | 28 | 33 |
| 1982, February | 10 | 10/15 | 10-17.2 | 28 | 38 |
| 1982, July | 10 | 10/15 | 10-17.2 | 28 | 50 |
| 1983, February | 10 | 10-28 | 12.7-21 | 28 | 55 |
| 1983, June | 10 | 10-28 | 12.7-21 | | 77 |
| 1984, February | 10 | 10-28 | 12.7-21 | | 140 |
| 1984, September | 10 | 10-28 | 21-60 | | 250 |
| 1985, February | 28 | 20-50 | 28-60 | | 500 |
| 1985, June | 28 | 20-50 | 28-60 | 650 | 700 |
| 1986, February | 70 | 20/70 | 70-188 | 770 | 1,150 |
| 1986, June | 70 | 20/70 | 685[c] | 1,300 | 2,200 |
| 1987, March | 70 | 20/70 | 1,680c | 3,300 | 4,700 |
| 1987, June | 70 | 70/170/370 | 2,785c | 5,500 | - |
| 1987, November | 70 | 70/170/370 | 5,035[c] | 20,000 | 55,000 |
| 1988, February[d] | 10 | 10 | 10- | 11 | 60 |
| 1988, June[e] | 80 | 80 | 80- | 80 | 150 |
| 1989· January[e] | 2,000 | 2,000 | 2,000- | 4,500 | 5,500 |
| 1989, June | 20,000 | 20,000 | 20,000- | 25,000 | - |

[a]From February 1981 until February 1988 different exchange rates for imports.
[b]After July 1979 multiple implicit exchange rates for exports, varying per product and per year; figures are estimations.
[c]An estimated average, based on the rate for non-traditional agricultural exports (changing 50 percent at official rate and 50 percent at parallel rate; see INIES 1987. *Boletín Socioeconómico* 5 (August-September):2.
[d]Monetary reform: one new cordoba = 1000 old cordobas.
[e]Black market rate of last day of previous month.

*Sources:* Compiled by the author from Inter-American Development Bank 1983. *Nicaragua Economic Report*; *Latin America Regional Report* April 1980; *Business Latin America* July 14, 1982; Pizarro, Roberto 1987. "The new economic policy: A necessary readjustment," *In The Political Economy of Revolutionary Nicaragua*, ed. Rose J. Spalding. Boston: Allen & Unwin, 217-32; Banco de Datos de INIES/CRIES 1985. "Coyuntura económica y Revolución, Nicaragua 1979–1985" (first draft); Cabieses, Hugo 1987. "La economía de Nicaragua 1979–1986", mimeo; Medal, José Luis 1988. Nicaragua: *Crisis, cambio social y política económica*, Managua: CINASE; ECLAC 1988. *Notas para el estudio económico de América Latina y El Caribe 1987: Nicaragua*; *La Prensa* June 12, 1989; ECLAC 1989. *Economic survey of Latin America and the Caribbean 1988.*

part of the export income on the parallel market. From 1986 onward, all exporters received part of their export income in dollars or received cordobas at the parallel rate for part of it. On average, the implicit export exchange rates have always been above the import rates. This caused the so-called exchange losses of the Central Bank. From 1985 onward, the high domestic inflation rate reduced the effect of guaranteed prices and export incentives, because domestic prices were still higher. Domestic consumption of, for example, coffee, increased, which reduced the export volume (Pilarte, Ubau, and Guevara 1988:14).

Table 5.7 also includes the changes in the parallel and black-market rates. In the first years after the Sandinista victory, the black market caused capital flight on a large scale. The government attempted to control this market by establishing an official parallel market controlled by the Central Bank. However, because of the fixed rate on this official parallel market, the black market soon reappeared. In June 1982 the official parallel market was abolished, to be opened again in June 1985 at a rate that, in principle, would fluctuate with market forces. But until 1988, black-market rates were much higher than the official parallel rate.[5]

Capital flight via the black and parallel exchange markets was probably limited—at least after the first few years. These markets functioned as an "escape valve" for production import needs not satisfied by official channels and for consumption needs of the middle and upper classes. One could also look upon them as a clearing market for redundant domestic money. As far as they satisfied consumption needs, however, they constituted, in a sense, capital flight, because potential savings were converted into consumption (World Bank 1981:48).

The monetary reform of February 1988 implied an official devaluation of 3,000 percent and a unification of the official exchange rates. But many exporters still received their export income at implicit exchange rates higher than the import rate. The government first abolished the parallel rate, but continuing inflation soon brought back a black market. From June 1988 onward, devaluations occurred more regularly and the differences between official, parallel, and black-market rates became much smaller.

The deficit in the balance of trade and services enlarged the already serious debt problem at the time of Somoza's overthrow (Table 5.1). But interest payments were limited relative to the size of the debt. The government was able to restructure the debt inherited from Somoza in negotiations with foreign commercial banks (Weinert 1981). Amortization and interest payments were reduced and postponed. According to this agreement, the government had to start interest and amortization payments on these debts in 1985 but could then postpone the major share again. Nevertheless, debt servicing constituted 46 percent of the export value in 1988 (ECLAC 1989a).

The new debts that accompanied the current account deficits were not commercial loans or loans from official multilateral organizations such as the Inter-American Development Bank or the World Bank. The U.S. government successfully blocked loans from the latter, even when they had been approved by the staff. From 1981 through 1984 this cost Nicaragua more than $160 million (FitzGerald 1987:201). Nicaragua received mainly official bilateral loans tied to the imports of goods. These were the real sources for state accumulation. Governments of such diverse countries as Mexico, France, the Soviet Union, and Argentina supported the Sandinistas. Although some of these credit lines were of a short- or medium-term nature, payment obligations remained limited. However, the amount of foreign loans from Western countries decreased after 1986, and socialist countries only partly compensated for this fall. This led to significant reductions in the level of international reserves in 1986–1988.[6]

### *Internal Sources*

A first source for financing state accumulation would be government taxation of private production, income, and exports. Table 5.8 gives an overview of government income and expenditure. Tax income relative to GDP increased enormously during the first years of Sandinista rule: from 11 percent in 1977 to 32 percent in 1984.[7] The government proclaimed some new taxes, but the most important reason for the increased government income was the improvement in the collection of taxes (Irvin 1983:130).

The nationalization of foreign trade did not result in the expected income growth for the government. Rather, falling world-market prices forced the state to give export subsidies instead of obtaining taxes. But more important was the difference between subsidized imports and the export rate, which led to the exchange losses of the Central Bank.

Within direct taxes, the share of the income tax increased in the course of 1981–1984, but not enough to compensate for the decreasing other direct taxes (Table 5.9). In 1985 the government increased the number of contributors to the income tax by including private traders and independent professionals. In 1987 cooperatives were also subjected to income taxes. These measures led to a remarkable increase of the income tax within total government income. The share of the turnover tax also remained large. The turnover tax is considered to be

TABLE 5.8 Indicators of Government Finance 1981–1988 (ratios in percent)

| | *1981* | *1982* | *1983* | *1984* | *1985* | *1986* | *1987* | *1988*[a] |
|---|---|---|---|---|---|---|---|---|
| Tax revenue/GDP | 19 | 21 | 25 | 31 | 28 | 28 | 25 | 17 |
| Total expenditure/GDP | 33 | 37 | 56 | 60 | 56 | 50 | 44 | 44 |
| Fiscal deficit/GDP | 12 | 13 | 28 | 25 | 23 | 18 | 17 | 26 |
| Fiscal deficit/total expend. | 36 | 35 | 49 | 41 | 42 | 35 | 38 | 59 |
| Domestic financing/deficit | 69 | 60 | 83 | 83 | 96 | 92 | 100 | 86 |
| External financing/deficit | 31 | 40 | 17 | 17 | 4 | 1 | 0 | 6 |

[a]Preliminary figures.

*Sources*: ECLAC 1985. *Notas para el estudio económico de América Latina y El Caribe 1984: Nicaragua* for 1981-1983; ECLAC 1986. *Notas para el estudio económico de América Latina y El Caribe 1985: Nicaragua* for 1984; ECLAC 1989. *Economic survey of Latin America and the Caribbean 1988* for 1985–1988.

a regressive source of tax income; in Nicaragua about half of turnover tax income came from so-called fiscal goods (INIES 1987b:14).[8]

Current budget expenditure increased more than government income. First there were the improvements in social services. Although much was accomplished by employing voluntary labor (in health and literacy campaigns, for example) and through external aid (for building hospitals and schools), such improvements implied a cost: Salaries had to be paid to workers in the field and to organizers and coordinators in the ministries. Expenses also increased in physical infrastructure projects (building highways and other communications projects) and in the production realm. The government speeded up its investment. Capital expenses represented 17 percent of the total budget in 1981 and 29 percent in 1984.

Government subsidies for basic items such as corn, beans, rice, milk, vegetable oil, public transport, and energy constituted a yearly increasing budget component until 1985. Subsidies for basic grains mounted to 652 million cordobas in 1983 (CIERA/PAN/CIDA 1984, 3:69). In 1984 total subsidies, including subsidies to enterprises, represented 11 percent of total expenditure and 16 percent of current expenditure.

After 1983 the share of defense in the national budget increased. In 1984, 40 percent of the government budget was spent on defense and for 1985–1988 it was estimated at 50 percent. This increase for defense was accompanied by falling real expenditure for other budget components.

The New Package of Economic Measures reduced government expenditure for, in particular, health, education, and some basic-item

TABLE 5.9 Composition of Current Government Income (in percent)

| | *1981* | *1982* | *1983* | *1984* | *1985* | *1986* | *1987*[a] |
|---|---|---|---|---|---|---|---|
| Tax revenue | 85 | 80 | 84 | 88 | 86 | 85 | 89 |
| Direct taxes | 22 | 18 | 18 | 20 | 20 | 22 | 21 |
| Income tax | 12 | 11 | 13 | 15 | 17 | 20 | 20 |
| Property tax | 6 | 5 | 3 | 3 | 2 | 2 | 1 |
| Export tax | 3 | 0 | 0 | 0 | 0 | 0 | 0 |
| Other | 2 | 2 | 3 | 2 | 1 | 0 | 0 |
| Indirect taxes | 63 | 62 | 65 | 67 | 66 | 63 | 68 |
| Tax on sales | 14 | 11 | 12 | 12 | 14 | 14 | 13 |
| Import tax | 13 | 10 | 7 | 7 | 8 | 8 | 5 |
| Turnover tax | 35 | 32 | 34 | 38 | 42 | 40 | 48 |
| Other | 2 | 9 | 13 | 10 | 1 | 1 | 1 |
| Nontax revenue | 15 | 20 | 16 | 12 | 14 | 15 | 11 |
| Total | 100 | 100 | 100 | 100 | 100 | 100 | 100 |

[a]Preliminary figures.

*Sources*: ECLAC 1985. *Notas para el estudio económico de América Latina y El Caribe 1984: Nicaragua* for 1981–1983; ECLAC 1988. *Notas para el estudio económico de América Latina y El Caribe 1987: Nicaragua* for 1984–1987.

subsidies in February 1985. The government abolished most subsidies for corn, beans, sorghum, milk, sugar, and rice but maintained those for public transport and energy. The measures were also intended to reduce expenditure on public investment, but this was difficult to accomplish because many large projects were under way. In 1985, 1986, and 1987 the proportion of gross investment within GDP did not diminish.

The government deficit increased from 12 percent of GDP in 1981 to 28 percent of GDP in 1983 and then decreased gradually to 17 percent in 1987 (Table 5.8). The austerity measures played some role, but also the fact that from 1984 onward, most public investment was no longer financed from the budget but by the FNI (Fondo Nicaragüense de Inversiones; Nicaraguan Investment Fund), which received its money from the Central Bank (Argüello, Kleiterp, and Croes 1988:18-19). Exchange losses were also excluded. The deficit was increasingly financed from internal sources, in particular from Central Bank credits (Table 5.8, last two rows).

The exchange losses of the Central Bank grew from 1,400 million cordobas in 1982 to 25,000 million cordobas in 1986 (INIES 1987a:2,6). From 1985 to 1986 they climbed from 2 to 7 percent of GDP, so that the sum of fiscal deficit and exchange losses remained unchanged in

TABLE 5.10 Distribution of Credit by Production Sector (in percent)

| | *1978* | *1979* | *1980* | *1981* | *1982* | *1983* |
|---|---|---|---|---|---|---|
| Commerce | 19 | 18 | 10 | 7 | 6 | 5 |
| Agriculture | 22 | 23 | 35 | 32 | 33 | 32 |
| Cattle-raising | 10 | 8 | 9 | 12 | 17 | 18 |
| Industry | 21 | 26 | 29 | 35 | 33 | 35 |
| Housing | 21 | 20 | 16 | 12 | 10 | 10 |
| Others | 7 | 5 | 1 | 1 | 1 | 1 |
| Total | 100 | 100 | 100 | 100 | 100 | 100 |

*Source*: Medal, José Luis 1985. *La revolución Nicaragüense: Balance económico y alternativas futuras*. Managua: CINASE, 35.

spite of a considerable reduction of the former (INIES 1987b:13). In 1987, exchange losses further increased to 9 percent of GDP. Exchange losses together with the monetary emission for the financing of public investment (10 percent of GDP) and for the fiscal deficit led to a global deficit of 36 percent of GDP (FitzGerald 1988:198 and Table 5.8). This global deficit was overwhelmingly financed by monetization.

Another source of domestic savings was bank profits resulting from interest on loans and credits given to the private sector. In practice, the banks experienced only losses. Real interest rates were always negative and there was a lack of control on the use of loans and credits.

After Somoza's overthrow, the pattern of credit allocation changed: The commerce share declined and the production share increased (Table 5.10). The National Financial System made large amounts of bank credits available to state and private producers. But many of these credits were not repaid. In 1983 many small farmers' debts as well as an even greater amount of debts of state agricultural enterprises had to be remitted (Enríquez and Spalding 1987:121).

Although state control over the use of bank credits improved somewhat in the course of time, the financial policy from 1979 onward was "passive" (FitzGerald 1984:9). In principle, bank credits financed 100 percent of most agricultural production. Policy stipulated that after February 1985 financing would be limited to 80 percent, but this restriction was not implemented. In all years, most requests for financing production met with a positive response.

The banking system could also provide resources for the state accumulation fund by attracting savings from the private sector. But savings hardly came about, partly because interest rates for deposits were always lower than the annual inflation rate.[9]

A third source for state investment could be the profits of state enterprises (enterprises of the APP, the Area of People's Property). A number of them seem to have become profitable after the first years of organization and reactivation, although profitability is difficult to calculate given the subsidized inputs. However, in 1985 there were apparently still many problems with the efficiency of state enterprises.[10]

## *Conclusion*

The government did acquire the external and internal resources to finance accumulation and defense, but at the cost of growing disequilibria. The nationalization of foreign trade allowed the state to control the acquisition of imported capital goods. Most foreign financing took the form of tied bilateral loans, also leading to easy government control of imported goods. The policy seemed directed at controlling the "real value of the surplus," that is, the imported (capital) goods (FitzGerald 1985a:8).

The government also obtained internal sources, but not by squeezing private surpluses. The dollar side of the economy was controlled fairly effectively, but the amount of domestic money was not. The fiscal deficit, the exchange losses, the financing of public investment, and the permissive credit policy led to a huge monetization. The government imposed forced savings on the economy by means of a high inflation rate.

This policy was dangerous for the stability of the mixed economy. The maintenance of markets requires that money have a stimulating function. So money must be scarce. In addition, it is doubtful whether a policy of controlling dollars but not controlling domestic money can be effective in a small, open economy. The first result of such a policy is a distortion of domestic prices relative to foreign prices, causing an increase in imports and a reduction of exports. When imports cannot grow any further because of balance-of-payments problems and the impossibility of lending more, domestic prices rise even more (see Ramírez Sánchez 1982). As a result, a large part of private profits in domestic currency is exchanged for dollars obtained on the black market, reducing state control also over the dollar side of the economy. Finally, the need to stimulate exports forces the government to give dollars to export producers, which implies more loss of control of the use of foreign exchange.

TABLE 5.11 Consumption and Investment 1981–1986 (annual growth rates)

| | *1981* | *1982* | *1983* | *1984* | *1985* | *1986* | *Accumulated 1981-1986* |
|---|---|---|---|---|---|---|---|
| GDP | 5.4 | -0.8 | 4.6 | -1.6 | -4.1 | -0.4 | 2.8 |
| Investment | 52.9 | -17.6 | 8.7 | 0.9 | -0.6 | 5.5 | 45.0 |
| Fixed inv. | 60.1 | -19.3 | 4.7 | 2.2 | 1.1 | 1.5 | 42.0 |
| Consumption | -8.8 | -5.7 | 7.1 | 3.5 | -1.6 | 3.2 | -3.2 |
| Public | 13.4 | 16.9 | 37.1 | 17.3 | 7.0 | 4.0 | 137.3 |
| Private | -14.1 | -12.9 | -5.6 | -5.1 | -8.1 | 2.5 | -36.8 |
| Basic | 3.0 | -5.0 | -9.7 | 0.0 | -6.6 | 6.4 | -12.1 |
| Non-basic | -41.7 | -35.3 | 11.4 | -1.1 | -12.9 | 28.8 | -53.4 |

*Source*: Arana, Mario et al. 1987. *Deuda, estabilización y ajuste: La transformación en Nicaragua, 1979–1986*. Managua: CRIES, Cuadernos de pensamiento Propio, 51.

## The Distribution of Income

At a global level, it is clear that increases in investment and public spending in general without accompanying increases in GDP occur at the cost of private consumption (Table 5.11). In Nicaragua, "nonbasic consumption" declined much more than "basic consumption," which indicates that the distribution of income improved—at least during 1981–1985. In 1986 the reverse took place, pointing to a loss of control of income distribution.

The improvement in income distribution during the Sandinistas' first years can probably be ascribed to the initial success of the policy of maintaining planned prices for basic-wage goods. Prices for some twenty-five, and later seventeen, basic products were kept low and controlled by MICOIN (the Ministry of Internal Trade). The result was that price increases of this "basic basket" were less than those of the total package of goods and services (Table 5.12). The state could also control nominal wages fairly effectively.

But the inflation rate rose to 50 percent in 1984 and climbed to astronomical rates in the years thereafter (Table 5.1). In this situation it was increasingly difficult to guarantee the availability of basic consumer goods at official low prices. Shortages started to appear: At the official prices goods were scarce.

In order to maintain planned prices for basic consumer goods it is necessary to control and expand their supply. This proved to be increasingly difficult in the context of Nicaragua's mixed economy which included private producers and private traders. Supply dimin-

TABLE 5.12 Wages and Prices 1980–1984 (1980=100)

| | *Average Wage*[a] | | *Basic Basket*[b] | | *Average Prices*[c] |
|---|---|---|---|---|---|
| | *Cordobas* | *Index* | *Cordobas* | *Index* | *Index* |
| 1980 | 2,340 | 100 | 1,402 | 100 | 100 |
| 1981 | 2,643 | 113 | 1,548 | 110 | 124 |
| 1982 | 2,929 | 125 | 1,753 | 125 | 155 |
| 1983 | 3,306 | 141 | 2,285 | 163 | 203 |
| 1984[d] | 3,933 | 168 | 3,298 | 235 | 275 |

[a]Of workers inscribed at INSSBI, the Nicaraguan Institute for Social Security and Welfare (public sector and larger industrial enterprises).
[b]A package of seventeen basic consumer goods distributed by MICOIN.
[c]Index of INEC.
[d]Preliminary figures.

*Source:* INEC 1985, Mimeo; and MICOIN 1985, Mimeo.

ished because of the war, the lower priority for consumer goods within the import allocation, and the negative effects of the subsidy policy.

The attacks of the counterrevolutionaries destroyed production capacity, and the fighting impeded the production and transport of many items (Table 5.3). In addition, the expansion of the army required large quantities of food, clothing, boots, and other goods that could not be used by the civilian population. As a result, the inflationary pressure on those goods intensified.

Until 1982, imports of consumer goods had to some extent filled the gap between insufficient domestic supply and increased demand. But after that the share of capital goods imports increased enormously at the cost of the share of consumer goods (see Table 3.3). The other component of imports that suffered a reduction was the inputs for manufacturing production, thus further reducing the availability of consumer goods (see also Argüello, Kleiterp, and Croes 1988:10).

The policy of maintaining official low prices for some seventeen basic goods could only be implemented by means of subsidies, which made official producer prices higher than official consumer prices. Officially, the government subsidized only seven products: corn, rice, beans, sorghum, sugar, milk, and vegetable oil. Grains were subsidized in the commercialization phase, and subsidies for the other products went to the processing plants, where prices did not cover production costs. In addition, the government financed part of production costs of the soap factories and the slaughterhouses, public transport and drinking water, as well as the costs of the popular shops (CIERA/PAN/CIDA 1984, 3:69).

Many other products were subsidized indirectly. Many directly subsidized items such as sugar, milk, and sorghum, served as inputs for the production of other consumer goods such as beverages, cheese, and pork and poultry, respectively. The state also gave indirect subsidies by conceding cheap credits, by allowing imports of inputs at below-market exchange rates, and by accepting losses of state enterprises.

Subsidized low prices for basic consumer goods not only caused relative scarcities because of increased demand but also had some undesired consequences for domestic production and marketing. Agricultural production did not diminish on average (with some exceptions, notably milk and cotton; see Table 5.4). However, production of corn and beans hardly kept up with population growth. Subsidies for corn, beans, and sorghum caused some producers to stop growing these crops and instead buy them at the state shop. This also occurred on state farms. Other producers preferred to grow crops for which no price controls existed, in particular horticultural crops. Better incomes in the countryside (lower rents, more credits) coupled with—in spite of the subsidies—often too low producer prices also resulted in reduced marketings of corn and beans. Although there are no data available, on-farm (human as well as animal) consumption probably increased.

In sum, the official producer prices did not stimulate production sufficiently, which reduced the supply of goods with a high priority. In addition, high demand stimulated private trading in these goods at much higher prices. This had severe consequences for the distribution of income.

Producers saw their incomes squeezed because of the low selling prices and the high inflation rate that increased their costs. This occurred in particular with small producers, and with medium and large producers in so far as they did not buy their inputs at subsidized prices. Wage earners also experienced a severe reduction in income because wages were controlled and consumer prices were increasingly out of control. Domestic traders, however, benefited from the high inflation rate and the scarcities.

The disequilibrium worked out differently for people in the cities and in the countryside. The shortages of many manufactures and the high demand in the cities caused high prices, although official prices were kept low. In the countryside the effect was worse. Many simple manufactures such as matches, boots, and vegetable oil were no longer available. Because good profits could be made in the cities, traders did not make an effort to sell a portion of their products in the countryside.

As a result, terms of trade for the countryside deteriorated, which in turn had negative consequences for the production of basic grains. People migrated from the countryside to the cities, especially to Managua. In general, an increasing share of the economically active population left production work and began to work in commerce. This caused shortages of labor in the production sector, for example, in industrial enterprises. These reactions of the working population intensified the imbalances of the economy.

A large private-trade sector reaped the difference between the low official prices and the market value of consumer goods. The high inflation rate caused an income transfer from the planned, taxable sector toward the unplanned and untaxable sector of the economy. So, part of the domestic surplus available for state accumulation was lost.

In response, the state could apply two different kinds of measures. It could attempt to increase its control over domestic trade, and it could also abolish subsidies and raise prices to stimulate production. To a certain extent, the Sandinistas attempted to do both.

### *Attempts at Control*

Already in July 1981, scarcities and speculation in sugar led to a nationalization of its wholesale trade. After floods in May 1982 destroyed part of the harvest of basic grains, the state expanded its control of domestic trade in other basic goods. It established a network of retail outlets to supply the population at official prices. But private trade still existed, also in subsidized products (Table 5.13).

In 1982 the government set up a rationing system for sugar. The neighborhood organization CDS (Comités de Defensa Sandinista; Committees for Sandinista Defense) registered families, and each family obtained a guarantee card. With this card it could buy sugar at the official price in little private neighborhood shops that received sugar from MICOIN. By early 1983 rationing expanded to include rice, vegetable oil, and soap. In addition, via a separate system, gasoline was rationed.

Wholesale trade in oil, refined sugar, rice, and soap was supposed to be controlled easily because these goods were produced in a limited number of factories. However, those products, and especially sugar, were still available in the private market at much higher prices. Probably, some goods disappeared illegally from the factories and others were sold by corrupt MICOIN officials. Sometimes MICOIN

TABLE 5.13 State and Private Trade of Foodstuffs 1982–1983 (in percent)

| | *Procurement* | | *Wholesale Trade* | | *Retail Trade* | |
|---|---|---|---|---|---|---|
| | *State* | *Priv.* | *State* | *Priv.* | *State*[a] | *Priv.* |
| Corn[b] | 38 | 62 | 50 | 50 | 61 | 39 |
| Beans[b] | 78 | 22 | 85 | 15 | 61 | 39 |
| Rice[b] | 95 | 5 | 95 | 5 | 61 | 39 |
| Sorghum | 95 | 5 | 95 | 5 | 72 | 22 |
| Beef | 30 | 70 | 20 | 80 | 22 | 77 |
| Milk | - | - | 25[c] | 75[c] | 20[d] | 80[d] |
| Cheese | 0 | 100 | 0 | 100 | 0 | 100 |
| Chicken | - | - | 19 | 81 | 28 | 72 |
| Eggs | - | - | 22 | 78 | 22 | 78 |
| Bananas | 70 | 30 | 70 | 30 | 2 | 98 |
| Potatoes | 7 | 30 | 70 | 30 | 2 | 98 |
| Yucca | 2 | 98 | 2 | 98 | 2 | 98 |
| Tomatoes | 5 | 95 | 5 | 95 | 2 | 98 |
| Onions | 70 | 30 | 70 | 30 | 2 | 98 |
| Cabbage | 5 | 95 | 5 | 95 | 2 | 98 |
| Meal/Bread | - | - | 100 | 0 | 20 | 80 |
| Oil[b] | - | - | 100 | 0 | 33 | 67 |
| Sugar[b] | - | - | 100 | 0 | 100 | 0 |

[a]Includes popular retail outlets.
[b]Rationed products.
[c]Crude milk.
[d]Pasteurized milk.

*Source:* CIERA/PAN/CIDA, *La estrategia alimentaria de Nicaragua.* Vol. 3, 79. Managua, 1984.

sold the controlled items, especially sugar, to small vendors for resale on the black market. It aimed to satisfy the grumbling of small traders and of consumers who complained about low quotas (Collins et al. 1985:217).

In 1984 popular dissatisfaction with hoarding and speculation on scarce goods mounted. In June of that year, the Council of State adopted the Law for the Protection of the Consumer initiated by the CDS. The government now officially nationalized trade in corn, beans, sorghum, and salt and included these products in the rationing system. The state distributed corn and sorghum only to producers (tortilla makers and fodder producers), and consumers could obtain salt and beans with the guarantee card. For distribution of these items to the public, MICOIN contracted 8,573 small outlets and the CDS began to control them.

The state also attempted to expand its control of transport and trade of eighteen nonrationed products. Manufacturers of these goods, such as machetes and boots, were obliged to sell to MICOIN, which carried out the distribution. Transporters and traders of other goods needed official permission. Those who could not show such a permission for their freight had to hand it over to MICOIN. In practice however, the government did not enforce this measure completely. For instance, only at night was there some control on the roads.

According to the law, government subsidies on basic grains would also be lowered. The state would equalize official consumer and producer prices and assume only transport and distribution costs. But implementing this law would conflict with the objective to maintain low consumer prices or it would reduce supply even more. In practice, subsidies continued to be fairly high, and the supply problem also persisted. In spite of the subsidies, producer prices were still not high enough to guarantee a 100 percent state procurement, especially of beans and corn. The announced nationalization of trade in these products could not be carried out, and private trade still played a role. Other problems were the lack of efficiency of the MICOIN distribution channels, and sometimes the corruptness of its workers. If MICOIN obtained goods from production centers, these goods were often lost during transport and distribution.

In February 1985 the government abolished many direct subsidies. This was followed by a tripling of consumer prices of rice, beans, corn, and sugar; the milk price rose more gradually. The February measures also aimed at stimulating production by other means. More industrial consumer goods would be made available in the countryside at the cost of the cities. The government attempted to increase labor productivity by implementing a material incentive policy. To reattract labor to the production sector, it improved supply of the commissaries. Several wage increases were proclaimed during the year, but they could not prevent real wages from deteriorating further in 1985. Wages in the lower SNOTS scales increased by about 175 percent compared to an inflation rate of 334 percent.

At the same time, the state tried to increase its control of internal trade. More and more industrial enterprises were obliged to sell their production to state trade organs. The state expanded its network of retail shops, especially in the countryside. An enormous propaganda war was waged against private "speculators" and "hoarders."

In 1985 the burden of accelerating inflation was still not equally distributed. Although the intention had been to reduce private-sector trade by giving incentives in the production sector, wage and producer price increases were not enough. In spite of the presumed greater government control, private trade could still florish. This improved the living conditions for the urban poor because, in general, at least one family member was involved in commerce. In the countryside the scarcities were still more severe and possibilities for trade were consequently absent (IHCA 1985b).

In 1986 and 1987 the government continued the policy of on the one hand trying to stimulate production and on the other aiming at more control of domestic trade. Early in 1986 MICOIN appointed some 1,000 inspectors to control official prices in the markets[11]. It proclaimed an "iron fist" system to control prices by means of police vigilance and social control by mass organizations. In spite of these efforts black markets expanded (Guevara 1987:20).

In 1985 the abolishment of subsidies was still accompanied by an attempt at trade controls for basic grains, but in 1986 the government liberated trade in corn and beans—at least within the regions. Between regions there was still control (Medal 1988:85). In 1987 the government extended the liberalization of trade in basic grains and eliminated the roadblocks for corn, beans, and sorghum (Guevara 1987:20). The policy of making more manufactures available in the countryside achieved some success in 1986. This led to an improvement of the terms of trade for the countryside. These measures seemed to have a favorable effect on corn and sorghum production (Table 5.4).

The urban workers' situation deteriorated further. They had to pay higher prices for basic foodstuffs, and shortages for other basic goods at official prices in MICOIN-controlled channels (neighborhood shops, commissaries, supermarkets) persisted. Between January 1986 and January 1987 the government did not increase nominal basic wages, and inflation was as high as 747 percent. But by then, incentives constituted an important part of the nominal wages. The impact of the incentive policy on workers' productivity was negligible because of the lack of available consumer goods. Similarly, the "economic brigades," promoted by the CST to increase worker productivity, had more ideological than economic impact (Arana et al. 1987:25). In 1987 wage increases followed more frequently, but again real wages fell by 34 percent (Table 5.1). More and more workers left their workplace completely or partially in favor of trading activities. The high inflation rate, the lagging behind of real wages, the consequent fall in labor productivity, and the maintenance of indirect subsidies (cheap credits, subsidized imports) were important causes of the persistent shortages.

Although the state attempted to increase its control of domestic trade in the course of 1984–1987, the economy remained mixed. Private trade existed—sometimes legally, sometimes illegally—along with state channels. In such a mixed economy, maintaining low consumer prices is possible only with subsidies, which must be large when desired prices are so much lower than market prices. From 1985 onward, the Nicaraguan government no longer had the capability or the will to grant the subsidies necessary for a decisive impact on prices.

The only way to maintain low prices is by complete state control of domestic trade. This is relatively easy to accomplish if there is only state production or if the number of private producers is limited. Also, the product must be fairly homogeneous. In Nicaragua, these conditions were fulfilled for some particular products such as vegetable oil, salt, rice, sugar, and many manufactures. However, the state proved unable to control trade of even these products. Private and black markets of sugar, for example, persisted. Due to the large differences between state-determined and market prices, government officials proved to be as difficult to control as private tradespeople. A complete nationalization of domestic trade could not be successful.

For the same reason, the attempt at controlling prices by means of administrative measures (appointing inspectors and imposing fines, for example) was doomed to failure. It was very costly and its result was a further reduction of supply and a further disappearance of goods from the official channels. Consequently, it was impossible to maintain state-determined prices as long as inflation was so high. So, implementing the price policy proved impossible as long as an internal macroeconomic equilibrium was not achieved.

Maintaining the mixed economy required revising the price policy. From 1985 to 1987, some government measures attempted to stimulate production by raising prices, but these were always combined with others that aimed at price and trade control. This combination was inconsistent and was not successful.

### *Evaluation*

The Sandinista government was not able to achieve all its objectives at the same time: state accumulation, maintenance of real wages, improvement of social services, maintenance of a sector of large private producers, and the maintenance of macroeconomic stability. In part, the failures were due to external factors, in particular, the costs of the war. But even without the war, it seems that it would have been impossible to achieve all these objectives.

In practice, the priorities were accumulation, defense, social services (at least until 1985), and the stimulation of production. Although the government abolished many direct subsidies in 1985, the economy could, in the years 1986 and 1987, still be characterized as a "subsidized mixed economy,"[12] because so many state and private producers received subsidies in the form of cheap imports and credits. Accumulation and subsidies were financed by external loans and, internally, by forced savings. The burden of these savings fell upon small private producers and wage earners.

Subsidized imports led to serious price distortions. Import-intensive production was stimulated at the cost of traditional production, more efficient in the use of foreign exchange. Microeconomic decisions were also distorted. For example, it was cheaper to import a new tractor than to repair one. Because of the complexity of the economy, "planned" import allocation decisions could not correct the wrong signals going out from these price distortions. The overvalued exchange rate caused producers to sell on the domestic market instead of exporting. In sum, the allocative efficiency of the economy was seriously reduced. This is an important cause of the persistent trade deficits. As a result, the policy controlling the dollar side of the economy was increasingly ineffective.

Another aspect of the subsidy policy was that many state and private enterprises experienced a soft budget constraint. This led in practice to a resource-constrained system in which the efficiency of enterprises was reduced. For that reason, shortages were apt to become a permanent phenomenon. But the effect was worse because there was no control of trade in these subsidized low-priced products. The internal disequilibrium was expressed in a high inflation rate *and* shortages. As consequences, real wages declined and private producers not receiving subsidized inputs were squeezed. Both consequences further reduced supply. The private-trade sector made large profits and was difficult to tax; thus, the state lost a significant source for accumulation. This internal disequilibrium had serious consequences for the stability of the mixed economy. Private producers were not stimulated enough due to a combination of the government's price policy and the high inflation rate. The same applied to wage earners: Controlled wages led to falling productivity and high job rotation. At the end of 1987 it was also clear that something had to be done to improve the relative price structure (the allocative efficiency) and to diminish the external disequilibrium.

## The 1988 Change

From February 1988 onward, the government carried out significant changes in the economic policy. The change started with a monetary reform, which implied the introduction of a new cordoba, worth

10,000 old cordobas. Ten new cordobas were equivalent to one dollar, which implied a devaluation of the official exchange rate of 3,000 percent. Holders of old cordobas could exchange them, but at a maximum of one million per family. In the process, 15 percent of the currency was eliminated, in particular cordobas held by counterrevolutionaries and large traders (IHCA 1988b:24).

The large devaluation was accompanied by a unification of the official exchange rates. This would bring an end to subsidized imports and to the exchange losses of the Central Bank. Because of the former diverging import and export exchange rates, unification meant for most imports a devaluation of 2,700 percent and for average exports a devaluation of only 43 percent (Medal 1988:118-120). At the new exchange rate many exports were not profitable, however. Within a few months the government conceded higher prices to exporters, leading to implicit exchange rates of up to fifty cordobas per dollar and to new exchange losses (IHCA 1988a:37). Parallel and black-market rates also went up. In June, the government proclaimed a new devaluation of the cordoba, among other measures (Table 5.7). From then on, devaluations followed more regularly. Gradually, the difference between official, parallel, and black-market rates diminished.

In February 1988 the government established prices for a basic basket of forty-six final products, including public transport, energy, and water. Imported products would be priced according to the new cordoba exchange rate; for other prices producers would simply do away with three zeros to get the new price (CIERA 1988:309). The intention was that consumers in general, and mass organizations in particular, would help in controlling these prices. In fact, people mobilized to protect their real wages, but prices proved to be unrealistically set and inflation reached 113 percent in the first five weeks after the montary reform (IHCA 1988a:34).

With the monetary reform, wages were raised by 500 percent. The value of the new average wage was equal to the value of the basket of forty-six basic consumer goods at the newly established prices. In practice, wages increased by only about 200 percent, because incentives were abolished.[13] However, the high inflation in the next months reduced workers' purchasing power below the December 1987 level.

The June economic package brought a change in the wage policy. From then on, the state fixed wages only for workers in the budget sector. For other sectors SNOTS was abolished and wages were left to negotiations between employers and workers. The wage increase for the budget sector was only 30 percent; the devaluation was 700 percent. In compensation, government workers received a monthly supply of rice, beans, and corn at highly subsidized prices (IHCA

TABLE 5.14 Purchasing Power of Salaries and Inflation Rate February 1988–February 1989 (by month)

| | *Average State Worker Salary* | *Average Wages in Production* | *Inflation Rate* |
|---|---|---|---|
| | *(% of a basic market basket of 46 products)* | | *(%)* |
| 1988 | | | |
| February | 100 | 100 | 47 |
| March | 88 | 88 | 82 |
| April | 76 | 76 | 29 |
| May | 70 | 70 | 19 |
| June | 19 | 19 | 66 |
| July | 18 | 17 | 83 |
| August | 15 | 27 | 20 |
| September | 19 | 34 | 48 |
| October | 19 | 35 | 61 |
| November | 19 | 31 | 12 |
| December[a] | 13 | 26 | 27 |
| 1989 | | | |
| January[b] | 26 | 34 | 92 |
| February | 25 | 32 | 46 |

[a]In December there was a double salary due to Christmas bonusses which is not reflected in the table.
[b]In January a new subsistence basket went into effect, estimated to be worth 75 percent of the old basket. But figures in this table are still based on the old basket.

*Source:* IHCA 1989. *Envío*, 8, no. 94(May):43.

1988b:25). During the year, the purchasing power of salaries diminished further, principally because wage increases were always smaller than devaluations (Table 5.14).

The credit policy was restricted, and this time the policy was enforced: The banks would finance only 80 percent of production costs. In keeping with the idea that inflation would be reduced, the government proclaimed a fixed interest rate. This was still not a positive real rate but it did imply an enormous increase. In the first months after the monetary reform, the banks conceded hardly any credit because of uncertainties about restrictions, interest rates, and other conditions. In May and June, just in time for the new agricultural cycle, the banks began conceding credits. By then, interest rates had been changed three times.

Together with the devaluation and salary measures of June, the government announced that interest rates would be indexed according to the consumer price index. In practice, the banks began using, but never publishing, a kind of "producer price index."[14]

In order to reduce the fiscal deficit, the government announced a *compactación* (contraction). The forty-two ministries combined into eight superministries. The objective was to achieve a 10 percent budget reduction by laying off 8,000 government workers. In practice, about 6,000 of these workers were reassigned to other ministries or state enterprises. However, even if the government had accomplished a large reduction in employment this would have diminished expenditure only slightly; because of the low real wage level, total government wages constituted only 9 percent of total government expenditure (IHCA 1988c:18).

The state also reduced public investment and announced a change in the orientation of investment. More investment would be directed to activities with a quick return and less to the big long-term state investment projects. For the first time, the state succeeded in its first objective, reducing the total investment rate to about 11 percent of GDP. But it did not accomplish the second goal. Most investment still went to the big projects (IHCA 1989b:37).

The state raised its income by setting domestic oil and gas prices at European price levels, which were higher than those in neighboring countries. The state also charged higher prices for services such as energy and water and introduced a progressive structure for these charges. Urban public transport was still subsidized, but fares on intercity buses were raised enormously.

By October 1988 estimates of the effect on production of these changes showed positive results in agriculture and negative ones in manufacturing (IHCA 1988c:14-15). Production of corn, beans, and rice was expected to grow by about 10 to 20 percent. As a result of the reduction in import subsidies, production of sorghum and irrigated rice—both with a high import content—went down, and production of "dry rice" increased by 60 percent. Exports of coffee were expected to increase in 1988–1989 as a result of higher profitability. Beef exports almost tripled in the year from August 1987 until August 1988 compared to the previous year. But the relative price of milk was still too low, so many small peasants sold their cows for slaughter, which was to have long-term consequences for herd size.

Between July 1987 and July 1988 industrial production fell by 47 percent. Here, the important cause was rising costs and the enterprises' lack of liquidity. Rising costs were converted into high prices, and the low wage level caused demand to fall heavily. Few enterprises succeeded in substituting home marketing for exporting. The problems were especially severe for small industrial enterprises.[15] The once large informal trade sector also suffered the consequences of falling demand. Open unemployment rose.

The positive estimates of agricultural production had to be revised after hurricane Joan struck Nicaragua on October 21. Total damage was estimated at $828.2 million, 12 percent of which represented direct production losses. The hurricane affected, in particular, the cattle herd, corn, beans, rice, and banana production. Twenty-four percent of total damage was in the economic infrastucture, roads and bridges. This was expected to have a negative impact on coffee exports because these damages were concentrated in some important coffee regions. The biggest damage, half of the total, was in the social infrastructure.[16]

Partly because of the hurricane but also because of the recession that followed the change in economic policy, GDP dropped by 8 percent in 1988. Inflation did not diminish. To the contrary, the inflation rate in 1988 was 33,600 percent (ECLAC 1989a). To a large extent, inflation was now cost-push inflation induced by the ongoing devaluations and the inefficiency of production methods, which could not be improved overnight. In addition, the lack of competition from imports meant that many producers operated in monopolistic or oligopolistic markets. For them, falling demand did not lead to price reductions. Instead, they reduced their supply and forced price increases. For this reason, the government began to control the prices of some industrial intermediate goods again in November 1988 (see also Chapter 4).

Another reason for the high inflation rate was that the fiscal deficit increased—to 26 percent of GDP (Table 5.8). Government expenses went up with every devaluation because a large share of expenses were for fuel and vehicle maintenance. Tax income decreased enormously because of the recession in general, and falling demand for the fiscal goods in particular. However, the state succeeded in reducing the exchange losses and the monetization for public investment financing.

In January 1989 the government announced the layoffs of 30,000 government workers. This time the measure included 10,000 workers of the Ministry of Internal Affairs and the Ministry of Defense. The state also reduced the ministries' investment programs to a minimum and again "promised" to reduce expenditure on the big investment projects. Inflation dropped significantly in February, March, and April but went up again in May and June as a result of the credit policy for the new agricultural cycle. Some debts of agricultural producers had to be remitted and the banks began conceding credits at lower rates to small producers to stimulate their production.[17] Although GDP still fell in 1989—by 3 percent—this fall was smaller than in 1988. Moreover, exports increased from U.S. $236 million in 1988 to U.S. $292 million in 1989. Estimated inflation was also significantly lower than in 1988, namely 3,452 percent.[18]

On the whole, the greatest success of the policy change was the reduction in price distortions, which certainly stabilized the mixed economy. Imports were no longer heavily subsidized and there was a growing awareness of real costs. This stimulated production that was efficient in terms of the overall economy. But the correction of relative prices could not bear fruit in one year because in many cases a fundamental change in production methods was needed. Nonetheless, in 1989 the trade balance improved significantly. There were, however, two exceptions to the improvement of relative prices. Prices of basic grains were still below Central American levels and wages were much lower.

Fewer subsidies and less state intervention in prices led to a growing income inequality. Producers who were able to adjust rapidly to the new prices or who operated in a monopolistic or oligopolistic market structure made large profits; wage workers in particular suffered the consequences of the high inflation rate. Unemployment increased and now had a more serious effect on incomes because of reduced opportunities for earning a living in the informal trade sector.

In general, it seems that the reform measures gave too much priority to restricting demand by restricting credits and holding down wages. In spite of this, the necessary devaluations and the slow reduction of government expenses continued to stimulate inflation. It must be recognized that the Nicaraguan adjustment package did not include an ingredient that is usual in other adjustment processes: the availability of foreign loans to prevent a recession. Another limiting factor was the ongoing, albeit decreasing, need to spend for defense.

## Notes

1. In Chapter 4, I analyzed the other aspects of a price policy: whether the state has the instruments to implement it and whether the policy leaves room for private accumulation.

2. In 1980 a great literacy campaign reduced illiteracy from 43 to 12 percent.

3. Figures on private investment are estimations based on the amount of long-term loans conceded; statistics for manufacturing are based on the annual surveys of INEC (Instituto Nicaragüense de Estadísticas y Census; Nicaraguan Statistics and Census Institute) of that sector. They do not include investment made with the enterprises' own resources, but in the public sector nonreported investment probably also existed.

4. Between 1980 and 1984, 75 percent of the contracted external debt was oriented toward investment financing. See Argüello, Kleiterp, and Croes 1988:16.

5. In 1987 the different offices of the parallel market attracted about $5 million from the free market and received about $20 million from the Central Bank via the export income changed at the parallel rate. It sold these dollars to producers with a special authorization. Estimates of the volume of the black market for the same year range from $50 to $130 million. See INIES 1987a:3.

6. International reseres were $194, $352, and $283 million, respectively; see ECLAC 1989a:465.

7. In reality, tax income relative to GDP was lower because by 1984, Nicaragua's GDP was probably underestimated. In the first place, only producer prices were taken into account and not the—much higher—consumer prices. In the second place, GDP did not include production of the so-called informal sector.

8. Fiscal goods are beer, rum, cigarettes, and soft drinks.

9. In general, however, other factors seem to have more influence on the amount of savings in developing countries; savings are not very sensitive to changes in the real interest rate. See Alberto Giovannini, 1985. "Saving and the real interest rate in LDCs." *Journal of Development Economics* 18, no. 1:197-217.

10. In a meeting with directors of state enterprises the minister of agriculture, Jaime Wheelock, threatened to close enterprises that could not become profitable. See *El Nuevo Diario*, March 7, 1985.

11. *Agencia Nueva Nicaragua*, February 26, 1986.

12. According to President Daniel Ortega, this "subsidized mixed economy" was necessary to maintain national unity during wartime (IHCA 1989b:36).

13. Incentives had constituted 190 percent of nominal basic wages in the productive sector and 140 percent in the nonproductive sector (IHCA 1988a:31).

14. This information came from a member of the CRIES economic team, November 1988.

15. Small industry production, which had constituted 24 percent of total industrial production in 1983 was down to 10 percent in 1988 (IHCA 1988c:15).

16. These official figures were presented by President Daniel Ortega on November 15, 1988. See *Barricada*, November 16, 1988.

17. Acording to the Instituto Histórico Centroamericano, this should be seen as a recognition that these producers were more efficient (IHCA 1989b:42).

18. ECLAC 1989. The inflation figure refers to changes in consumer prices between November 1988 and November 1989.

# 6

# The Mixed Economy and Industrialization

This chapter deals with the sectoral distribution of investment and the outward or inward orientation of Nicaragua's economic strategy—what I called earlier the industrialization strategy "in a strict sense." It is also a discussion of the willingness of private producers to continue producing and investing, another stability condition for the mixed economy that I mentioned in Chapter 2. My focus here is on the industrial sector.

As Table 6.1 shows, a large private sector remained active in the manufacturing industry. In addition, almost all the foreign companies in Nicaragua were manufacturing enterprises (Chapter 3). In agroindustry, private and state ownership also coexisted. In the processing of coffee, rice, and sugar, each sector handled roughly 50 percent of production. Most cotton- and sesame-processing was in private hands; the majority of slaughterhouses and dairy plants were state-owned.

## The Industrialization Strategy

According to the economic plans for 1980 and 1981, the Nicaraguan government aimed at building up an economy that would be less externally dependent and would meet the basic needs of the majority of the population. Greater economic independence did not mean complete self-sufficiency. Instead, the aim was to diversify export products and export and import markets. In the long run, the government intended to spread trade relations equally over four "blocks": the United States, the Latin American countries, Western Europe and Japan, and the socialist countries.

The objective of meeting the basic needs of the population meant that the agricultural sector took priority in Nicaragua's industrializa-

TABLE 6.1 Private Ownership in Manufacturing Industry per Branch 1980–1987 (in percent of total GDP)

| | *1980* | *1981* | *1982* | *1983* | *1984* | *1985* | *1986* | *1987* |
|---|---|---|---|---|---|---|---|---|
| Food | 94 | 92 | 91 | 90 | 84 | 84 | 86 | 86 |
| Beverages | 49 | 53 | 61 | 62 | 51 | 58 | 61 | 62 |
| Tobacco | 100 | 100 | 100 | 100 | 100 | 100 | 100 | 100 |
| Textiles | 65 | 52 | 3 | 4 | 4 | 2 | 3 | 3 |
| Clothing ) | | | | | | | | |
| | 97 | 93 | 91 | 84 | 74 | 73 | 71 | 74 |
| Shoes ) | | | | | 95 | 93 | 85 | 83 |
| Wood and cork | 64 | 48 | 48 | 48 | 0 | 0 | 0 | 0 |
| Furniture | 96 | 94 | 94 | 94 | 0 | 0 | 0 | 0 |
| Paper & paper products | 95 | 97 | 98 | 98 | 100 | 89 | 55 | 35 |
| Printing & publishing | 91 | 92 | 90 | 90 | 63 | 74 | 69 | 74 |
| Leather & leather products | 95 | 86 | 85 | 91 | 79 | 82 | 79 | 72 |
| Rubber products | 100 | 100 | 97 | 96 | 85 | 88 | 89 | 26 |
| Chemicals | 94 | 95 | 92 | 92 | 72 | 73 | 69 | 70 |
| Construction materials | 27 | 17 | 6 | 5 | 3 | 4 | 4 | 3 |
| Metal products | 49 | 50 | 16 | 13 | 17 | 17 | 15 | 15 |
| Electr. and non-el. machin. | 77 | 62 | 50 | 41 | 41 | 58 | 41 | 43 |
| Transport materials | 100 | 100 | 100 | 100 | 0 | 0 | 0 | 0 |
| Other | 76 | 53 | 52 | 51 | 44 | 37 | 33 | 50 |
| Total | 79 | 76 | 71 | 67 | 61 | 61 | 59 | 58 |

*Source:* Ministry of Industry, General Division of Planning 1988. Mimeo.

tion strategy, principally to stimulate food production. But developing the agricultural export sector was also a high priority, as this was expected to provide foreign exchange for investment. In the long run, the aim was to develop agroindustry, increasing the value added of exports by processing more agricultural crops within the country.

Manufacturing took a lower priority within Nicaragua's development strategy. This sector would be promoted only insofar as it produced basic consumer goods and necessary inputs (intermediate goods, capital goods) for other important sectors: agriculture, construction, transportation, and priority branches of manufacturing itself. An important objective was to establish more integration between different branches of manufacturing and between manufacturing and other sectors. Furthermore, manufactured exports would be promoted (MIPLAN 1980).

In 1982–1983, the Ministry of Industry elaborated the Strategy for Industrial Development, which by 1989 still functioned as medium-term industrial strategy (MIND 1983a and 1984c). It established the same hierarchy of objectives as in the 1980 and 1981 plans except that defense production now took precedence over the promotion of exports. In the 1985 Industrial Program, the production of goods for defense became a top priority. Nicaragua did not produce weapons; defense production included the production of boots, uniforms, and other goods for the army.

The government's decision to give a lower priority to the manufacturing industry and stimulate only certain of its branches was based on a then generally accepted diagnosis of this sector (see, for example, Wheelock Román 1980). The most important aspects of this diagnosis were that manufacturing production made a relatively unimportant contribution to GDP and employment, that the sector was highly import intensive, and that it produced mainly luxury goods for a small elite and had very few linkages with agricultural production.

As shown in Chapter 3, this diagnosis was not correct. Manufacturing was an important sector of the national economy in 1978 (see Table 1.2). Many manufacturing enterprises produced basic consumer goods, used domestic raw materials, or supplied inputs to other domestic sectors. The few enterprises that did not fulfil any of these functions were often important exporters to the Central American market. This should have justified a higher priority for manufacturing as a whole. In addition, the objectives for manufacturing as defined in the 1980 and 1981 plans and in the Ministry of Industry's medium-term strategy amounted to stating that *all* existing manufacturing industry had to be promoted. Obviously, this created problems, in particular because the overall priority for the sector was low.

Nicaragua's industrialization objectives were remarkably constant between 1980 and 1986 (see also Argüello, Kleiterp, and Croes 1988:28). At the global level, the first priority was to meet basic needs; second came production for export. In third place was the integration of the domestic economy through producing more inputs for domestic production and processing more domestically produced raw materials. The only change was that production for defense gradually became more important.

### *The Investment Program*

Most investment outlined in the 1980 Economic Plan was designed to speed up the recovery and improvement of the social and economic infrastructure (48 percent and 37 percent of total state investment, respectively) (MIPLAN 1980). This was not accomplished. The production sector took a much higher share than planned (35 percent instead of 15 percent) (MIPLAN 1981). More imports of machinery and equipment were necessary to reactivate production than was expected, and construction capacity was reduced dramatically during the liberation war.

Much higher public investment was planned for 1981 and the plan gave a more detailed breakdown of spending (MIPLAN 1981). Production investment's share increased to 36 percent of the total. Most production investment (69 percent) was directed at the agricultural sector. Total investment in 1980 and 1981 was lower than planned, partly because the state was inexperienced in designing production investment projects. It did not commission enough feasibility studies or technical documentation and did not have the capacity to control implementation of investment projects (Argüello, Kleiterp, and Croes 1988:22).

Production investment further increased in 1982, with less money being dedicated to social infrastructure. The government initiated some new large-scale projects, for example, the Timal sugar production and refinery project and the Chiltepe dairy plant. These projects were highly capital intensive and had a long maturation period.

In 1983 the government defined a medium-term investment policy (JGRN 1983). Agriculture and livestock still constituted the most important sectors (Table 6.2). Investment plans included expanding production of traditional commodities such as coffee, sugar, cotton, tobacco, and cereals and the promotion of livestock for beef and milk production. In line with the diversification objective, there was also investment in vegetables, citrus, and African palms production.

A second investment goal was agroindustry. The five-year program defined nineteen agroindustrial investment projects including African palm oil, salt, peanuts, coffee, processed cocoa, flour, and starch. Manufacturing played a minor role in this medium-term investment strategy, receiving only 7.8 percent (including forestry 11.2 percent) of total investment.

In 1983 and 1984 the production sector's share increased further, to an average of 58 percent (Argüello, Kleiterp, and Croes 1988:23). The government initiated other large investment projects in 1983, even though feasibility studies for many of them had not yet been completed. Because of the huge scale of many projects initiated in 1982 and 1983, existing projects absorbed 75 percent of total production investment in 1983 and 90 percent in 1984. Although the country's financial and economic situation was already very unfavorable in 1984 and it was clear that the total investment package exceeded the country's financing capacity, the government initiated more large projects in that year.

Argüello and Kleiterp made a detailed analysis of forty production investment projects under way in 1985, referring only to the public investment program and excluding investment financed directly from

TABLE 6.2 Investment Program 1983–1987 (in millions of $ 1982 prices and in percent)

| *Sector* | *Investment* | *% of Total* | *% of Group* |
|---|---|---|---|
| Productive investment | 1,789 | 55.8 | 100.0 |
| Agroindustry | 426 | 13.3 | 23.8 |
| Agriculture | 804 | 25.1 | 44.9 |
| Industry | 250 | 7.8 | 14.0 |
| Forestry | 110 | 3.4 | 6.2 |
| Mining | 58 | 1.8 | 3.2 |
| Fisheries | 142 | 4.4 | 7.9 |
| Economic infrastructure | 929 | 29.0 | 100.0 |
| Energy | 460 | 14.3 | 49.5 |
| Transportation | 469 | 14.6 | 50.5 |
| Other econ. infrastruct. | 66 | 2.1 | 7.1 |
| Social infrastructure | 479 | 15.0 | |
| Preinvestment | 7 | 0.2 | |
| Total | 3,205 | 100.0 | |

*Source:* National Reconstruction Government of Nicaragua (JGRN) 1983. Economic Policy Guidelines 1983-1988. Managua. Mimeo.

the budget or by the banking system (Argüello and Kleiterp 1985; Argüello, Kleiterp, and Croes 1988:33-36).[1]

The forty projects they examined represented 87 percent of total production investment in 1985. This meant that only 13 percent of production investment was in smaller projects or in maintaining existing capacity, which shows that the latter was accorded a very low priority. The government apparently aimed to change the production structure from above by adding new projects but not by reforming existing production capacity.

Many of the projects Argüello and Kleiterp examined were very large. Thirteen of them absorbed 70 percent of the total amount invested. These all had a maturation period of on average nearly six years, and many were very capital intensive. Projects initiated in 1984 and 1985 had on average a slightly shorter maturation time. Those in manufacturing, fishing, and mining were, on average, also smaller scale and had a shorter maturation period.

The sectoral distribution of the forty projects was very different from that outlined in the plan. First, agroindustry received a much larger amount than agriculture and cattle-breeding together (40 percent and 31 percent of the total, respectively). Furthermore, agroindustrial projects were not planned to use existing agricultural production or to provide it with inputs. The new agroindustry seemed to be an independent sector of the economy. The projects generally demanded very advanced technology compared with that existing in Nicaragua at the time, and most production was geared to exports.

Second, investment in cattle-breeding almost doubled that in agriculture, although for meeting basic needs of the population dairy products were relatively less important. The projects in cattle-raising also made use of advanced technology; their major effects would not be visible until the mid-1990s. According to the same study, investment funds geared to promoting exports equaled the amount devoted to producing for basic needs. It follows that the public investment program was more outward oriented than had been intended.

Another of Argüello and Kleiterp's conclusions was that there were many problems with the implementation of investment projects. From 1983 onward, annual evaluations of the public investment program repeatedly referred to these problems. Sometimes there was a lack of construction materials, sometimes of skilled labor, and in other cases of financing (Argüello and Kleiterp 1985:65). Contra attacks were another problem, for example, they hindered completion of two large forestry projects. Yet despite these problems, the government continued to initiate new large-scale projects annually.

Long-term bank credits accounted for only a small proportion of the state investment budget. Their function proved to complement the public investment program because they were mainly used for the maintenance, expansion, and improvement of existing capacity (Argüello, Kleiterp, and Croes 1988:38-9). In agriculture, they benefited state enterprises and cooperatives in particular. In the industrial sector, the distribution of these credits pointed to a serious decapitalization in certain branches such as chemicals, construction materials, rubber, and oil refining. There was also an outflow of capital from much existing agroindustry—dairy plants and slaughterhouses, for example. The already relatively low amount of long-term bank credits declined by 38 percent between 1983 and 1985, indicating a further deterioration of existing production capacity.

Within manufacturing, investment was higher in 1980 and 1981 than in later years (Table 6.3). Machinery and equipment were imported in order to rebuild manufacturing capacity. At this time, investment was distributed to branches more or less in line with each branch's share of value added. Largely because of the foreign-exchange crisis, manufacturing investment fell to a minimum in 1982. Only 48 percent of total investment was directed at buying machinery and equipment (MIND 1984c). The Ministry of Industry undertook

TABLE 6.3 Manufacturing Industry: Value Added 1983 and Investment 1980–1984 per Branch (in percent)

| | Value Added | Investment | | | | |
|---|---|---|---|---|---|---|
| | 1983[a] | 1980 | 1981 | 1982 | 1983 | 1984 |
| Food | 41.3 | 23.1 | 20.7 | 9.5 | 9.6 | 8.7 |
| Beverages | 12.0 | 11.7 | 30.6 | 4.5 | 3.5 | 2.0 |
| Tobacco | 5.2 | 4.3 | 9.9 | 1.7 | 0.0 | 0.0 |
| Textiles and clothing | 12.5 | 16.2 | 6.7 | 5.7 | 13.1 | 19.7 |
| Leather and shoes | | 5.9 | 5.5 | 4.3 | 3.4 | 2.5 |
| Wood and cork | 2.0 | 1.8 | 1.7 | 15.0 | 39.9 | 34.3 |
| Furniture | 0.5 | 2.0 | 0.5 | 0.0 | 0.0 | 0.0 |
| Paper & paper products | 1.8 | 0.1 | 0.2 | 1.7 | 14.6 | 8.7 |
| Printing & publishing | 2.4 | 1.5 | 2.3 | 0.0 | 0.4 | 2.4 |
| Rubber products | 0.9 | 0.0 | 0.0 | 0.0 | 0.0 | 0.0 |
| Chemicals | 6.9 | 18.8 | 12.4 | 34.4 | 9.3 | 8.6 |
| Oil products | 3.5 | 0.0 | 0.0 | 0.0 | 0.0 | 0.0 |
| Non-metallic minerals | 4.9 | 3.6 | 3.9 | 4.5 | 1.3 | 0.9 |
| Metal products | 3.9 | 7.8 | 3.5 | 15.4 | 3.7 | 10.7 |
| Electr. & non-el. machinery | 0.7 | 0.6 | 0.8 | 0.2 | 0.2 | 0.2 |
| Transport materials | 0.2 | 0.3 | 0.1 | 0.0 | 0.1 | 0.0 |
| Plastics & other manufact | 1.1 | 2.2 | 1.2 | 3.1 | 1.0 | 1.4 |
| Total[b] | 100.0 | 100.0 | 100.0 | 100.0 | 100.0 | 100.0 |
| Total in millions of current cordobas | - | 240.4 | 345.6 | 66.7 | 598.9 | 793.6 |

[a]Source: Table 3.6.
[b]Total may not sum to 100%, due to rounding.

*Sources:* For 1980–1983: Ministry of Industry 1984. Cinco años de gestión. Managua. Mimeo; for 1984: MIND 1985. Sector industrial: Evaluación año 1984. Managua. Mimeo.

several feasibility studies for new investment projects to be carried out in the following years (MIND 1984a).

In 1983 the ministry initiated several new investment projects, including a textile plant, a cardboard plant, and plants for salt and ice production. The biggest projects involved wood extraction. Total investment was now much higher than in 1982. Machinery and equipment constituted 79 percent of total investment expenditure, of which two forestry projects, the private enterprise Gracsa (foodstuffs) and the new textile and cardboard projects, absorbed the largest proportion.

In 1984, investment in machinery and equipment represented 56 percent of the total, 56 percent of which was directed toward acquiring new plants. As well as continuing projects initiated in 1983, the ministry began some new projects, such as a serum plant and an ampoule plant, a plant for metal packing, and a central maintenance workshop for spare-part construction and equipment repair.

To a large extent the breakdown of industrial investment in 1983 and 1984 reflected the new investment projects. Large wood extraction projects meant the wood and wood products sector received the highest proportion of investment, although it accounted for only 2 percent of total manufacturing value added in 1983. The expansion of this sector reflected the government's priority of improving the use of domestic resources. However, both wood projects were geared toward the export market and no funds were allocated to expanding production for the local market or to the urgently needed reforestation of some zones (Argüello, Kleiterp, and Croes 1988:35-6).

The paper and paper products, metal products, and textiles sectors also absorbed high levels of investment. This suggested that many manufacturing investment projects had a role in improving linkages within manufacturing and with agriculture. Few were directed at substituting imports in the provision of basic consumer goods (medicines, foodstuffs). Foodstuffs production was very important in manufacturing value added, but its share in investment was relatively low (Table 6.3), which suggested that improving basic needs had a lower priority.

According to the 1983–1987 investment program, 62 percent of manufacturing investment would be financed by external sources and 38 percent internally. Figures on the actual financing of manufacturing investment are so far available only for 1982–1984. Table 6.4 shows that the majority of manufacturing investment was financed by internal sources, and most of it from firms' own resources. So manufacturing's priority in assigning foreign exchange for investment was even lower than planned. In 1984 the proportion financed by the banking system (National Financial System) increased; the contribution of "own resources" decreased after 1982. Credit lines from foreign countries became important after 1983.

Investment in manufacturing, already lower than that in agriculture and agroindustry, fell from an average of $27,000 in 1983 and 1984 to $17,000 in 1985, $19,000 in 1986, and $6,000 in 1987.[2]

On the whole, the Nicaraguan government's investment policy gave a higher priority to long-term industrialization than to improving the supply of basic consumer goods. By constructing large agroindustrial projects geared to export markets, it attempted to build up "heavy industry," which in due course was expected to provide foreign exchange to pay for imports of capital goods. But the new projects had a long maturation time, often bore no relation to existing

TABLE 6.4 Sources of Financing for Manufacturing Investment (in percent)

| Source | *1982* | *1983* | *1984* | *1984* S | *1984* P[a] |
|---|---|---|---|---|---|
| Internal Sources | 80 | 56 | 59 | 57 | 91 |
| Own resources | 61 | 48 | 30 | 25 | 85 |
| S.F.N.[b] | 19 | 8 | 26 | 29 | 6 |
| Government budget | | | 2 | 2 | |
| Other | | 0 | 1 | 1 | 0 |
| External sources | 20 | 44 | 41 | 43 | 9 |
| Loans | 11 | 4 | 1 | 1 | 9 |
| Credit lines | 6 | 41 | 36 | 41 | |
| Donations | | | 4 | 2 | |
| Other | 3 | | 0 | 0 | |
| Total | 100 | 100 | 100 | 100 | 100 |

[a]The FSLN newspaper "Barricada" is excluded.
[b]S.F.N: Sistema Financiero Nacional (National Financial System).

*Sources:* For 1982 and 1983: Ministry of Industry 1984. Cinco años de gestión. Managua. Mimeo; for 1984: MIND 1985. Sector industrial: Evaluación año 1984. Managua. Mimeo.

production, and were afflicted by many implementation problems. So new projects were not bearing fruit and the relative neglect of maintenance and repair activities led to a deterioration of the economy's production capacity. This affected, in particular, consumer goods production. Manufacturing—very important for consumer goods production—had a low priority in the investment strategy. The few investments being carried out in the sector were of a "heavy industry" nature (promoting exports or improving internal linkages).

The experiences of Nicaragua during 1983–1985 can to a certain extent be compared with those of other countries with socialist industrialization strategies: for example, the Soviet Union after 1929 and Cuba during the 1960s. During the USSR's industrialization drive, Soviet leaders officially stated that the objective of increasing the supply of consumer goods was important—but in practice the emphasis was on heavy industry.[3] From 1963 onward, Cuba gave top priority to sugar production, also a kind of "heavy industry." A fairly high investment rate was accompanied by a rather low level of investment productivity (Mesa-Lago 1981:44). This was due to a lack of consumer goods to stimulate worker productivity and to insufficient planning and control in the implementation of investment projects.

It seems that after a revolution it is difficult to avoid this "growth optimism" accompanied by the relative neglect of consumer goods production. All socialist governments appear to be subject to "megalomania," to a wish to show with a few large prestigious projects that they are working on the development of their country. In addition, it probably seems easier to plan and implement a few big projects than to improve existing production capacity. At least in Nicaragua, the dependence on foreign aid to finance investment also played a role. Foreign donors often preferred their aid to be visible in a big project.

From 1985 onward the Sandinista government attempted to change the direction of investment. More short-term projects and more projects directed at increasing consumer goods production were to be put into effect, the government said. However, because ongoing projects absorbed a large share of resources, it was difficult to put this change into practice. Even maintaining discontinued investment projects absorbed some of the investment budget. Furthermore, the factors that had stimulated Nicaragua's "megalomania" and the higher priority accorded to export production over basic consumer goods still had an impact on specific investment decisions.

In spite of the verbal recognition of the importance of repair and maintenance and of providing inputs for peasant production, the 1985 and 1986 economic plans still devoted more than 80 percent of state investment to highly sophisticated long-term projects (IHCA 1986:22b). New projects absorbed 24 percent of the 1986 public investment program. In 1987 this share had diminished to 1 percent (IHCA 1987:18). For the first time, the 1987 plan included a program of medium-term credits for the maintenance and recovery of agricultural production capacity. This program would benefit private producers as well as state enterprises and cooperatives. In 1987 the program absorbed 28 percent of total state investment funds (INIES/SPP 1987:145); by 1988 this share had increased to 35 percent; it reached 65 percent in 1989 (IHCA 1989b:37).

### *The Manufacturing Industry*

Table 5.5 shows that production diminished enormously in 1979. The losses caused by the liberation war had more than short-term consequences. Part of the industrial capacity had been destroyed during the war and many owners of enterprises had decapitalized their factories, taking as much working capital abroad as they could. The reactivation of industry required extensive imports of raw materials, inputs, and machinery and equipment. In addition, the fall

TABLE 6.5 Imports of Raw Materials, Inputs, and Spare Parts for Manufacturing 1977 and 1980–1987 (in millions of $)[a]

| | 1977 | 1980 | 1981 | 1982 | 1983 | 1984 | 1985 | 1986 | 1987 |
|---|---|---|---|---|---|---|---|---|---|
| Imports | 176 | 161 | 120 | 160 | 147 | 145 | 140 | 146 | 112 |

[a]These figures are only indications.

*Source:* Ministry of Economy, Industry, and Commerce, General Division of Planning 1988, Mimeo.

in agricultural production caused a shortage of domestically produced raw materials (cotton-seed, hides) and increased import requirements.

But in reality, imports of raw materials and inputs diminished, as Table 6.5 shows. Insufficient import capacity was one obstacle to the reactivation and growth of the manufacturing industry. Nonetheless, until 1983–1984 the manufacturing industry did grow and almost regained 1977 levels (see also Table 6.6). In 1985 manufacturing value added fell by 4.7 percent. The U.S. government's trade embargo probably played a role in this, as did the temporary elimination of pay in kind (Castillo 1988:237). In 1986 and 1987 industry achieved small growth rates, but in 1988 it experienced an enormous decline. Manufacturing suffered first from energy conservation measures adopted in the first months of 1988 as a result of successful contra attacks on electricity installations. More serious was the general recession that followed the monetary reform of February 1988.

If we look at the results of manufacturing industry per branch, consumer goods producers recovered relatively well during the first years after the Sandinista victory (Table 5.5). The price controls on these products and the general improvement in the distribution of income increased demand for soft drinks, cigarettes, clothing, and shoes, in particular. In leather and shoes, production had fallen enormously by 1987. The insufficient availability of domestically produced raw materials was probably the most important cause. Some other branches continued to grow after 1981, for example, textiles and printing and publishing (Table 6.6). This growth was probably due to relatively high investment in these branches.

Production of intermediate goods did not recover well. In the important chemicals sector, import dependence was high and decapitalization had been fairly extensive. Furthermore, the fall in regional demand affected production. Problems with the Central American Common Market were also in part responsible for the slow reactivation of the metal products and transport materials industries.

TABLE 6.6 Indexes of Manufacturing Value Added 1980–1987 (1980=100)

| | *1980* | *1981* | *1982* | *1983* | *1984* | *1985* | *1986* | *1987*[a] |
|---|---|---|---|---|---|---|---|---|
| Food | 100 | 100 | 113 | 111 | 111 | 97 | 94 | 89 |
| Beverages | 100 | 101 | 95 | 100 | 104 | 108 | 108 | 111 |
| Tobacco | 100 | 96 | 83 | 92 | 106 | 110 | 115 | 114 |
| Textiles | 100 | 129 | 134 | 160 | 159 | 153 | 185 | 190 |
| Clothing | 100 | 104 | 92 | 94 | 84 | 80 | 90 | 111 |
| Leather | 100 | 94 | 102 | 91 | 84 | 80 | 61 | 52 |
| Shoes | 100 | 98 | 83 | 85 | 68 | 64 | 57 | 51 |
| Wood | 100 | 104 | 91 | 88 | 88 | 62 | 65 | 102 |
| Furniture | 100 | 102 | 90 | 91 | 87 | 76 | 86 | 99 |
| Paper | 100 | 143 | 181 | 228 | 244 | 247 | 360 | 417 |
| Printing | 100 | 137 | 145 | 154 | 184 | 191 | 179 | 174 |
| Chemicals | 100 | 104 | 94 | 118 | 118 | 113 | 110 | 105 |
| Oil products | 100 | 101 | 99 | 88 | 72 | 80 | 84 | 82 |
| Rubber | 100 | 124 | 128 | 108 | 125 | 123 | 133 | 94 |
| Nonmetal. minerals | 100 | 94 | 90 | 123 | 127 | 117 | 125 | 140 |
| Metal products | 100 | 99 | 111 | 132 | 126 | 133 | 149 | 151 |
| Mach. & electr. art. | 100 | 137 | 108 | 137 | 112 | 99 | 117 | 148 |
| Transport materials | 100 | 109 | 81 | 109 | 112 | 144 | 150 | 118 |
| Plastics and other | 100 | 123 | 113 | 106 | 100 | 112 | 106 | 119 |
| Total | 100 | 103 | 103 | 109 | 109 | 104 | 106 | 107 |

[a]Preliminary figures.

*Source:* Elaboration of ECLAC 1988. *Notas para el estudio económico de América Latina y El Caribe, 1987: Nicaragua,* 39.

However, investment and the availability of raw materials supplies from Eastern European countries meant metal products could achieve considerable growth. Low production results in electric and nonelectric machinery, compared to 1977 levels, were in keeping with the objective of not stimulating the production of consumer durables.

The interviews presented in Chapter 4 show that factories producing basic consumer goods (the first category) received more dollars to import raw materials and inputs than other enterprises. Enterprises of that category could also import relatively more spare parts. Exporting enterprises received the fewest dollars, although differences between categories were not very substantial.

Manufacturers' answers to some other questions may throw more light on the causes of growth or stagnation of certain branches. I first asked whether or not the enterprise was using 100 percent of production capacity; if not, I asked how much was in use and why not all production capacity was being used.[4] The average capacity utilization in the whole sample was 62.1 percent. Seven enterprises used 95

TABLE 6.7 Sample of Enterprises: Capacity Use

| | *S* | *N,C*[a] | *T* | *Subtotal P* | *Total* |
|---|---|---|---|---|---|
| More than 95% capacity use | 4 (25) | 1 (11) | 2 (22) | 3 (17) | 7 (21) |
| Less than 95% capacity use | 12 (75) | 8 (89) | 7 (78) | 15 (83) | 27 (79) |
| Total enterprises | 16 (100) | 9 (100) | 9 (100) | 18 (100) | 34 (100) |
| Causes for less than 95% capacity use: | | | | | |
| Imported raw materials | 9 (75) | 6 (75) | 4 (57) | 10 (67) | 19 (73) |
| Domestic raw materials | 4 (33) | 3 (38) | 1 (14) | 4 (27) | 8 (31) |
| Spare parts | 4 (33) | 3 (38) | 0 (0) | 3 (20) | 7 (27) |
| Labor | 0 (0) | 1 (13) | 2 (29) | 3 (20) | 3 (12) |
| Energy failure | 0 (0) | 0 (0) | 1 (14) | 1 (7) | 1 (4) |
| Machinery[b] | 1 (8) | 0 (0) | 0 (0) | 0 (0) | 1 (4) |
| Market | 0 (0) | 0 (0) | 1 (14) | 1 (7) | 1 (4) |
| Total enterprises[c] | 12 (100) | 8 (100) | 7 (100) | 15 (100) | 27 (100) |

[a]In this and some of the following tables, a distinction is not only made between state (S) and private (P) enterprises, but within private the last group also between transnational (T), nationally owned (N), and Central American (C) companies.
[b]If there are, for instance, two production lines and one is dependent on the other.
[c]Sometimes one director mentioned more than one factor, so the total of factors exceeds the total amount of enterprises in the sample.

*Source:* Interviews.

or 100 percent (Table 6.7). State enterprises recorded a higher average utilization rate than private enterprises: 68.9 percent versus 56.2 percent. Basic consumer goods producers mentioned a higher average utilization rate (71.8 percent) than producers in the other categories, and intermediate goods producers (the third category) mentioned the lowest (53.5 percent). The averages for the other categories, exporting enterprises and nonbasic consumer goods producers, were 60.7 percent and 62.7 percent, respectively.

As to why businesses were running below full capacity, see again Table 6.7. The most important reason proved, as could be expected, to be a lack of imported raw materials (and inputs). Other important factors were a lack of spare parts and of domestically produced raw materials, in particular cotton seed, hides, and wood. In one case, the "domestically produced" raw material was bunker oil, which is only indirectly produced nationally, because Nicaragua imports crude. As I showed in Chapter 3, a low rate of capacity utilization has always been a structural feature of the manufacturing industry in Central America. But the reasons for low utilization in 1984–1985 seemed to be different from those during the 1960s and 1970s, which was a period of growth. Demand before that growth period had increased more gradually than production capacity, which usually expanded in big jumps. At the time of my investigation, production was not constrained by demand but by supply.

The shortage of imported raw materials was mentioned most by exporting enterprises (the fourth category): eighty-six percent cited this as a cause of low utilization, followed by the second category (nonbasic consumer goods) with 75 percent. Sixty-seven percent of the first category (basic consumer goods) listed and 50 percent of the third (intermediate goods) cited a raw materials shortage as the cause of low productivity. Raw materials imports were completely state controlled. My interviews, then, confirmed that the government accorded a higher priority to the first and the third categories. Exporting enterprises here again seemed to take the lowest priority.

The only major difference between causes cited by state and private enterprises for underutilization was the lack of labor, which more affected private enterprises, in particular transnational enterprises. But transnational enterprises apparently did not have problems obtaining spare parts. Perhaps they could still obtain spare parts from other subsidiaries in the region or from their parent company. No enterprise mentioned a lack of liquidity as a factor. Only one director, in this case of a foreign enterprise, pointed to an insufficient market, the Central American market in particular.

I used two indicators to investigate the quality of the existing equipment.[5] One was the average age of the equipment as estimated by the director. The average age of machinery was higher in the state sector than in the private sector (Table 6.8). But across the whole sample, machinery proved to be very old. There were wide differences between categories in this respect. Equipment in the first and the fourth categories was, on average, much older (19.6 and 18.2 years, respectively) than that in the second and third categories (10.5 and 14.8 years).

My second indicator was the director's explicit evaluation of the quality of equipment. I asked whether the existing machinery and equipment were sufficient. As the majority of the enterprises were not using 100 percent of installed capacity, their answers generally referred to the quality of the equipment rather than the quantity. Most directors said the quality of their equipment was not sufficient (Table 6.8). More directors of transnational enterprises were satisfied with the quality of their equipment. Given that they had already said they did not experience a lack of spare parts, this response was consistent.

All directors of first category enterprises (basic consumer goods producers) said their equipment was not sufficient. Of the other

TABLE 6.8 Sample of Enterprises: Evaluation of Existing Equipment

| | *Average Age (in years)* | *Is the Equipment Sufficient?* | | |
|---|---|---|---|---|
| | | *Yes* | *No* | *Total* |
| State | 18.13 | 5 (31) | 11 (69) | 16 (100) |
| Private | 13.38 | 7 (47) | 8 (53) | 15 (100) |
| N,C[a] | 13.33 | 2 (28) | 7 (78) | 9 (100) |
| T[b] | 13.43 | 5 (83) | 1 (17) | 6 (100) |
| Total | 15.64 | 12 (39) | 19 (61) | 31 (100) |

[a]National and Central American enterprises.
[b]Transnational enterprises.

*Source:* Interviews.

categories this proportion was much lower, probably because average capacity utilization was lower. This result indicated that it was necessary to give first category enterprises not only a high priority in the assignment of foreign exchange for raw materials and inputs but also in (replacement) investment.

Directors were asked where the existing machinery and equipment came from. The United States and the Federal Republic of Germany were mentioned most frequently. West Germany was an important supplier for private enterprises in particular. The fact that so much machinery came from the United States had serious consequences for its maintenance after the U.S. trade embargo in May 1985. Much Nicaraguan equipment was so old that spare parts could be obtained only from the firm that had originally supplied the machine. Part of the machinery originating from the United States probably did not function anymore by 1989 because of the impossibility of repair. According to the data in Table 6.9, this problem affected the state and the private sectors equally.

Almost all enterprises had problems finding skilled labor; many also found it hard to secure unskilled labor (Table 6.10). This was probably because official wages were low; many industrial laborers were instead attracted to the informal trade sector (see Chapter 5). However, only three enterprises cited the lack of labor as a reason for not using 100 percent of capacity (Table 6.7). Apparently, the other problems were more severe. Private enterprises seemed to be in a better position to recruit unskilled labor, probably because some paid wages much higher than the official SNOTS wages (Chapter 4). The

TABLE 6.9 Sample of Enterprises: Origin of the Equipment

| *Country* | *State* | *Private* | *Total* |
|---|---|---|---|
| Western Europe | 9 | 14 | 23 |
| FRG | 7 | 14 | 21 |
| Spain | 3 | 1 | 4 |
| Italy | 2 | 2 | 4 |
| France | 0 | 2 | 2 |
| Great Britain | 0 | 2 | 2 |
| The Netherlands | 0 | 2 | 2 |
| Belgium | 1 | 0 | 1 |
| Switzerland | 1 | 0 | 1 |
| United States | 11 | 11 | 22 |
| Eastern Europe | 3 | 1 | 4 |
| Latin America | 2 | 0 | 2 |
| North Korea | 2 | 0 | 2 |
| Taiwan | 0 | 1 | 1 |
| Total enterprises[a] | 15 | 17 | 32 |

[a]One director could mention more than one country of origin, so the total of countries of origin exceeds the total amount of enterprises.

*Source:* Interviews.

TABLE 6.10 Sample of Enterprises: Problems with Labor Recruitment

| | *Skilled Labor* | | | *Unskilled Labor* | | |
|---|---|---|---|---|---|---|
| | *Yes* | *No* | *Total* | *Yes* | *No* | *Total* |
| State | 13. (93) | 1 (7) | 14 (100) | 10 (77) | 3 (23) | 13 (100) |
| Private | 12 (75) | 3 (25) | 15 (100) | 5 (55) | 4 (45) | 9 (100) |
| N,C[a] | 6 (67) | 3 (33) | 9 (100) | 3 (60) | 2 (40) | 5 (100) |
| T[b] | 6 (100) | 0 (0) | 6 (100) | 2 (50) | 2 (50) | 4 (100) |
| Total | 25 (86) | 4 (14) | 29 (100) | 15 (68) | 7 (32) | 22 (100) |

[a]National and Central American enterprises.
[b]Transnational enterprises.

*Source:* Interviews.

TABLE 6.11 Sample of Enterprises: Profits

| | *Preceding Years*[a] | | | *This Year*[b] | | |
|---|---|---|---|---|---|---|
| | *Yes, All Years* | *Not All Years* | *Total* | *Yes* | *No* | *Total* |
| State | 7 (45) | 9 (55) | 16 (100) | 15 (94) | 1 (6) | 16 (100) |
| Private | 10 (67) | 5 (33) | 15 (100) | 14 (82) | 3 (18) | 17 (100) |
| Total | 17 (55) | 14 (45) | 31 (100) | 29 (88) | 4 (12) | 33 (100) |

[a]Because some interviews were held in 1984 and others in 1985, this means 1980 through 1983 or 1984, respectively.
[b]1984 or 1985, see above.

*Source:* Interviews.

labor recruitment problem probably grew in the course of time. In the first semester of 1987, for example, labor turnover in manufacturing was as high as 34 percent (Castillo 1988:241).

Directors of transnational enterprises had the most problems finding skilled labor. These enterprises probably demanded more skills from their workers than did others. Directors who mentioned problems finding skilled workers cited in particular a lack of technical personnel (seventeen directors) and of professionals (bookkeepers, etc.; six directors).

Directors were also asked about profitability since 1979. Most firms had booked profits in every year since 1980 (Table 6.11). More state than private enterprises had experienced losses in some years, particularly immediately after the Sandinista victory. Apparently, neither state nor private enterprises had been threatened with closure as a result of losses in previous years. This is consistent with my conclusion in Chapter 4, that the availability of sufficient cordobas was not decisive for the possibility of producing.[6] Three private-sector directors and one of a state enterprise said when I interviewed them that the enterprise was not profitable. These firms operated in the third (intermediate goods) and the fourth (export goods) categories. More firms in these categories had also not recorded profits in some preceding years.

My interviews show the most important bottleneck for manufacturing production was a lack of imported inputs and raw materials. No enterprise director mentioned a lack of liquidity as a limiting factor on production, which confirmed that the manufacturing industry was a "resource constrained system" as pointed out in Chapter 4.

Even though there was a large private sector, the government planned manufacturing production centrally. It assigned most inputs at subsidized prices according to criteria other than market efficiency. This gave the government a high degree of control of what was to be produced and how.

In terms of industrial strategy, a centrally planned system is compatible with carrying out an import substitution strategy, which in fact was dominant in Nicaragua during 1980–1987. But the dilution of market forces opens the possibility of wrong allocation decisions and leads to lower efficiency and a lower quality of production within an enterprise. These factors in turn reduce the possibility of promoting exports (see further on).

The 1988 reform measures brought more realistic import and export exchange rates and interest rates, reduced price controls and state intervention in domestic markets, and abolished wage controls. Except for wages, which still were very low by Central American standards, the reforms led to more realistic prices in general. The government still assigned imported inputs and raw materials centrally, but because the discrepancy between official and black-market exchange rates almost disappeared, the power of state control on manufacturing production diminished. Enterprises could buy dollars on the black market.

Manufacturing results show that reactivation had come to an end by 1984. By that time, investment in replacement and maintenance of machinery was urgently necessary. But, although imports of spare parts increased as a proportion of total imports for manufacturing after 1985, the latter's decline (Table 6.5) meant there was no absolute improvement.

In its last years, the Sandinista government seemed more conscious of the importance of manufacturing for the Nicaraguan economy. Comandante Luis Carrión, minister of economy, industry, and commerce, for example, said in an interview with *Barricada* that domestic consumption of nationally produced goods saved $500 million annually in import costs (IHCA 1989c:14). But by 1989, the possibilities of improving the foreign-exchange assigment for manufacturing were limited. The sector was mainly dependent on credit lines, in particular from Eastern Europe, which were tied to certain products. The share of freely spendable dollars for imports for manufacturing sank from 49 percent in 1984 to 10 percent in 1987.[7] Eastern European credit lines tended to benefit only certain branches, such as metal products, and could not contribute to the repair and maintenance of old equipment.

### *Manufactured Exports*

The objective of stimulating manufacturing exports was not very successfully fulfilled, as Table 5.6 shows. In fact, manufacturing exports shrank enormously during the liberation war and continued to fall afterward. In 1985 they were reduced to one-fifth of their 1977 value. The reason for this drop is usually said to be the reduced demand from CACM countries and the crisis of the CACM in general (Brundenius 1984; Weeks 1985b).

This was of course an important factor, in particular in the first years after the Sandinista victory. However, some other factors also seem to have been important. For example, in 1984 several other economies in the region began to show positive growth rates, but Nicaragua did not succeed in increasing exports to the region. Supply problems were probably the main reason (ECLAC 1986:14).

Insufficient foreign exchange for imports was already mentioned in the Industry Ministry's annual evaluations of 1981 and 1982 as a cause for diminished exports (MIND 1982; MIND 1983c). In the 1984 evaluation, also listed were the poor quality of imported inputs and the fact that export contracts with the German Democratic Republic and Cuba were not signed in time. Exports of wood had been hindered by the contra attacks (MIND 1985b).

Eleven of the thirty-four enterprises I examined exported part of their production. These included all firms in category 4 (goods for export) and three in category 1 (basic consumer goods). If I had approached them before the revolution, this figure would have been twenty-six. Twenty firms, eight of the twelve state enterprises and twelve of the fourteen private enterprises, had seen a drop in exports since the revolution. I asked eighteen of them what had caused this reduction (Table 6.12). Only one private-sector director said it was due to the decline of the CACM market. Many directors, in particular in the private sector, pointed to a lack of foreign exchange for imports. There were also many directors, particularly in the state sector, who said "the internal market is now more important." Directors of state enterprises apparently had more comprehension of the government preference for supplying the domestic market instead of producing for exports.

Table 6.13 shows the markets of the exporting enterprises in the sample. All exported to the CACM but many also to other countries. Two of the four state-sector directors said their export market had changed since 1979; no private-sector director reported this. The state did not seem to exert a direct influence on the export policy of private enterprises beyond that of the foreign exchange policy on exportable quantities.

TABLE 6.12 Sample of Enterprises: Reasons for Export Reduction

| Decision | *Reduced Market* | *Decision P.C.*[a] | *Internal Market*[b] | *Lack of Dollars* | *Lack of Dom. Raw Mater.* | *State* |
|---|---|---|---|---|---|---|
| State | 0 | 0 | 5 | 2 | 0 | 1 |
| Private | 1 | 1 | 1 | 6 | 1 | 1 |
| Total[c] | 1 | 1 | 6 | 8 | 1 | 2 |

[a]P.C. = parent company.
[b]The director said supplying the internal market was more important than exporting abroad.
[c]One director mentioned two causes.

*Source:* Interviews.

So it seems that stimulating manufacturing exports was not accorded high priority, although this had been one of the official objectives of Nicaragua's postrevolutionary industrial policy. Both in investment policy[8] and in foreign-exchange assigment the government awarded privileges to producers for the domestic market (import substitution). In addition, despite export-stimulating measures like allowing the exchange of 40 percent of export income on the parallel market (Chapter 5), the exchange rate for manufactured exports did not constitute an incentive. Especially from 1985 onward, domestic prices were higher—favoring local sales above exports (Castillo 1988:242).

A first reason for the discrepancy between practice and official objectives is that not all enterprises enjoyed a high priority. In practice, exporting enterprises received relatively less foreign exchange for current production than those producing basic consumer goods for the domestic market and inputs for other domestic sectors.

The problems with the CACM might have indirectly influenced the low priority accorded to manufactured exports. In the first years after the Sandinista victory, Nicaragua imported large amounts of goods from its neighboring countries—this created huge trade deficits with them.[9] As a result, the Central American payment clearing system (Cámara de Compensación Centroamericana) stopped working. The other countries required immediate payment for exports to Nicaragua, but Nicaraguan exports were only credited against outstanding debts. This reduced the value to Nicaragua of exports to the CACM. At the same time, the practical impossibility of importing from neighboring countries meant domestic firms were forced by necessity to supply the internal market.

TABLE 6.13 Sample of Enterprises: Export Markets

| | CACM | Latin America | Cuba | Other Third World | United States | Western Europe | Japan | Total Enterpr.[a] |
|---|---|---|---|---|---|---|---|---|
| S[b] | 4 (100) | 2 (50) | 2 (50) | 0 (0) | 0 (0) | 1 (25) | 0 (0) | 4 (100) |
| P[c] | 6 (100) | 2 (33) | 0 (0) | 1 (17) | 2 (33) | 1 (17) | 1 (17) | 6 (100) |
| T | 10 (100) | 4 (40) | 2 (20) | 1 (10) | 2 (20) | 2 (20) | 1 (10) | 10 (100) |

[a]One director could mention more than one export market, so the total of countries exceeds the total number of enterprises.
[b]S = state enterprises.
[c]P = private enterprises.

*Source:* Interviews.

Because of the problems with CACM exports, from 1983 onward the Ministry of Industry attempted to establish export contracts with other countries, for example, with the United States and Japan for soluble coffee (involving a private enterprise). Most were barter contracts. Nicaragua received imports of raw materials or equipment and supplied manufactures in exchange. In this manner the value of manufactured exports to, for example, Cuba, increased.

But many enterprises were still dependent on the CACM for their market. To overcome the payment problems, some firms in the region started to organize direct barters, *trueques*, without using dollars. Trueques normally involved three or four companies. Within Nicaragua, the importing firm paid in cordobas to the exporting firm. For the former, this meant an opportunity to import without dollars. The exporting firm received requests from many companies to participate in a trueque. Enterprises could organize these contracts directly, but they had to be approved by MICE (Ministerio de Comercio Exterior), the Ministry of External Trade. It only checked whether exports and imports involved were included in the annual plans. The share of trueques in Nicaragua's total exports increased from zero in 1980 to 9 percent in 1984.[10]

The fact that all exports had to be included in the annual plan hindered enterprises from seeking new export markets. If they found new markets during the plan year they could not guarantee supply to their potential buyers: Companies received dollars only for buying inputs for production included in the plan. Potential buyers could be expected to be unwilling to wait until new exports were approved and planned.

To make the system more flexible, exporting enterprises were allowed to maintain 40 percent of the value of their exports in CDDs (foreign exchange certificates). CDDs were introduced after the—temporary—abolition of the parallel market in 1983 (Chapter 5).[11] CDDs were a kind of dollar account at the Central Bank. But they were not a real dollar account because companies had to request permission to use them. In many cases, the Central Bank did not give that permission, saying that no dollars were available.

So in practice, Nicaraguan manufacturing still operated in a centrally planned system. For that reason, the country experienced the same problems as did, for example, Eastern European countries in stimulating exports (Dijkstra 1988). Central planning leads to a reduction of the efficiency of production and implies an emphasis on quantity instead of quality. In addition, the foreign trade monopoly of the state uncouples domestic prices from international prices. This creates an overvalued exchange rate and relative domestic prices do not reflect international scarcities. This impedes an effective adjustment to changes in international demand and costs. The experiences of Eastern European countries showed that reforms of the centrally planned system in these aspects are necessary.

In 1986 a partial decentralization of production decisions came about with the introduction of an Export Promotion Fund, partly financed by Western donors. Exporting enterprises could retain part of their export income in dollars, with which they could buy inputs abroad. After 1985 the downward trend in manufacturing exports seemed to have ended, with their value remaining more or less constant from 1985 to 1987.[12]

Following the February 1988 monetary reform, there came an end to the overvalued exchange rate and to the deviations from relative prices in the world market. In principle, exports again became profitable. But the unrealistic import and export exchange rates of previous years and the till then existing system of central planning had reduced the efficiency of the enterprises and had diminished product quality. As a result, manufactured exports could be expected to recover only gradually. Nevertheless, a first increase in these exports was registered in 1989.

## Cooperation in the Private Sector

Some authors expressed severe doubts about the cooperativeness of the Nicaraguan private sector, saying that loss of political power would make the bourgeoisie reluctant to continue producing (see, for example, Coraggio 1986; also Chapter 4). They would attempt to get hold of as large a share as possible of credits and foreign exchange and then transfer it abroad. According to Weeks (1985b) this was in fact happening in the industrial sector. If Weeks was correct, then the stability of the mixed economic order would have been endangered because the state would have been confronted with a dilemma: To take over private possessions or to let manufacturing production collapse.

When I interviewed directors of manufacturing enterprises (1984–1985), the state was using the foreign-exchange instrument to influence the quantity of production; it determined wages and many prices. So the industrial private sector not only lost political power but also a great deal of its economic decision-making power. It seems that there was reason to suppose that private producers in manufacturing were not willing to maintain production.

Private producers in Nicaragua are organized in the Superior Council of Private Enterprise, COSEP. This council explicitly acted as a political organization in opposition to the Sandinista government; in 1984 it was, for example, a member organization of the Coordinadora Democrática, along with political parties and some labor unions.[13] In 1990, COSEP supported the opposition coalition UNO (Union Nicaragüense de Oposición; Nicaraguan Opposition Union), which won the elections.

Before starting interviews with company directors, I interviewed the executive secretary of the Chamber of Industry of Nicaragua, one of the integrating organizations of COSEP. He said it was clear that the government intended to eliminate private enterprise from industry. Many unjustified nationalizations had occurred. He referred, among other cases, to those carried out on the basis of Decree No. 38.[14] Another indicator of the approaching end for private industry was that the state had curtailed the decision-making power of private enterprises to a minimum. Directors could not raise their workers' wages, for example, and the state often carried out firms' sales. In addition, he alleged that in distributing foreign exchange and domestically produced raw materials the Ministry of Industry always favored state enterprises. However, from the results of the interviews presented in Chapter 4, I concluded that the state did not differentiate between state and private enterprises, at least not in distributing inputs for production.

## *Opinions and Expectations*

In my interviews with company directors, I asked some of them their opinions about several aspects of the industrial policy Nicaragua was following: foreign-exchange assignment, price, wage, and export

TABLE 6.14 Sample of Enterprises: Opinions on the Assignment of Foreign Exchange for Raw Materials, Inputs, and Spare Parts

| | Good | Not Good, Not Bad | Bad | Total |
|---|---|---|---|---|
| State | 2 (33) | 0 (0) | 4 (67) | 6 (100) |
| Private | 2 (14) | 4 (29) | 8 (57) | 14 (100) |
| Total | 4 (20) | 4 (20) | 12 (60) | 20 (100) |

*Source:* Interviews.

policy. In a few cases, a director refused to give his opinion on an issue. If this happened, it is explicitly mentioned.

Seven of the twelve directors of private enterprises complained that state enterprises received preferential treatment with respect to foreign-exchange assignment for imports of raw materials, inputs, and spare parts. The other five saw no differentiation between the two ownership sectors. However, most state-sector directors said there was no difference in the assignment of foreign exchange to state and private enterprises. Two directors expressed the opinion that state enterprises rightly received favorable treatment and one thought it unfair that even though his company belonged to the state sector, it was not more favorably treated than private enterprises. Table 6.14 shows that not all directors of private enterprises were fully negative on the foreign exchange assignment issue. In addition, there was no major difference between the two ownership sectors.

I also asked how directors viewed the likelihood of their firm receiving sufficient dollars in the next year. Not all directors were pessimistic, and again, there were no important differences between the state and the private sector (Table 6.15). These results confirmed my earlier conclusion (Chapter 4) that the state did not differentiate between state and private enterprises in assigning foreign exchange for production.

The state determined the prices of the products, or part of the products, made by fifteen state and eleven private enterprises (Chapter 4). As could be expected, more state-sector directors (eight of the ten) than private-sector directors (three of the nine) considered the price sufficiently high. However, it is surprising that some private-sector directors were satisfied with the state-determined price. This can probably be explained by the subsidized prices at which they could buy their inputs or by the reduced meaning of money in the Nicaraguan economy.

TABLE 6.15 Sample of Enterprises: Expectations to Receive Foreign Exchange Next Year

| | Good | More Difficult | Better | Don't Know | Total |
|---|---|---|---|---|---|
| S | 3 (23) | 5 (38) | 2 (15) | 3 (23) | 13 (100) |
| P | 2 (17) | 5 (42) | 3 (25) | 2 (17) | 12 (100) |
| Total | 5 (20) | 10 (40) | 5 (20) | 5 (20) | 25 (100) |

*Source:* Interviews.

With respect to wage policy, the majority of directors in both the state and private sectors judged the official wages according to SNOTS as too low. Only one state-sector director thought wages were high enough. Two (one of a state and one of a private company) refused to give their opinion on this issue. Four private-sector directors said they were against state control of wages. I only asked this question of directors who actually applied SNOTS. Those who did not could be assumed to be against state control of wages too.

Three of the four state-sector directors and six of the seven directors of private enterprises were negative on the export policy. They wished to export more but depended on the state for foreign exchange.

Private-sector directors also answered some more general questions. The first was whether they thought the Ministry of Industry gave equal treatment, in general, to state and private enterprises. Five of the nine directors answered that there was no difference and four said it favored the state sector.

I asked eleven of these directors whether they still felt that they were managing a private enterprise. Four answered they were civil servants, in fact. They spent a large part of their time participating in meetings in several state institutions and could no longer make their own decisions. One of them was pleased with that situation. The majority of private-sector directors (seven of the eleven) responded positively to this question; each still felt like a manager of a private enterprise. This is rather high given the high degree of state intervention these enterprises experienced.

Fourteen private-sector directors gave their opinion on the "revolutionary process" in general, and in particular on Nicaragua's economic policy. I did not ask three directors; one refused to give his of the fourteen, six had a very negative opinion. One said "the government must talk with the private sector" (i.e., with the representative of

TABLE 6.16 Private Enterprises of the Sample: Opinions on the Revolutionary Process

| | N + C[a] | T[b] | Total |
|---|---|---|---|
| No answer | 1 (13) | 0 (0) | 1 (7) |
| Bad | 5 (63) | 1 (17) | 6 (43) |
| Not good, not bad | 3 (38) | 4 (67) | 7 (50) |
| Good | 0 (0) | 1 (17) | 1 (7) |
| Total | 9 (100) | 6 (100) | 15 (100) |

[a]National and Central American enterprises.
[b]Transnational enterprises.

*Source:* Interviews.

the private sector, the COSEP). Others affirmed "there is too much state control of the economy" or "there is a more severe dictatorship than before the revolution."

Seven directors were not very pleased with the situation but said they understood, for instance, that "the extent of control in the economy is necessary because of the war," or that the government made mistakes but had good intentions. One was very positive about the revolutionary process: "There is more equality now, and more participation."

In Table 6.16 the first group of opinions is classified "bad," the second as "not good, not bad" and the third as "good." The table shows also that directors of transnational enterprises (T) on average were more positive about the revolutionary process and the economic policy than directors of national and Central American (N, C) enterprises.

In sum, many directors of private enterprises complained about the industrial policy and about half of them thought the state sector received preferential treatment. However, on foreign-exchange assignment there was a negative view from almost as many directors of state enterprises. Concerning the price policy, it was surprising that some private-sector directors were content with the state-determined prices. On the revolutionary process in general, the opinions were not as negative as could be expected from COSEP declarations. In particular, directors of foreign enterprises showed a large degree of comprehension of government policy.

TABLE 6.17 Industrial Investment 1980–1984 per Ownership Area (in percent)

| | 1980 | 1981 | 1982 | 1983 | 1984 |
|---|---|---|---|---|---|
| State | 57 | 51 | 71 | 85 | 89 |
| Private | 43 | 49 | 29 | 15 | 11 |
| Total | 100 | 100 | 100 | 100 | 100 |

*Sources:* Ministry of Industry 1984. Cinco años de gestión. Managua. Mimeo; and for 1984: MIND 1985. Sector industrial: Evaluación año 1984. Managua. Mimeo.

### *Private-Sector Investment*

Most private enterprises in my sample had invested after the Sandinista victory (Chapter 4). Fewer private than state enterprises, however, had received foreign exchange to import machinery and equipment. The sectoral figures on the amounts of state and private investment are in line with this finding (Table 6.17). During 1980 and 1981, investment by the public and private sector was roughly equal. During these years, investment was predominantly geared to reactivating existing capacity. Yet the 1981 Evaluation of the Ministry of Industry pointed to a "limited willingness" of the private sector to invest. Evaluations of later years no longer mentioned this. As of 1982, industrial investment in general was very low, and the rate of private investment fell below that of the state sector. Over the period 1980–1987, the state sector accounted for 90 percent of investment in manufacturing.[15]

A reason for the difference between the 1980–1981 period and later years in this respect could be that during 1980 and 1981 private-sector investment was often financed by loans from the World Bank and the Inter-American Development Bank. In later years, applications for credits continued to be directed to these banks, but the U.S. administration prevented them from being approved. As a result, several private-sector investment projects could not be carried out.

However, from 1983 onward the government managed to acquire credit lines from other countries, which made it possible to buy some new machinery and equipment for manufacturing. The government used these credit lines exclusively for state enterprises and new state investment projects, as the last columns of Table 6.4 show for 1984. This table also indicates that the private sector did not receive funds

TABLE 6.18 Sample of Enterprises: Investment Plans and Expectations to Receive Foreign Exchange

| | *Investment Plans* | | | *Expectation to Receive $* | | | |
|---|---|---|---|---|---|---|---|
| | *Yes* | *No* | *Don't Know* | *Yes* | *No* | *Don't Know* | *Not Necessary* |
| S | 11 (85) | 2 (15) | 0 (0) | 7 (64) | 0 (0) | 3 (23) | 1 (9) |
| P | 11 (65) | 5 (29) | 1 (6) | 1 (9) | 1 (9) | 9 (82) | 0 (0) |
| T | 22 (73) | 7 (23) | 1 (3) | 8 (36) | 1 (5) | 12 (55) | 1 (5) |

*Source:* Interviews.

from the state budget and received only a small proportion of bank loans. Private enterprise financed most investment with its own resources and seemed willing to risk its own money.

This finding agrees with the results of my interviews. Sixty percent of the private enterprises in the sample had used their own money for investment, as shown in Chapter 4. In addition, all fifteen private-sector directors said they used their profits for reinvestment. It must be noted, however, that companies were unable to transfer profits abroad. It was not forbidden, but the Central Bank did not release dollars for that aim.

I also asked whether companies had further investment plans. Most did, but there were more plans in state enterprises than private ones (Table 6.18). Directors of state enterprises were also more certain that they would get the necessary dollars. This was to be expected, because they had received more foreign exchange for investment in the past.

Having investment plans probably depended not only on a company's willingness to maintain production in Nicaragua but also on several other factors: whether existing capacity was fully utilized and whether the director of an enterprise was content with existing equipment. Furthermore, given the high inflation rate in Nicaragua—which made saving useless—and the practical impossibility of transferring profits abroad, it can be assumed that most enterprises would opt to reinvest their cordoba profits, albeit in not-directly-necessary construction activities.

The interview results confirm these assumptions. Those five private enterprises without investment plans all used a very low proportion of their production capacity: 22 percent on average. This is much lower than the 56 percent average for all private enterprises. Furthermore, four of the five directors who did not have investment plans considered their existing equipment sufficient (the fifth director was not asked). And three of the five were the three companies that were not profitable at the time of my interview.

In sum, most private enterprises had investment plans and had been willing to spend their own money on investment. Private-sector directors had fewer investment plans than did state enterprises, but this did not mean they were less willing to maintain production in Nicaragua. However, the private sector accounted for a very small proportion of the already limited level of manufacturing investment. The government clearly prioritized state enterprises and new state investment projects. Even though there were difficulties in obtaining multilateral loans, this prioritization seemed to be a deliberate policy decision. The Ministry reserved *strategic investment* for the state sector and for that reason rejected some investment proposals made by private enterprises.[16]

### *Private-Sector Willingness to Continue Production*

I also asked the directors of private enterprises what they saw as the future of their enterprise within the Nicaraguan mixed economy. Did they think they would be able to maintain production? Only two of the sixteen directors said that it had been a mistake to stay. These directors said they would wait one more year and if the situation did not improve, they would leave. These two directors both were large shareholders in the companies they worked for. Their firms were working at a low capacity-utilization rate—one at 50 and the other, at 25 percent. Strangely, one of them did have investment plans. This could imply that his threat to leave should not have been taken too seriously.

All the other directors said they would go on producing, although seven added "it depends on the government." Six of these had already experienced many problems in maintaining operations, particularly because they lacked imported raw materials and inputs, and in one case because of a lack of domestically produced raw materials. Those directors who said it depended on the government did not imply that they expected their businesses to be promptly expropriated. Nor could they be deemed less likely to invest, or call for investment, in continued production. All the directors of the eight transnational enterprises said they would maintain production; three added the "it depends on the government" rider.

I was also interested in the opinion of the shareholders or owners of a firm or, in foreign enterprises, of a parent company, but I had to depend on the directors' perceptions of shareholder opinion. Most directors said shareholders wanted to continue production, although

TABLE 6.19 Private Enterprises of the Sample: Opinions of Shareholders

| | *N* | *C* | *T* | *Total* |
|---|---|---|---|---|
| Wants to retire (probably) | 1 (17) | 1 (50) | 1 (14) | 3 (20) |
| Continues, "no alternative" | 1 (17) | 1 (50) | 0 (0) | 2 (13) |
| Lost interest, but continues | 0 (0) | 0 (0) | 2 (29) | 2 (13) |
| Continues and invests | 4 (67) | 0 (0) | 4 (57) | 8 (53) |
| Total | 6 (100) | 2 (100) | 7 (100) | 15 (100) |

*Source:* Interviews.

some for a negative reason: They did not have an alternative for their invested capital in Nicaragua (Table 6.19). But according to the directors, the majority of owners were willing not only to maintain production but also to invest. Only three owners probably wanted to retire. Two of them owned the same enterprises of which the directors said they would quit in one year if the situation did not improve. With respect to the third enterprise, a transnational company, the local director wanted to maintain production; the company was already 10 percent state owned. The foreign company that owned the remaining 90 percent had completely lost interest in the firm's Nicaraguan operation and wished to sell it. The state had offered a bid on these shares, which the company had turned down. At the time of the interview, a decision from the Nicaraguan court was expected.

Clearly, some of my questions aimed to find an explanation for the willingness of directors and shareholders to maintain production in Nicaragua. As pointed out, the two directors who wanted to leave if the situation did not improve possessed shares in their company. But this could not be considered a determining factor: Five other directors possessed shares in their companies and all wanted to maintain production.

I also asked some directors whether shareholders had other fixed assets or alternative sources of income, either within or outside Nicaragua. I supposed that not having alternatives, particularly within Nicaragua, would make them more willing to maintain production. It appears that having alternatives was a necessary but not sufficient reason to consider stopping industrial production in Nicaragua (Table 6.20).

I also asked fourteen private-sector directors what they thought of their relationship with the Ministry of Industry. Most said it was "good." Two added there was "too much bureaucracy" and said that

TABLE 6.20 Private Enterprises of the Sample: Position of Shareholders and Alternatives

| | *Continue* | *Not continue* | *Total* |
|---|---|---|---|
| Alternatives in Nicaragua | 3 (60) | 2 (40) | 5 (100) |
| Alternatives only abroad | 6 (86) | 1 (14) | 7 (100) |
| No alternatives | 2 (100) | 0 (0) | 2 (100) |
| Total | 11 (79) | 3 (21) | 14 (100) |

*Source:* Interviews.

their relationship with MIND was "not good, not bad." That so many private-sector directors were positive about their relation with MIND probably had a positive impact on their willingness to maintain production. But there seemed to be no direct link here, because one of the two who said he might give up producing also said he had a good relationship with the ministry.

I also supposed a firm's profitability would be important in the decision about maintaining production, particularly for shareholders. But two of the three companies whose owners were thinking of quitting had posted positive financial results in all years after the change in power. The third had experienced losses only in the year before the interview. This again shows that having profits in cordobas did not have much significance.

Another assumption was that there was a link between a director's opinion of Nicaragua's industrial policy and the decision to maintain production. As pointed out, many private-sector directors complained about most aspects of industrial policy, as did state-sector bosses. There were some exceptions; some private-sector directors were content with the foreign-exchange assignment and with the prices established for their products. Indeed, about half were more or less neutral on economic policy in general. The two who indicated that they wanted to leave within a year if the situation did not improve voiced negative opinions on all aspects of the country's industrial policy and on its economic policy in general.

Finally, I asked the directors of private enterprises why they wanted to continue production. In the transnational enterprises the answers were, for example, "there is always demand," "we make profits and we hope to be able to repatriate them some day," "in other countries the situation is worse than in Nicaragua," or "continuing the firm's name and technology in the country is important." In the case of the one transnational enterprise that had lost interest in its Nicaraguan subsidiary, the director wanted to repay a debt to the parent company. Another reason to maintain production was that he felt responsible for the maintenance of employment. In the group of Nicaraguan and Central American private enterprises, I asked this question only three times. The answers were "I am a Nicaraguan and I am responsible for employment here," "there is no alternative," and "I make the best of it, in whatever situation."[17] Thus, many private-sector directors had positive reasons for maintaining production.

In conclusion, many directors of private enterprises in manufacturing complained about industrial policy, particularly of the insufficient amount of foreign exchange assigned to them. But directors of state enterprises also complained, and almost to the same degree. The most important survey result is that the overwhelming majority of private industrial enterprises of the sample were willing to maintain production in Nicaragua. Most private enterprises had invested in preceding years and used their own money. Most also had investment plans at the time of the interview. This was an unexpected finding.

Some factors do seem to explain this willingness to continue production. The first is that, contrary to COSEP allegations, the Ministry of Industry did not seem to discriminate against private producers in its most important policy instrument, the assignment of foreign exchange for current production (Chapter 4). Another factor was the small scale of the Nicaraguan industrial sector. The Ministry of Industry, and particularly the branch directors, had very frequent contacts with all company directors in their branch. Most directors of private enterprises said their relationship with the ministry was a good one. This probably increased their sympathy for the industrial policy.

For some enterprises the most important reason for maintaining production proved to be a negative one—namely that they had no alternative for their invested capital within Nicaragua. However, there were some factors that made production in Nicaragua attractive: All production could be sold—there were no competing imports and internal demand was growing; firms could always obtain financing (in cordobas) on easy conditions; the state kept workers' wages at a low level and salaries of higher personnel could be freely determined; and almost all the companies were profitable. Although profits were in general not sufficient to replace equipment, they could be used for consumption needs of the director or the owners.

Transnational enterprises seemed to have some additional reasons for maintaining a subsidiary in Nicaragua. The continuation of the enterprise appeared to be more important than the possibility of transferring profits in the short term. The profits of the subsidiary in

Nicaragua were generally small compared with those of the company as a whole, considered an advantage because the survival of the latter was not dependent on the profits made in Nicaragua. In addition, the Nicaraguan government did everything to avoid conflicts with transnational enterprises. Many were not subjected to wage control, for example.

My conclusion that the private sector in industry was willing to maintain production in Nicaragua is confirmed by a study of forty multinational corporations in Nicaragua published in the Harvard Business Review (Austin and Ickis 1986). Austin and Ickis found that these enterprises could not only survive the revolution but could also grow and generate profits. The objective of their study was to find out how these enterprises had achieved this.

Most of the companies experienced problems, first resulting from the liberation war, later from government bureaucracy, and some also from contra guerrilla warfare. Foreign exchange restrictions also limited their activities. But managers considered it an advantage that they could sell anything they produced (Austin and Ickis 1986:105). The directors of these enterprises adjusted production processes and products to the reduced availability of dollars. In addition, they adapted their style of management to take account of the stronger position of workers since the revolution.

Although all enterprises were affiliated with COSEP, they preferred to have contacts with the government on an individual basis. "COSEP is outspokenly critical of the government," said one (Austin and Ickis 1986:107). If there was a common interest, they would form a coalition with other enterprises to negotiate with the government.

The enterprises did experience difficulties in expatriating their profits but some had found inventive ways to achieve this. In sum, Austin and Ickis concluded that multinational enterprises could survive after the Nicaraguan revolution because the government had left room for a private sector.

### *Opinions in Agroindustry*

I held only three interviews with directors of private agroindustrial enterprises. Almost all agroindustrial plant owners also produced the primary materials for these plants and were big producers in agriculture. In this sense, these three were typical. In addition, they belonged to the big agricultural bourgeoisie that not only owned, for example, coffee farms, but also had cotton production and possessed cattle ranges. The results of these three interviews lead only to tentative conclusions.

The situation in agroindustry was very different from that in manufacturing. Production was not influenced by imported inputs but by the agricultural raw materials themselves. State and private processing plants had excess capacity and competed with each other for obtaining the harvest of small and medium producers not having their own processing installation.

As pointed out in Chapter 4, the three interviewees complained that the state used its ability to establish processing tariffs and crop prices before and after processing to guarantee a larger share of the raw crops for state processing plants. They also complained about the foreign-exchange assignment for spare parts and about the high interest rate and the small amount of credits received, particularly for their agricultural activities. Furthermore, they said that SNOTS was a bad system and that wages were too high.

Only one of the three private producers made profits on agroindustrial activity. But he complained that he could not buy anything with the cordobas he made. He said that he was investing now but that he would not maintain production in the country if he could not get part of his profits in dollars.[18] The other two were not making profits and they alleged that they only maintained production to avoid confiscation of their plant. They had to subsidize their agroindustrial activity with income from other sources. One said he used only state-provided credits to maintain production in agriculture and agroindustry: None of his own money was invested. But he added that state credits were not sufficient, in fact admitting that he was decapitalizing.

All three mentioned recent cases of expropriations in agriculture or agroindustry that they considered unjustified. For example, they cited the case of an expropriated enterprise that was more productive than the country's average, even though the government had said that nationalizations would only affect unproductive enterprises. This unjustified expropriation policy created an uncertain climate for private producers, they said.

These three private producers in agroindustry and agriculture generally complained much more about government policy than did private producers in manufacturing. But they probably had more reason to complain. Functionaries of MIDINRA admitted that it was possible the state favored state enterprises in agriculture and agroindustry above private enterprises, especially in distributing imported inputs.

The most important problems for these private producers seemed to be a lack of incentives for production (they registered losses or complained about not making *hard currency* profits) and the nationalizations that were still occurring in this sector. It is obvious that continuing expropriations in agriculture and agroindustry resulted in a deterioration of the relationship between the state and the private sector. The mixed economy—at least the division of ownership between the state and large private producers—was here much more unstable than in manufacturing. The state appeared to discriminate against private producers and sometimes confiscated their businesses. Some large private producers were reducing their production or decapitalizing.

How can the difference between the manufacturing industry and agroindustry be explained? The attitude of large private agricultural and agroindustrial producers is the more surprising because state influence on agroindustrial and agricultural production was less strong than on the manufacturing industry because the former was not as dependent on imported raw materials and inputs. One reason could be that two of the three agroindustrial producers ran unprofitable plants, whereas most manufacturing enterprises did make profits. However, agroindustrial entrepreneurs could compensate for these losses with profits on their agricultural production. In addition, there was no relationship between having cordoba profits and the private manufacturers' decision to maintain production.

A more important reason for the reluctance of private producers in agroindustry probably was that the state did seem to discriminate against private enterprises in agroindustry and that nationalization still occurred in this sector. This suggests that the state adopted a different attitude toward this sector. The government had defined agriculture and agroindustry as sectors with a higher priority than manufacturing. Consequently, it was more important to achieve the objective that the state be the "pivot of the accumulation process" (Chapter 5). So the government would be more likely to give a higher priority to state enterprises and to nationalize. But this reduced the possibility of maintaining the mixed economic order.

However, the attitude of big producers in agriculture and agroindustry also seemed to be different from that of large producers in manufacturing. This can be explained by the different historical role of the few big producers in agriculture and agroindustry compared with that of most large manufacturing producers. As shown in Chapter 3, most manufacturing producers have always been dependent on the state for tax exemptions, import subsidies, and protective tariffs. To finance investment they were dependent on finance companies established by the big agricultural bourgeoisie. Manufacturing producers therefore exchanged their former dependence on the Somocista state and the agricultural bourgeoisie for dependence on the Sandinista government. For that reason, they were more likely to adjust to the new situation.

In agriculture, a small group of large producers had always controlled the processing and the distribution of inputs and had dominated the financial institutions. But they lost the latter two powers to the state. In addition, they had constituted a political power along with the Somoza family, using the state and its institutions for their own interests. For example, when world-market prices for agricultural crops declined they intensified the exploitation of the workers to guarantee their profit margins, if need be with the help of Somoza's National Guard. Under the Sandinistas, these producers lost their political and economic power to an important degree. They were for the first time dependent on a state that did not automatically act in their interests.

### *Developments in Later Years*

At the time of my interviews, most large producers in the manufacturing industry were willing to maintain production. However, as far as investment was concerned, the government gave priority to state enterprises. This could have endangered the stability of the mixed economy in manufacturing, particularly because of the age of equipment and the urgent need for maintenance and replacement. As pointed out, manufacturing investment fell during the years 1985–1987, and the foreign-exchange assignments for spare parts did not increase. So what happened to the willingness of the private sector to produce, especially after the economic reforms of February and June 1988?

In November 1988 I attempted to investigate what had become of the two enterprises whose directors had threatened to quit after one year if the situation did not improve. One director was not available.[19] The other enterprise had invested $4.5 million in past years, had expanded production enormously, and now also produced its own inputs and raw materials. The director said he had bought dollars for investment on the black market and had used bribes to get things done by government institutions or to obtain goods from other enterprises. According to this director, his plant was "an island of efficiency." He said his company was not suffering from a lack of demand for his main product (a consumer good) because it was of high quality and, according to him, Nicaraguan consumers had become sensitive again to quality standards. To maintain his highly qualified technical personnel he paid wages of up to $2,000 a month. He said that he transferred part of his profits abroad. If what he said was true, this case shows that the new market rules allowed some enterprises to be highly profitable, which probably enhanced their willingness to continue production.

The attitude of the Sandinista government toward the private sector does not seem to have become more negative in the years 1985–1989. No nationalizations occurred and the Ministry of Industry (Economy, Industry, and Commerce) continued to handle relations with manufacturing enterprises on an individual, nonpolitical basis (see also Castillo 1987). If anything, the government attitude appeared to have become more favorable toward private enterprise—at least toward foreign investors. At the end of 1987 the National Assembly approved the long-awaited new Foreign Investment Law. According to this, the contract that establishes the conditions for the investor could include the possibility of repatriating capital and remitting profits. The Central Bank had to release dollars for that aim. However, this possibility only applied to *new* investment from abroad (Guevara 1988).

By 1988 a change had also come about in the institutional representation of private manufacturing enterprises. For a long time, COSEP had been the only organization representing their interests. But many industrial entrepreneurs had felt COSEP had not successfully done so, because it acted much more as a political organization in opposition to the government than as an interest group. In 1988 two new organizations appeared to fill in the gap. One was CORDENIC (Comisión para la Recuperación y el Desarrollo en Nicaragua), the Commission for Recovery and Development in Nicaragua (IHCA 1989b:50-1). This was a group of Nicaraguan entrepreneurs and intellectuals institutionally linked to INCAE (Instituto Centroamericano de Administración de Empresas), the Central American Business Administration Institute, which in turn is affiliated with the Harvard Business School. CORDENIC's activities included preparing studies that propose solutions to the economic crisis, organizing forums and seminars, and encouraging economic agreement between the state, private enterprise, workers, and political parties. Although CORDENIC still had fewer members than COSEP, according to the Central American Historical Institute it represented the more efficient producers who were capable of working under the new market rules.

The other new organization was AENIC (Associación de Empresarios Nicaragüenses), the Nicaraguan Entrepreneurial Association. According to a newspaper announcement, it aimed to unite directors of private, mixed, cooperative, and state enterprises in order to express their needs and opinions to the government. It wanted to strengthen the mixed economy by allowing these directors to participate in decision-making.[20] Both new organizations seemed to offer an opportunity for private producers in manufacturing to strengthen their position with respect to the government, without having to adhere to COSEP.

To conclude, it seems that after 1985 the peaceful coexistence of the state and private sectors in manufacturing continued in spite of the limited assignments of foreign exchange to private enterprises. The economic reform measures of 1988 seemed to open new profit opportunities to the private sector.

## Notes

1. But in fact, the public investment program was dominant. In 1983 total public investment was 3,839.5 million cordobas (Argüello and Kleiterp 1985), and total state investment mounted to 4,052.9 million cordobas according to figures released by the Secretary of Planning and the Budget. The public investment program therefore represented 95 percent of total state investment. For 1982 this figure was 83 percent.

2. General Division of Planning of the Ministry of Economy, Industry, and Commerce, June 21, 1988.

3. See, for example, Weissenburger (1983) and Zaleski (1980).

4. The answers to the first question were probably not very reliable: The percentages were an oral estimation by the director. Nevertheless, they may give an indication.

5. Some other problems mentioned by the directors, such as the impact of the foreign-exchange policy on raw materials and spare parts and the impact of of the distribution policy on national raw materials, were discussed in Chapter 4.

6. That most enterprises were making profits did not have much significance for another reason. Most enterprises were not able to replace their equipment because their accounting was based on a severe underestimation of fixed capital. Sometimes the existing equipment had already been depreciated; in other cases it was written off at cordoba prices of 1979, not including the cordoba devaluations that had occurred since then. It was only in 1989 that fiscal laws permitted a revaluation of the book value of equipment.

7. Ministry of Economy, Industry, and Commerce 1988, Mimeo.

8. See note 7, with the exception of the big forestry projects.

9. Trade deficits in 1980, 1981, and 1982 were $225, $171, and $129 million, respectively (Brundenius 1984).

10. Information obtained in an interview with a functionary of the Central Bank of Nicaragua, 1985.

11. An enterprise could also exchange 40 percent of the value of its exports at the former parallel rate.

12. Manufacturing export value was U.S. $22 million in 1985, 1986, and 1987 according to figures provided by the General Division of Planning of the Ministry of Economy, Industry, and Commerce of June 21, 1988. The 1985 figure is lower here than in Table 5.6 because it includes a smaller range of industrial products.

13. The Coordinadora Democrática refused to participate in the November 1984 elections.

14. But the government withdrew this decree soon after announcing it (Chapter 4).

15. General Division of Planning of the Ministry of Economy, Industry, and Commerce, 1988. Mimeo.

16. Interview with a vice minister of industry, May 1985.

17. This director referred to the fact that his enterprise had already survived the earthquake of 1972 and the liberation war of 1978–1979.

18. At the time of this interview, agricultural producers did not yet receive part of their income in dollars, with the exception of beef producers.

19. The head of the Planning Division of the Ministry of Economy, Industry, and Commerce did not know what happened to the firm. I was unable to get in touch with the ministry's branch director involved. It is probable that the enterprise stopped functioning.

20. *Barricada*, November 11, 1988.

# 7

# Summary and Conclusion

Although Nicaragua experienced high growth rates in the 1950s, 1960s, and 1970s and both the manufacturing industry and agroindustry grew rapidly, industrialization prospects were not very good in 1979. First, the country's growth and accumulation model was still based on an unequal distribution of income. The agricultural export sector had made high profits because of the concentration of land and the existence of a large reserve of semiproletarians providing cheap labor. The state bureaucracy was small and served the interests of capitalist producers efficiently; social services were virtually absent. Any change in these conditions would probably affect the basis for the growth model. In addition, although the limited market for manufactured goods had to some extent caused lower manufacturing growth rates in the 1970s, changes in the distribution of income were soon likely to lead to supply problems in the manufacturing industry. Second, imports by the manufacturing industry were high and increased as a result of the effects of the liberation war. So the development of industry would depend to a large extent on the agricultural export sector.

The industrialization strategy after 1979 was also restricted by the new government's decision to establish a mixed economy. To date, mixed economies in transition to a socialism like that in Nicaragua had always been a temporary phenomenon. They either evolved toward socialism (with state ownership of the means of production and central planning) or returned to capitalism. On the basis of the first historical mixed economy, the New Economic Policy (NEP) of the Soviet Union, I deduced in this book five *stability conditions*—factors that influenced the introduction of central planning in the Soviet Union and that I expected to also play a role in the abandonment or retention of the Nicaraguan mixed economy. These stability conditions are:

1. The ideology of the leaders and the reasons they opt for a mixed economy.
2. The accumulation policy, that is, the rate of desired state accumulation and the kind of contributions needed from the private sector.
3. The price policy. A government in a mixed economy can control prices, but only under three conditions:
   a. It must have the necessary instruments to maintain these prices;
   b. It must allow for a minimum level of private accumulation;
   c. The government must maintain macroeconomic stability.
4. The willingness of private producers to continue producing.
5. External factors.

I concluded that the first and the fourth factor were not likely to affect the stability of Nicaragua's mixed economy. There were strong reasons for the FSLN to maintain a mixed order, especially because of the geopolitical position of the country. With respect to the private-sector willingness to continue producing, my interviews with large private producers in the manufacturing industry revealed that they were willing to maintain production, and most were also willing to invest. But in agriculture and agroindustry the situation seemed different. Both the attitude of the state toward these large producers and the attitudes of large producers themselves proved to be different from in manufacturing. The producers' attitudes could have been influenced by external factors, for example, the war situation. Given that the Reagan administration supported the contras, these producers probably anticipated a change in power, which reduced their willingness to maintain production. But these large producers in agriculture and agroindustry were small in number, so their attitude did not greatly threaten the stability of the mixed economy.

The second and the third factors, the accumulation policy and the price policy, more affected the stability of the Nicaraguan mixed economy. During 1980–1987, the government maintained a rather high investment rate. The intention was to finance state investment by capturing surpluses from the private sector, in particular from large private producers. But instead, an overvalued exchange rate brought about subsidies for many private producers in agriculture and industry. In spite of that, producers saw their profit margins squeezed by the high inflation rate from 1984 onward. In fact, state investment was financed by foreign loans and by domestic forced savings.

The Sandinista price policy aimed at guaranteeing minimum profit margins for private producers and, like the NEP, at maintaining low consumer prices to protect real wages. With respect to large producers, both state and private, the state had sufficient instruments to enforce prices. In fact, these sectors of the economy were centrally planned without the state being juridical owner of the majority of the means of production. So the state achieved some control over production, but at the cost of lower efficiency. Both the allocative efficiency and the X-efficiency diminished. This affected agricultural export production and manufacturing production in particular.

My interviews with manufacturing policymakers and enterprise directors revealed that the state did not discriminate against private producers—at least with respect to the distribution of inputs for current production. In agriculture and agroindustry, favoring of state enterprises seemed to occur. State enterprises in both sectors enjoyed a higher priority with respect to investment than did private enterprises. This could have endangered the stability of the mixed economy in the medium term.

My investigation of the Nicaraguan experience shows that it is much more difficult to control sectors in which small producers are dominant. The Sandinista government did not have the instruments to implement a price policy in the rest of the economy, particularly in agricultural production for the domestic market and in internal trade. Low official producer prices reduced production of essential consumer goods such as beans and milk in spite of large subsidies. In addition, as happened in the NEP period, government policy encouraged private traders who bought at much higher prices from small producers in the countryside and sold manufactures at much higher than the official producer prices. This meant a double loss from the state accumulation viewpoint: Profits made in private trade were lost for state accumulation purposes, and trading attracted labor away from production activities. The high demand responsible for the profits in trading originated from the large macroeconomic disequilibrium: Purchasing power, especially in the cities, was much higher than the amount of goods supplied at official prices.

So the Sandinista government also did not fulfill the third condition for successfully carrying out a price policy in a mixed economy: Macroeconomic equilibrium was not maintained. This was because of a permissive credit policy and because of a large government deficit, increasingly financed by printing money. A restrictive credit policy often seems to be a problem for socialist states in a decentralization process.[1] Although production decisions were decentralized in Nicaragua, many firms did not apply appropriate cost accounting, and if they did, prices on which the accounting was based did not reflect real costs. In addition, fulfilling production plans was more important than calculating profitability.

The government deficit was caused by the relatively high state accumulation rate and by the fact that the Nicaraguan government pursued some additional objectives that increased government spending. In this sense, the objectives of the Nicaraguan government were even more ambitious than those of the NEP. Additional objectives included improving social services such as health and education and providing subsidies to maintain real wages. Government revenues did not increase sufficiently to carry out these ambitions. The fact that governments in transition to socialism often pursue too many objectives seems to be an important danger for the viability of mixed economies in transition. In addition, it is normally necessary that these countries allocate funds for defense against an external threat.

In Nicaragua, the need to defend the country against contra attacks exacerbated the problems related to the accumulation policy and the price policy. The government needed more taxes from the private sector not only for accumulation but also for defense. It was also necessary to collect food and other basic products for the army. Some of these goods could be delivered by state enterprises (boots, uniforms) or could easily be obtained through state trade channels (sugar, vegetable oil, gasoline). But the state's need to obtain nonstate-controlled foodstuffs (rice, corn, and beans) increased its problems with controlling prices. Meanwhile, supply diminished because of contra attacks and because small peasants were unwilling to produce. Prices for peasants' crops were low; many industrial goods were more scarce in the countryside than in the cities; and there was no land reform in the peasants' favor. Especially during 1983–1985, many small peasants went over to the ranks of the contras.

With respect to the industrialization strategy, the Sandinista government attempted to combine growth with the production to meet basic needs. Growth would be achieved through new investment projects in agroindustry geared toward exports to the extraregional market. This implied a deviation from the industrialization model related to the Central American Common Market. The government attempted to satisfy basic needs mainly through subsidies and through expansion of state-provided services in health, education, and housing. Although manufacturing was very important for the production of basic consumer goods, the government gave a low priority to this sector.

Export production officially had a high priority but in practice the volume of exports diminished. Most of the new agroindustrial investment projects were large projects with a long maturation time, which increased inflationary pressures and did not increase export production in the short term. There were also many implementation problems, and maintenance of existing production capacity in the agricultural export sector was neglected. In general, it seems difficult for socialist oriented governments to avoid "growth optimism" and "megalomania" in the initiation of investment projects.

Apart from the effects of the war, export production also declined as a result of state intervention. The insecurity about land ownership reduced large farmers' willingness to produce and to invest. Gradually, small and medium farmers increased their shares. But their limited access to capital goods and, in some cases, output prices that were too low, made it difficult for them to maintain production. Furthermore, the provision of subsidized inputs coupled with guaranteed output prices lowered their efficiency of production. In manufacturing, private firms experienced more security of ownership and they did not suffer directly from contra attacks. They maintained production, but manufactured exports went down dramatically. The collapse of the Central American Common Market played a role; also, the state controlled all imported inputs. Enterprises did not have any freedom to decide what to produce and how. In addition, guaranteed output prices and the fact that all production could be sold in the domestic market lowered the efficiency of production and the quality of the product.

During 1980–1983 the Nicaraguan economy still experienced growth. After 1983 growth rates were, on average, negative. Macroeconomic imbalances such as the balance-of-payments deficit and the government deficit were large. As a result, it was increasingly difficult to achieve the objectives of (more or less in historical sequence) maintaining real wages, stimulating private production, improving social services, and continuing state investment.

From 1984–1985 onward the Nicaraguan government took adjustment measures. First, it addressed loss of support from the peasants. It attempted to improve the terms of trade for the countryside and changed the land reform policy, giving more land to small individual producers. This land came mainly from state farms. So, contrary to Soviet policy in the 1920s, Nicaragua abandoned the collective model in favor of one dominated by small and medium individual producers.

But at the same time, the government attempted to achieve more control over private trade and in some cases made efforts to restrict it. These measures were not successful and they contradicted the general policy of maintaining market relations. According to the stability conditions, in a market environment a government can regain control over the economy by abandoning price controls or by reestablishing macroeconomic equilibrium. In practice, the government *revised* prices, for example, by adjusting the exchange rate, by increasing interest rates, and by abolishing subsidies. But these reforms were only partial and were never sufficient to achieve the desired effects. The attempt to restore macroeconomic equilibrium was not successful either. The accumulation rate continued to be fairly high and it was impossible to eliminate the government deficit because the contra war continued.

By 1988, the accumulation policy and the price policy were still largely unaltered and the imbalances had increased. Other countries with mixed economies, for example, the Soviet Union under the NEP, would have abandoned the mixed system under the combined influence of imbalances and external threat, but Nicaragua did not. It seemed that maintaining a mixed economy was more important for the Sandinista government than achieving basic economic objectives—growth and basic-needs fulfillment.

This mixed-economy priority was probably reinforced by the war. Because of Nicaragua's mixed economy, many Latin American and Western European countries did not support the U.S. government's anti-Sandinista policy, which was important in preventing a direct U.S. invasion. In addition, these countries, along with Eastern European countries, supplied Nicaragua with loans and aid. However, due to the country's ever more disastrous economic situation, every year it needed more foreign loans. Latin American countries were not capable of increasing their support for Nicaragua because of their own external debts. West European countries' willingness to provide loans did not increase either. So the Sandinista's dependence on socialist countries increased in the course of time. This had consequences for the *kind* of industrialization strategy (in a strict sense) Nicaragua could pursue. Except for Cuba, socialist countries were less able to supply goods that supported an agroindustrial strategy in a tropical country. But they could provide inputs for many branches of the manufacturing industry, and because of this the Sandinista government might have gradually given more priority to the manufacturing industry had it stayed in power.

In the peace optimism following the Esquipulas accords of August 1987, the Sandinistas made another attempt at economic reform in February 1988. This time, state accumulation and defense expenditure really diminished and the price policy reforms were more substantial. The market environment was restored for large and small producers in manufacturing and handicrafts. But the government maintained some guaranteed prices for agricultural export producers and still attempted to control prices for basic grains.

In fact, with the exception of these export subsidies and the price policy for basic grains, Nicaragua carried out IMF-like adjustment measures directed at promoting exports at the cost of an income loss for many domestic sectors. But the country lacked the financial injection that usually accompanies IMF compliance, which made income consequences more serious and threatened the very success of the measures.

Purchasing power of salaries diminished by 70 percent in 1988. In spite of this, there were no riots or strikes, which would have accompanied such a real wage fall in other countries. Firms producing for the domestic market suffered a fall in demand. The reform measures did have positive effects on agricultural and industrial exports, but these were largely lost in 1988 because of a damaging hurricane in that year. The combined result of reform measures and a natural disaster was a 1988 GDP fall of 8 percent.

In 1989 the Sandinista willingness to negotiate peace with the contras and to set general elections for February 1990 still did not lead to the expected inflow of foreign aid. Although exports increased, GDP fell again by 3 percent in 1989. Real wages improved a little in comparison with 1988 but were still far below the 1987 level.

The Nicaraguan experience with a mixed economy shows that it is not necessary to nationalize all of Lenin's "commanding heights" to achieve control over the most important sectors of the economy. By nationalizing the banking system and foreign trade, it is possible to introduce some kind of central planning in export agriculture–very important for small developing countries–and in almost all manufacturing production. However, apart from giving private producers a guaranteed profit margin (which was not always fulfilled in the case of Nicaragua's small and medium farmers), it is necessary to provide them with foreign exchange so they can maintain their production capacity.

Obviously, another condition for subjecting state and private firms alike to central planning is that private producers are willing to maintain production. In Nicaragua, this was not the case with a small group of large agricultural and agroindustrial producers. It seems that it would have been preferable to expropriate these large producers.

Central planning has its negative consequences. Firms operate in a resource-constrained system and experience a soft budget constraint, which reduces the economy's allocative efficiency, the X-efficiency of producers, and the quality of the product. For a small country that is very dependent on exports, these are serious consequences. They appear to be more harmful for the manufacturing industry than for agriculture and agroindustry. This is due to a greater degree of product diversification in the manufacturing industry. The efficiency and quality losses in manufacturing as a result of the price controls will prevent exportation and reduce growth possibilities. Given the Cuban experience, it seems possible to achieve economic growth based on a centrally planned agricultural and agroindustrial export sector.

## Notes

1. A restrictive credit policy was, for example, the reason that Yugoslavia returned to more central planning after registering a large balance-of-payments deficit. See, for example, J. Mencinger, 1985. "Yugoslav economic system and performance of the economy in the seventies and early eighties." In P. Gey, J. Kosta, and W. Quaisser, eds. *Sozialismus und Industrialisierung, die Wirtschaftssysteme Polens, Jugoslawiens, Chinas, und Kubas im Vergleich*. Frankfurt/New York: Methuen, 197-210. In China it also seemed one of the factors that brought about the balance-of-payments deficit in 1985 after a partial liberalization of foreign trade. See W. Tims, 1987. "De economische hervormingen in China." Paper delivered at Ecozoekdag, Amsterdam, May 22.

# Epilogue

Because this book is being published about two years after the change in power by which President Chamorro of the Unión Nacional Opositora (UNO) took over the government, some remarks are in order regarding the changes in the economic policy and industrialization strategy.

After the 1988 reforms Nicaragua remained a mixed economy, although it had more capitalist features than before. State intervention in prices, for example, diminished. Many small and medium-sized enterprises operated again in a demand-constrained system and began to bring production output and production methods in line with more realistic exchange rates and prices.

In order to reduce inflation and restore a balance-of-payments equilibrium, however, two ingredients are virtually indispensable: (1) a willingness of the population to suffer large income reductions and (2) foreign aid. Given the consequences of the reform measures on income, it is rather surprising that the Sandinistas were able to keep salaries down without causing public riots or strikes. (Although the FSLN lost the February 1990 general elections, it still received 40 percent of the votes.) Foreign aid was lacking, however, and this seriously hindered the Sandinistas from restoring macroeconomic equilibria.

The UNO had promised to end inflation within two months. To do so, it planned to forcefully reduce the volume of domestic credits and of government expenditure. It also wanted to phase out the mixed economy, liberalizing foreign trade and privatizing banks and other state enterprises. With respect to the industrialization strategy, the UNO seemed to expect that these liberalizations would lead to a recovery of agricultural exports.

However, the new government lacked sufficient political support to carry out this program. The UNO itself is a loose coalition of fourteen parties, which sometimes have contrasting ideologies. This coalition has to confront a more coherent FSLN opposition in Parliament and the large Sandinista-based trade unions and other popular organizations. More and more, the Conservative party of President Chamorro has become dominant within the government coalition. The party is rather moderate and seeks to cooperate with the Sandinistas. The ups and downs of this attempt at cooperation are reflected in the economy.

In fact, the year 1990 meant in many respects a step backward in the stabilization and adjustment process. First, the government deficit increased, partly for reasons beyond the control of the new government. During the election campaign and in the two months between elections and the change in power, the Sandinistas increased expenditures, in particular the salaries of government officials. The UNO attempted to lower salaries and to reduce the number of officials but was prevented from doing so by large strikes in May and July 1990. In addition, the new government appointed its own officials in higher posts, so the wage bill even increased.

The Chamorro government did restrict the credit policy. Peasants and small industrial producers were the first to be deprived of credits. Larger industrial firms continued to receive financing, mainly to allow them to pay arrears. But the budget constraint seemed to become "hard" for these enterprises also (see chapter 4): In December 1990 the first large manufacturing firm had to close. Credits for the large state investment projects were stopped altogether. Agricultural exporters were most favored among credit receivers, but the overvalued exchange rate meant that only 30% of them could repay their loans.

Gradually, the government began privatizing some state enterprises. In 1991 the first private bank began operations, competing with the four state banks. In 1990 it became much easier to import, and private exports were permitted for the first time in 1991. The import liberalization, together with the overvalued exchange rate, had a negative impact on production for the domestic market, in particular for products such as food, clothing, and shoes.

Inflation increased again, to 13,000%, in 1990. In spite of weekly devaluations of the cordoba, the exchange rate was overvaluated by more than 100% by the end of the year (IHCA 1991a). This overvaluation made export incentives disappear and stimulated imports.

In 1990, Nicaragua's gross national product declined by 5.5% and its manufacturing production diminished by 8%. The personal income distribution became more skewed but shifted a bit. Owners and workers in small enterprises in agriculture and industry were confronted with further income reductions and many of them lost their jobs. But tradespeople (importers) and government officials were able to improve their real incomes. At the same time, education and health services deteriorated rapidly under the new government, especially in the countryside.

Although the government was not very successful in its economic policy in 1990, politically it registered some gains. First, increased unemployment and the threat of more unemployment, especially in the public sector and state enterprises, diminished the labor unions' power. Thus it became easier to reduce real wages. Second, the availability of foreign aid had increased. Although the U.S. government promised $300 million in aid for 1990, most of it became available in 1991.

In March 1991 the government announced a new package to fight inflation and to achieve adjustment. The measures included a large devaluation and a reduction of government expenditure, mainly by real wage reductions. The prices of some twenty-five basic consumer goods and services were centrally fixed. Although the IMF and World Bank played a role in defining these policies, an agreement with these institutions was not reached until September of that year, after the measures had shown some success.

The tight credit policy was continued, as evidenced by high real interest rates and strict credit conditions. This not only affected small enterprises, but it also undermined the government's export recovery aim. Agricultural credits in May 1991 were 36% lower than in 1990, for example (Neira 1991). As a result, agricultural production and agricultural exports are expected to diminish in 1991/1992.

This time, the government succeeded in reducing real wages in the public sector by about 20%. Due to the large devaluation, prices increased by 297% in March. But in the following months stabilization was achieved. By early 1992, the nominal exchange rate of the cordoba had been maintained without causing a significant overvaluation of the real exchange rate.

Three factors seem to have enhanced this monetary stabilization. First, the UNO government was much more successful in attracting foreign aid. In particular, dollars supplied by the United States helped to keep the exchange rate fixed. Second, the UNO succeeded in establishing an agreement with the Sandinista labor unions: They would refrain from making wage demands for two months. This gave the measures a chance and cleared the way for an agreement with the IMF and World Bank. Afterward, the government continued to be more or less on good terms with the Sandinistas. Third, direct state intervention kept prices from rising, but partly at the cost of lower government revenues and higher expenditures. For the time being, the resulting deficit was financed by foreign (U.S.) aid (IHCA 1991b).

Given this dependence on foreign aid and on the relative "social peace," one might doubt whether the achieved stabilization will be a lasting one. Reduced attention from the U.S. government to the region is leading to lower aid levels. At the same time, UNO policies are increasing the income differences and provoking a rapid deterioration of basic social services. Both results are likely to increase social tensions.

With respect to the industrialization strategy, the new government appears to base its hope on large private producers and, in particular, agricultural export producers who, attracted by the liberalizations, return their capital into the country and produce and invest again. This reinvestment does not seem to occur on a large scale. On the other hand, the tight credit policy prevents small and medium-sized agricultural producers from contributing to export recovery.

At the same time, UNO policies have a negative impact on production for the domestic market. First and to some extent inevitably, stabilization policies lead to shrinking domestic demand and reduced financing possibilities. However, the liberalization of foreign trade makes the situation worse. Food production is hampered by low food prices induced by cheap imports and food donations that are sold at low prices on the domestic market. Although the 1991 devaluation reduced the import flow of manufactured consumer goods from neighboring countries, lowering import tariffs has caused this flow to swell again, leading to massive bankruptcies in the textiles and clothing and leather and shoes sectors.

In fact, UNO policies seem to be leading to "deindustrialization" (Gatica Barros 1989). After so many years of very low investment levels (because of its low priority in the Sandinista investment strategy), only a very small proportion of manufacturing enterprises is likely to be able to shift production to export markets. Most firms will need large-scale investments, which are unlikely given the financial tightening. Although a recovery of export production is crucial for both adjustment and a lasting stabilization, UNO policies do not further that aim consistently.

# Appendix 1: The Methodology for the Fieldwork

The fieldwork concentrated on medium and large industrial enterprises, defined as enterprises with thirty or more workers. In 1980, such enterprises represented 82 percent of total gross industrial production (see Chapter 3). I excluded the smaller enterprises, cooperatives, and collectives, because the character of the planning with respect to these smaller enterprises is very different. In addition, these enterprises were the subject of another study (Laenen 1988).

According to the Nicaraguan national accounts and the industrial statistics of, for example, INEC (Instituto Nicaragüense de Estadísticas y Census; Nicaraguan Institute for Statistics and Census), manufacturing includes all industrial production except the first processing of agricultural crops such as coffee, cotton, and sesame. Other industries carrying out the first processing of primary products, such as slaughterhouses, the dairy industry, and sugar mills are included, as are industries carrying out the second or third stage processing of agricultural products, such as vegetable oil production or textiles.

However, policymakers in Nicaragua distinguished between the "manufacturing industry" under MIND (Ministry of Industry) and "agroindustry," under MIDINRA (Ministry of Agriculture). Agroindustry in this distinction is more than just the first processing of coffee, cotton, and sesame and includes slaughterhouses, the dairy industry, sugar mills, factories mixing cattlefodder, and some factories producing (or mixing) fertilizers. Meat processing, vegetable oil production, and textile factories fall under MIND.

For practical reasons, I first limited the investigation of the industrial sector to manufacturing, defined as industrial production administered by the Ministry of Industry. Later, I conducted some research in agroindustry, under MIDINRA.

### The Research Questions

Interviews with directors of state enterprises and general managers of private enterprises were conducted to investigate both the "objective impact" and the "subjective impact"—opinions and expectations—of state planning on the enterprises. The second objective was to determine the most important problems confronting manufacturing enterprises and, in particular, enterprises that represented different industrialization strategies.

The investigation of the subjective impact of the different state-planning instruments was exploratory. With respect to the objective impact of the instruments, the aim was to test the hypothesis that these planning instruments did not discriminate between private and state enterprises but were selective according to enterprise priority. This hypothesis reflected the official policy of the Ministry of Industry as deduced from its policy documents (MIND 1983a, 1983b, 1984a, 1984c) and from statements of its functionaries. According to these documents, industrial production could be broken down into six priority categories.

1. Basic consumer goods, defined as goods satisfying the basic needs of the population.
2. Intermediate goods and capital goods for sectors with a high priority: agriculture, construction, transport.
3. Goods for defense.
4. Goods for export.
5. Other consumer goods.
6. Other intermediate and capital goods.

Categories 1, 2, and 4 were a high priority for policymakers in manufacturing, the latter two a lower priority. Category 3 did not have a high priority in 1980, but it became most important from 1985 onward.

With respect to the second objective of the interviews, I compared enterprises representing different industrialization strategies. For the Nicaraguan situation, I distinguished four groups of enterprises:

1. Production of consumer goods.
2. Production of intermediate goods and capital goods.
3. Production of manufactured goods for export, not including agroindustry.
4. Agroindustry.

Categories 3 and 4 reflect an outward-oriented strategy. Industrial exports are stimulated in category 3 and processed agricultural exports are stimulated in category 4. Categories 1 and, in particular, 2 reflect an inward-oriented strategy. According to the policy documents of MIND, the Nicaraguan industrial policy was both outward and inward oriented, because both 2 and 3 had a top priority. The broader economic policy appeared to be outward oriented, as it prioritized agroindustry.

In the interviews I aimed to find out whether, and how, this policy was implemented. The experiences of the enterprises could throw light on the results of the policy and on the extent to which the results depended on the existing economic order.

I supposed that various factors could have an influence on the enterprises' results:

- The industrial policy.
- The availability of qualified and nonqualified workers.

- The quality and quantity of existing machinery and equipment.
- The technology.
- The quality and quantity of available raw material and inputs, both of domestic and foreign origin.
- The availability of markets, both internal and external.
- The work efforts of the labor force and their motivation.
- The role of the labor union.
- The financial results in preceding years.
- The expectations of the director.

## The Interviews

The first aim of the interviews was to test the hypothesis on the objective impact of policy instruments. This required a structured interview method with, if possible, standardized response categories. The investigation of the subjective impact, reflected by opinions and expectations, was exploratory, which required a more unstructured questioning. The investigation of problems of the enterprises was more or less intermediate in this respect.

I conducted open, half-structured interviews, using a checklist that contained the minimum of questions to be answered. Questions addressed the objective and subjective impact of policy instruments and the impact of external factors. I also asked some qualitative questions on financial results as well as on another type of "result," the directors' opinions and expectations. Background data on the firm and its director, such as whether the director possessed shares in the enterprise, served to determine possible intervening factors in the impact of instruments and external factors. Appendix 2 contains the list of questions. The sequence of these questions was not maintained during the interviews, and the interviewees could expand on a question and bring in other themes.

Compared to a structured interview, open, half-structured interviews create a more informal atmosphere in which opinions and expectations can be expressed. They also gather more information: Material that is relevant but not included in the questionnaire may be obtained. Third, they increase the validity of the answers by minimizing misunderstandings due to potential language problems and to cultural differences, concerns in this case.

The disadvantage of open interviews is that the results are, in principle, less suitable for the testing of the hypothesis. In general, open interviews increase the validity of the answers but lower the reliability (Gadourek 1972:1-82). In this case, however, the reliability was enhanced because I performed all interviews myself and interpreted all results. I used the analysis-of-contents method to construct a systematic classification of the responses.[1]

The intention was to hold interviews with the highest manager of the enterprise: the "director" in the case of state enterprises and the "general manager" in the case of private enterprises. In seven private enterprises this was not possible and I interviewed the "production manager" (twice), the "financial manager" (twice), the "vice-manager" (twice) and once the bookkeeper. This probably was a disadvantage, as their vision of what happened in the enterprise was less complete and they were less likely to have strong opinions. In this book, I use the word "director" to denote all interviewees.

I made the appointments for the interviews by telephone from INIES (Instituto de Investigaciones Económicas y Sociales; Institute of Economic and Social Investigations) in Managua. In contacts with state enterprises, I said I cooperated with the Department of Planning of the Ministry of Industry. At the beginning of the interview, I showed a letter from the director of that department. In private enterprises I introduced myself as a researcher financed by a Dutch government-sponsored foundation and working at INIES, in Nicaragua known as an independent research institute.

In general, it was not difficult to make the appointments for the interviews. There was one exception, but this did not appear to be an active refusal to cooperate. One director of a private enterprise made his cooperation dependent on a letter from the INIES director in which the objectives of the interview were explained. Another director stopped the interview before it was finished and refused to make another appointment. All other interviewees were very willing to answer the questions and spoke with great candor about their problems.

The average finished interview lasted 80 minutes, with a range of 50–125 minutes. The average interview with directors of private enterprises was a little longer than with directors of state enterprises: respectively 85 and 76 minutes.

During the interview I noted as much as possible and completed these notes immediately afterward. The same day or the next I wrote a complete report of the interview. The list of questions provided the structure for these reports. The elaboration of the data consisted of constructing categories for classifying the responses. Sometimes I discovered that I had not asked a question or that the answer did not fit in any of the categories. For this reason, the number of responses is sometimes smaller than the total number of enterprises in the sample.

Given the apparent great willingness to answer questions and the frank and often critical responses, it is likely that the results of the interviews are fairly reliable. Although there were limits to press freedom in Nicaragua under the Sandinistas and the activities of opposition parties were sometimes curtailed, people were generally not afraid to criticize the Sandinista government openly, be it in discussions in the street or in a more formal situation. All opposition groups, for example, were free to receive foreign journalists and politicians, and often did so, venting frankly their grievances.

Two additional factors enhanced the reliability of the interview results: my affiliations and the timing of the investigation. I was a foreigner, my research was sponsored by a Dutch foundation, and I was working at an independent research institute in Managua. The interviews were held in the months just before and after the elections of November 1984, which was a period of relative political openness in Nicaragua; there was more freedom of maneuver for political parties and less press censorship.

## The Sample

It was impossible to interview the directors of all industrial enterprises of thirty or more workers. In view of the objective of comparing enterprises with different characteristics, I drew up a stratified sample. The first distinction was between state and private enterprises. If the state had the majority of the shares, the enterprise qualified as "state." Next, the enterprises were classified according to their degree of priority within the industrial policy and according to the type of industrialization strategy they reflected (see previous priority and strategy categories.

However, some kinds of production appeared in both classifications, and in any case it would have been too complicated to have ten different stratification categories. For these reasons, I made a combination of the two classifications. I left out priority 3, because many enterprises produced partly for defense. I also left out strategy category 4, agroindustry, because I would carry out a separate investigation of these enterprises. I combined priority categories 2 and 6 in order to simplify. Including the distinction per type of ownership this resulted in the following eight strata:

1S. Production of basic consumer goods, state enterprises.
1P. Production of basic consumer goods, private enterprises.
2S. Production of other consumer goods, state enterprises.
2P. Production of other consumer goods, private enterprises.
3S. Production of intermediate and capital goods, state enterprises.
3P. Production of intermediate and capital goods, private enterprises.
4S. Production of goods for export, state enterprises.
4P. Production of goods for export, private enterprises.

I made the stratification exclusive in the following ways: Enterprises appearing in 1 or 4 were always included in 1 or 4 although they might appear in 2 or 3 as well; and enterprises appearing in 1 and 4, or in 2 and 3, were assigned to only one of these strata on the basis of the relative shares of their gross value of production that fell into one or the other category.

This stratification allowed investigation of whether there were differences between state and private enterprises. It also permitted comparing enterprises with a high priority (categories 1 and, to a lesser extent, 3 and 4) to enterprises a low priority (category 2). In addition, it allowed investigation of whether it was feasible to stimulate category 3, representing an inward-oriented strategy, and category 4, reflecting an outward-oriented strategy, at the same time.

I established the population of industrial enterprises on the basis of *Industrial Program 1984* (MIND 1984a). In particular, I used the tables "Volúmenes y valores de producción 1982-1984 por sección, rama y empresa," including 133 enterprises, and "Valor bruto de producción y empleo de las principales empresas, por area de propiedad," including 188 enterprises.[2] I supplemented this information with data from other sources, such as interviews with functionaries of the Ministry of Industry. The final number of industrial enterprises employing thirty or more workers was 141: 71 state enterprises and 70 private enterprises.

*Industrial Program 1984* was also the basis for assigning the enterprises to the different strata. Within the eight strata I chose the enterprises at random according to the systematic method. Within the category of private enterprises, I intended to include a number of transnational enterprises in order to draw separate conclusions about this type of ownership. For this reason, I sometimes passed over a national enterprise in favor of the next foreign enterprise on the list. This procedure is not likely to have brought about a systematic sampling bias.

The sample consisted of forty-six enterprises: twenty-two state enterprises, fourteen private domestic enterprises, and ten transnational enterprises. All strata included at least five, and generally six, enterprises. For practical reasons, I first approached the enterprises in the city of Managua or with offices in Managua. Later on I established contacts with enterprises outside Managua. When a lack of time precluded interviewing the directors of all forty–six enterprises, I gave priority to the completion of the strata: All eight strata had to include at least four enterprises. The procedure of first holding interviews in Managua and later in enterprises further away may have led to an overrepresentation of Managua enterprises in the sample (see further on).

There were thirty-three completed interviews: sixteen in state enterprises, nine in foreign enterprises, and eight in domestic private enterprises. In two of these domestic enterprises, citizens of other Central American countries held the majority of the shares. Some questions involved distinctions between national and foreign enterprises; "Central-American enterprises" (C) are classified as "National" (N) or as "Transnational" (T) depending on the nature of the question. To guarantee the anonymity of the enterprises, this book does not include a list of the enterprises involved.

If we compare the sample of thirty-three enterprises with the population at large, transnational enterprises are overrepresented, as could be expected. The relative share of private and state enterprises was more or less the same in the sample and in the population (Table A.1).

Table A.2 shows the comparison of the sample and the population with respect to the eight strata. As a consequence of the aim to include a certain number of enterprises with a high priority in the industrial policy, enterprises of categories 1S and 1P were overrepresented.

Table A.3 gives some gross alue of production and employment figures for the enterprises in the sample and in the population (as far as data are available). The average employment level of state enterprises was approximately twice that of private enterprises both in the population and in the sample. The average private enterprise had a higher production than the average state enterprise. In the sample, the larger state enterprises appear to be slightly dominant, and the average private firm in the sample is a little smaller than in the population as a whole.

There was no list of industrial enterprises that specified their place of business. I obtained addresses only for the sample enterprises. With respect to the population, it was known that 57 percent of total gross value of manufacturing production came from enterprises registered in the Third Region,

TABLE A.1 Comparison of Sample and Population by Type of Ownership

| | *Sample* (1) | *Population* (2) | (1)/(2) |
|---|---|---|---|
| State | 16 | 71 | 22.5% |
| Private | 17 | 70 | 24.3% |
| National, Central American | 8 | 48 | 16.7% |
| Transnational | 9 | 22 | 40.9% |
| Total | 33 | 141 | 23.4% |

*Sources:* Ministry of Industry 1984. Programa industrial 1984. Managua. Mimeo; and the author's research.

TABLE A.2 Comparison of Sample and Population by Stratum: Categories 1–4; and State (S) or Private (P)

| | 1 | | 2 | | 3 | | 4 | |
|---|---|---|---|---|---|---|---|---|
| | *S* | *P* | *S* | *P* | *S* | *P* | *S* | *P* |
| Sample | 4 | 4 | 4 | 4 | 4 | 4 | 4 | 5 |
| Population | 7 | 14 | 23 | 15 | 23 | 27 | 18 | 14 |

*Sources:* Ministry of Industry 1984. Programa industrial 1984. Managua. Mimeo; and the author's research.

which included the city of Managua (MIND 1984b). Of the sample of thirty-three enterprises, twenty-two were located in the city of Managua (67 percent). This figure cannot be easily compared with the figure on gross value of production for the population. In the first place, the average enterprise in Managua might have been smaller or larger than that in other regions in terms of GVP. And second, the Third Region includes more than the city of Managua. It is possible that sample enterprises classified as "outside Managua," were still within the Third Region.

Although the data are insufficient, it is possible that enterprises located in Managua were overrepresented in the sample. This would affect the conclusions if the policy toward enterprises in Managua was different from that toward other enterprises. It can be expected that the enterprises in Managua, because of their proximity to policymakers, had more chances to influence the industrial policy in their favor. However, after 1983 the Ministry of Industry

TABLE A.3 Comparison of Sample and Population: Gross Production, Employment, and Productivity of State (S) and Private (P) enterprises[a]

| | *Production (thousands of cordobas) (1)* | | *Employment (2)* | | *Productivity (cordobas) (1)/(2)* | |
|---|---|---|---|---|---|---|
| | *S* | *P* | *S* | *P* | *S* | *P* |
| Sample | 88.9 | 72.2 | 324 | 140 | 340 | 601 |
| N | (14) | (15) | (16) | (17) | (14) | (15) |
| Population | 68.2 | 82.4 | 249 | 129 | 269 | 562 |
| N | (67) | (55) | (71) | (70) | (67) | (55) |

[a]Figures represent average values per enterprise. N is the number of enterprises for which data are available.

*Sources:* Ministry of Industry 1984. Programa industrial 1984. Managua. Mimeo; and the author's research.

had offices in all regions where industrial enterprises were established. The enterprises in the other regions stood in a double hierarchy under the ministry: one status according to branch and another according to region. Several directors of enterprises outside Managua considered this to be an advantage.

In conclusion, it can be expected that *if* there was an overrepresentation of enterprises of the Third Region, on the whole this is not likely to have led to a systematic distortion of the interview results.

The size of the sample in absolute terms was not very large. Relatively, however, it was fairly large; almost a quarter of the industrial enterprises employing thirty or more workers was included (Table A.1). Within the eight strata, the sample was drawn at random, so it can be expected that no systematic bias existed. No systematic distortions are found in the comparison of sample and population with respect to certain characteristics such as production level and employment.

For these reasons, the sample as a whole can be considered large enough to be representative of the population of industrial enterprises. However, the investigation aimed to compare different strata. It can be doubted whether the number of enterprises per stratum (four) is sufficient. However, combinations of strata are compared: state with private enterprises, transnational with national enterprises, and priority categories with other priority categories. On the basis of the eight strata for different types of enterprises it is probably possible to infer conclusions about the population with a reasonable amount of confidence.

## Agroindustry

The investigation of MIDINRA's agroindustry was not as extensive as that of manufacturing. In addition to a study of documents, two interviews were held with functionaries of MIDINRA, three with private enterprise directors, and one with a state enterprise director. The three directors of private enterprises were all large producers as far as their direct agricultural production was concerned. I chose them because they represented the large private producers in the national production commissions, advice commissions to the government for each agricultural crop (see Chapter 4). The number of interviews with producers certainly is too small to infer general conclusions, for example, to compare private with state enterprises. But if these interview results are supplemented with other data, such as the results of interviews with functionaries of MIDINRA and some secondary material, it is possible to induce some tentative conclusions, in particular to compare agroindustry with manufacturing.

## Notes

1. If this procedure is followed, it is generally considered possible to test hypotheses with open interviews. See, for example, Gadourek (1972:146).
2. The translations of titles of these tables are Production Volumes and Values 1982–1984 by Section, Branch, and Enterprise; and Gross Production and Employment of the Most Important Enterprises, by Ownership Sector.

# Appendix 2: List of Questions

## 1. General

- Name of the enterprise.
- What does it produce? What did it produce (1978, 1981)?
- Since when has the enterprise existed?
- Ownership: What proportion of shares is in foreign hands, what in state hands? Does the director have shares?
- Since when in state hands, and why was it nationalized?
- Title and name of interviewee.
- Since when have you worked in the enterprise and since when in this function?
- Do shareholders have other enterprises in Nicaragua or abroad?

## 2. Imported inputs and raw materials

- What proportion of raw materials and inputs is from Nicaragua and what proportion is imported? Did this change in the past five years?
- Did your product or the assortment of products change in the past five years?
- Where do imported inputs and raw materials come from?
- Did this change in the past five years?
- Do you receive foreign exchange to import raw materials and inputs? Is it sufficient?
- Do you experience bureaucratic problems in applying for foreign exchange?
- Does a central importation of raw materials or inputs exist for your branch? How does it function?
- Do you have other problems related to imports?
- Do you think state enterprises can obtain more imported raw materials and inputs? Or less?
- What is your opinion on the assignment policy of imported raw materials and inputs?
- What do you think is the possibility of receiving imported raw materials and inputs next year?

3. Local raw materials and inputs

- Can you obtain sufficient local raw materials and inputs?
- From what suppliers do you purchase: state organs, wholesale trade, retail trade, "buhoneros," other? In what proportions? How was this before?

4. Capacity; machinery and equipment

- Is your machinery and equipment sufficient?
- Where do your machines come from?
- How old are they?
- Can you obtain sufficient spare parts?
- Do you need imported spare parts?
- Do you receive foreign exchange for the imports of spare parts?
- What do you do if you do not have sufficient spare parts ("innovadores," domestic market, "buhoneros")?
- What proportion of your capacity is in use?
- If this is not 100 percent, why not?
- What is your opinion on the assignment policy with respect to spare parts?
- What do you expect of this policy for next year?

5. Labor

- How many workers does the enterprise have?
- Is that sufficient?
- Who decides on the number of workers?
- Do you experience problems as a result of military service or mobilizations?
- Do you experience problems in finding qualified workers? What skills are especially difficult to find?
- Do you experience problems in finding unskilled workers?
- Do you have problems with the motivation of the workers, absenteeism, labor discipline? How was this before?
- Is there a union? To what federation does it belong?
- How does it function?
- Does a "central agreement" exist? When was the first? Since when is the current agreement applied?
- Do you apply SNOTS? Since when?
- Did you experience problems with the introduction of SNOTS in your enterprise?
- What are the wages according to the agreement (if not applying SNOTS); minimum, average, maximum?
- Are wages high enough?
- How are the secondary labor conditions? Does a commissary exist?
- Do you give pay in kind?
- Does the enterprise have an incentive system?

- Has this system been approved by the Ministry of Industry or the Ministry of Labor?
- What is your opinion on the wage policy?
- Do you think there are differences in wages between state and private enterprises? In what sense?
- Does the enterprise have an "enterprise committee" or "production Council"? Since when?
- How does it function?
- Do you have other regular contacts with the workers or with the union?
- What kinds of problems are discussed in these different meetings?

6. Prices

- Who decides on the prices of your products?
- If there were changes in the prices during the last couple of years, how did these changes come about?
- If the state decides on the price, is it sufficient?
- Is it easy to change prices that have been determined by the state?

7. Sales

- What proportion of production is sold in the domestic market?
- To whom or what do you sell: state organs, state enterprises, private enterprises, wholesale or retail trade, commissaries? In what proportions?
- Did this change in the past five years?
- What is your opinion on the commercialization policy of the state?

8. Exports

- What proportion of production is exported? Has this changed since 1978? How?
- How do you bring about exports: contacts of the enterprise, via the state, "trueques"?
- To what countries do you export? Has this changed since 1978?
- If you export less than before, for what reason? (market problems, lack of imported inputs, quality of the product, other problems)
- Do you have plans for (more) exports?
- Do you expect to find markets?
- What is your opinion on the export policy of the government?

9. Credits

- Do you need credits for current production?
- Do you receive sufficient credits?
- Did you receive long-term credits in the past five years?
- Do you experience problems in applying for credits?
- Are you able to remit credits you received?

- If the enterprise has an old debt (from the former owner or from before the revolution), is it repaying that debt now?
- Do you think it is easy to postpone repayment if necessary?
- Do you think you will receive sufficient credits in the next year?

10. Taxes

- Did taxes increase after the revolution?
- What is your opinion on the tax policy?

11. Results of the firm

- Did the enterprise make profits in the past five years?
- Is the enterprise profitable now?
- What is the destination of the profits: dividends to shareholders, bonuses for workers, reinvestment?
- In state enterprises: who decides on the destination of profits? Do you have to hand over a part to the Ministry or the Branch?

12. Investment

- Have you carried out investment since 1979?
- In state enterprises: who decides on investment?
- What part of investment was in machinery and equipment; what in construction?
- Did you receive foreign-exchange assignments for investment?
- Did you have investment plans that could not be carried out because of a lack of foreign exchange?
- Did you finance investment with own funds or with credits?
- Do you have investment plans for the coming years?
- Do you need credits and/or foreign exchange for these plans?
- Do you expect to receive sufficient?

13. Opinions, expectations, etc.

- How do you describe your relation with the Ministry of Industry and with the director of the Branch?
- Do you think the Ministry discriminates between state and private enterprises?
- What do you expect of the economic situation in the coming years?
- What is the future of your enterprise in the mixed economy of Nicaragua? Do you think you can maintain production?
- Do you still feel a director of a private enterprise, or more like a public servant?
- What is the attitude of the owners or shareholders of the firm with respect to the maintenance of the firm in Nicaragua?
- Why do you maintain production?
- What is your opinion on the revolutionary process?

# Acronyms

AENIC Associación Empresarial Nicaraguënse/Nicaraguan Entrepreneurial Association, 180

AGROMAQ Maquinaria para el Agro/Machinery for Agriculture, 88

APP Area de Propiedad del Pueblo/Area of People's Property, 77

ATC Associación de Trabajadores del Campo/Agricultural Labour Union, 85

BND Banco Nacional de Desarrollo/National Development Bank, 93

CABEI Central American Bank for Economic Integration, 35

CACM Central American Common Market, 34

CAS Cooperativa Agraria Sandinista/Sandinista Agrarian Cooperative, 78

CDDs Certificados de Divisas/Foreign Exchange Certificates, 164

COIP Corporación Industrial del Pueblo/Industrial Corporation of the People, 84

CORDENIC Comisión para la Recuperación y el Desarrollo en Nicaragua/Commission for Recovery and Development in Nicaragua, 179

COSEP Consejo Superior de la Empresa Privada/Superior Council of Higher Enterprise, 69

CCSs Cooperativas de Crédito y Servicios/Credit and Service Cooperatives, 78

CST Central Sandinista de Trabajadores/Sandinista Labor Union, 85

ECLAC Economic Commission for Latin America and the Caribbean, 33

ENABAS Empresa Nacional de Abastecimiento/National Procurement Enterprise, 98

ENIA Empresa Nacional de Insumos Agrarios/National Enterprise of Agricultural Inputs, 88

ERAIN Empresa Regional de Abastecimiento Industrial/Regional Enterprise of Industrial Supply, 97

GVP Gross Value of Production, 201

FAO Frente Amplio Opositor/Broad Opposition Front, 71

FNI Fondo Nicaraguënse de Inversiones/Nicaraguan Investment Fund, 125

FPN Frente Patriótico Nacional/National Patriotic Front, 71

FSLN Frente Sandinista para la Liberación Nacional/Sandinista Front for National Liberation, 1

IDB Inter-American Development Bank, 103

INCAE Instituto Centroamericano para la Administración de Empresas/Central American Institute for Business Administration, 180

INCA Industria Centroamericana/Central American Industry, 35

INEC Instituto Nicaragüense de Estadísticas y Census/Nicaraguan Institute for Statistics and the Census, 195

INIES Instituto de Investigaciones Económicas y Sociales/Institute of Economic and Social Investigations, 198

INFONAC Instituto de Fomento Nacional/National Development Institute, 60

INRA Instituto de Reforma Agraria/Agrarian Reform Institute, 82

MDN Movimiento Democrático Nacional/National Democratic Movement, 72

MICE Ministerio de Comercio Exterior/Ministry of External Trade, 164

MICOIN Ministerio de Comercio Interior/Ministry of Internal Trade, 98

MIDINRA Ministerio de Desarrollo Agropecuario y Reforma Agraria/Ministry of Agricultural and Livestock Development and Agrarian Reform, 79

MIND Ministerio de Industria/Ministry of Industry, 85

MITRAB Ministerio de Trabajo/Ministry of Labor, 100

MPU Movimiento del Pueblo Unido/United People's Movement, 71

NEP New Economic Policy, 11

PROAGRO Provisiones para el Agro/Provisions for Agriculture, 88

SIECA Secretaría de la Integración Económica Centroamericana/Secretary of Central American Economic Integration, 49

SNOTS Sistema Nacional de Ordenación de Trabajo y Salarios/National System Ordaining Work and Wages, 100

SPP Secretaría de Planificación y Presupuesto/Secretary of Planning and the Budget, 86

SUCA Sistema Uniforme de Control Administrativo/Uniform Administrative Control System, 83

UNO Union Nicaraguënse de Oposición/Nicaraguan Opposition Union, 165

UPE Unidad de Producción Estatal/State Production Unit, 83

# Bibliography


Arana, Mario, Richard Stahler-Sholk, Gerardo Timossi, and Carmen López. 1987. *Deuda, estabilización y ajuste: La transformación en Nicaragua: 1979–1986*. Managua: CRIES, Cuadernos de Pensamiento Propio, Serie Ensayos 15.

Argüello, Alejandro, and Nanno Kleiterp. 1985. "Inversiones 1979–1985: Análisis del proceso inversionista Nicaragüense de 1979 a 1985." Managua: Fondo Nicaragüense de Inversiones. Mimeo.

Argüello, Alejandro, Nanno Kleiterp, and Edwin Croes. 1988. *Acumulación y transformación: Nicaragua 1979–1985*. Managua: INIES, Cuadernos de Investigación 3.

Austin, James E., and John C. Ickis. 1986. "Managing after the revolutionaries have won." *Harvard Business Review* 64, no. 3 (May-June):103-9.

Austin, James, Jonathan Fox, and Walter Kruger. 1985. "The role of the revolutionary state in the Nicaraguan food system." *World Development* 13, no. 1:15-40.

Balassa, B., G. M. Bueno, P. P. Kuczynski, and M. H. Simonsen. 1986. *Towards renewed economic growth in Latin America*. Mexico City: Colegio de Mexico.

Baran, Paul A. 1973. *The political economy of growth*. Harmondsworth: Pelican Books.

Barry, Tom, and Deb Preusch. 1986. *The Central America fact book*. New York: Grove Press.

Baumeister, Eduardo. 1985a. "Un balance del proceso de reforma agraria Nicaragüense." *Polémica* 17/18:47-60. San José.

______. 1985b. "The structure of Nicaraguan agriculture and the Sandinista agrarian reform." In *Nicaragua: A revolution under siege*, ed. R. L. Harris, and C. M. Vilas, 10-35. London: Zed Books.

Bettelheim, Charles. 1975. *The transition to socialist economy*. Hassocks, Sussex: Harvester.

Biderman, Jaime. 1983. "The development of capitalism in Nicaragua: A political-economic history." *Latin American Perspectives* 36 (Vol. 10, no. 1):7-44.

Black, George. 1981. *Triumph of the people: The Sandinista Revolution in Nicaragua*. London: Zed Press.

Borge, Tomas. 1981. *Los primeros pasos: La RPS*. Mexico City: Siglo Veintiuno.

Bornstein, M. 1989. "The comparison of economic systems: An integration." In *Comparative economic systems: Models and cases*. 6th ed., ed. M. Bornstein. Homewood, Ill.: Irwin.

Brahim, John, and Claudine Correia. 1983. *Centraal-Amerika: Ontwikkeling van de produktieverhoudingen*. Tilburg, The Netherlands: Instituut voor Ontwikkelingsvraagstukken.

Brundenius, Claes. 1984. *Industrial development and strategies in revolutionary Nicaragua*. Lund, Sweden: Research Policy Institute, University of Lund.

______. 1987. "*Industrial development strategies in revolutionary Nicaragua.*" In *The political economy of Revolutionary Nicaragua*, ed. Rose J. Spalding, 85-104. Boston: Allen & Unwin.

Bukharin, N. [1928] 1964. "Notes of an economist at the beginning of a new economic year." In *Foundations of the Soviet strategy of economic growth*, ed. N. Spulber, 258-65. Bloomington: Indiana University Press.

Bulmer-Thomas, Victor. 1983. "Economic development over the long run: Central America since 1920." *Journal of Latin American Studies* 15:269-94.

______. 1987. *The political economy of Central America since 1920*. Cambridge: Cambridge University Press.

Cable, Vincent. 1976. *Foreign investment, economic integration, and industrial structure in Central America*. Glasgow: Glasgow University, Institute's Occasional Papers 21.

Carr, E. H. 1966. *The Bolshevik Revolution: 1917–1923*. Vol. 2, *The economic order*. Harmondsworth: Penguin Books.

______.[1958] 1978. *Socialism in one country: 1924–1926*. Vol. 1. London: MacMillan.

Carr, E. H., and R. W. Davies. 1969. *Foundations of a planned socialist economy: 1926-1929*. Vol. 1, Parts 1-2. London: Macmillan.

Carrión, L. 1981. *El patriotismo: base de la unidad nacional*. Managua: Unidad Editorial.

Castillo, Melba. 1987. "El papel de los empresarios industriales en la economía mixta Nicaragüense." Managua. Mimeo.

______. 1988. "Implicancias de un reajuste monetario en el sector industrial." In *El debate sobre la reforma económica*, ed. CIERA, 235-45. Managua: MIDINRA.

Castillo Rivas, Donald. 1980a. *Acumulación de capital y empresas transnacionales en Centroamérica*. Mexico City: Siglo Veintiuno.

______. 1980b. Nicaragua: Situación económica y alianzas políticas, *Revista Mexicana de Sociología* 42:501-21.

Catalán Aravena, O. O. 1981. "De economische achtergrond van de Midden-amerikaanse crisis." *Internationale Spectator* 25, no. 6:319-28.

Central Bank of Nicaragua. 1978. *Estadísticas básicas del sector industrial 1960–77*. Managua.

Chenery, H. B. 1979. *Structural change and development policy*. New York: Oxford University Press.

CIERA (Centro de Investigaciones y Estudios de la Reforma Agraria). 1988. "La reforma monetaria de 1988: 'Operación mártires de Quilalí': resumen." In *El debate sobre la reforma económica*, ed. CIERA, 302-19. Managua: MIDINRA.

CIERA/PAN/CIDA (CIERA/Programa Alimentario Nicararagüense/Centro de Información y Documentación Agrarias). 1984. *La estrategia alimentaria de Nicaragua*. Parts 1-4, Managua.

CIERA/UNRISD (CIERA/United Nations Research Institute on Security and Development). 1984. *Managua es Nicaragua: El impacto de la capital en el sistema alimentario nacional*. Parts 1-4, Managua.

Cline, William R. 1978. "Benefits and costs of economic integration in Central America." In *Economic integration in Central America*, ed. W. R. Cline, and E.

Delgado, 59-124. Washington, D.C.: Brookings Institution/SIECA.

Cline, William R., and Alan I. Rapoport. 1978. "Industrial comparative advantage in the Central American Common Market." In *Economic integration in Central America*, ed. W. R. Cline, and E. Delgado, 267-316. Washington, D.C.: Brookings Institution/SIECA.

Cohen, I., and G. Rosenthal. 1983. "The dimensions of economic policy space in Central America." In *The future of Central America*, ed. R. R. Fagen and O. Pellicer, 15-34. Stanford, Calif: Stanford University Press.

Collins, Joseph, Frances Moore Lappé, Nick Allen, and Paul Rice. 1985. *What difference could a revolution make? Food and farming in the new Nicaragua*. San Francisco: Institute for Food and Development Policy.

Coraggio, José Luis. 1985. "Política económica y revolución popular en Nicaragua: Los costos políticos de la política económica." Paper presented at ANICS Conference. Managua.

______. 1986. "Economía y política en la transición: Reflexiones sobre la Revolución Sandinista." In *La autodeterminación en los pequeños países periféricos*, ed. J. L. Coraggio and C. D. Deere, 257-85. Managua: Editorial Vanguardia.

Cruz Sequeira, Arturo. 1983. "Nicaragua: Crisis económica, radicalización o moderación?" In *Centroamérica: Mas allá de la crisis*, ed. D. Castillo Rivas, 137-61. Mexico City: Editorial SIAP.

Deere, Carmen Diana. 1981. "Nicaraguan agricultural policy: 1979–1981." *Cambridge Journal of Economics* 5:195-200.

Delgado, Enrique. 1978. "Institutional evolution of the Central American Common Market and the principle of balanced development." In *Economic integration in Central America*, ed. W. R. Cline and E. Delgado, 17-58. Washington, D.C.: Brookings Institution/SIECA.

Díaz, Alvaro. 1984. "La acumulación en Nicaragua 1980–1985: Balance y perspectivas." Managua. Mimeo.

Dijkstra, Geske. 1988. *Industrialization in a mixed economic order: A system-comparative study of the industrialization policy of Nicaragua*. Ph.D. diss., State University of Groningen, Groningen, The Netherlands.

Dijkstra, Geske, Ted van Hees, and Marnix Krop. 1983. "Nicaragua: Revolutie en mensenrechten." *Socialisme en Demokratie* 11:3-11,14.

Dobb, M. [1948] 1966. *Soviet economic development since 1917*. London: Routledge & Kegan Paul.

______. [1963] 1980. *Economic growth and underdeveloped countries*. London: Lawrence & Wishart.

Dumas, Isabel. 1988. "La política de desarrollo industrial." In *Nicaragua: Cambios estructurales y políticas económicas 1979–1987*, ed. INIES, 111-41. Managua: INIES.

ECLAC (Economic Commission for Latin America and the Caribbean). 1979. "Nicaragua: Antecedentes económicos del proceso revolucionario." *Comercio Exterior* (September):1020-6.

______. 1982. *Características principales del proceso y de la política de industrialización de Centroamérica: 1960 a 1980*. Mexico City.

______. 1986. *Notas para el estudio económico de América Latina y El Caribe 1985: Nicaragua*. Mexico City.

______. 1988. *Notas para el estudio económico de América Latina y El Caribe, 1987: Nicaragua*. Mexico City.

______. 1989a. *Economic survey of Latin America and the Caribbean 1988*. Santiago.

______. 1989b. *Preliminary overview of the economy of Latin America and the Caribbean: 1989*. Santiago (December).

Elenbaas, Kees, and Patricio da Silva. 1983. "De Middenamerikaanse gemeenschappelijke markt: Economische integratie als ontwikkelingsmodel." Amsterdam. Mimeo.

Ellman, Michael J. 1975. "Did the agricultural surplus provide the resources for the increase in investment in the USSR during the First Five-Year Plan?" *Economic Journal* 85 (December):844-63.

______. 1980. *Socialistische planning in theorie en praktijk*. Alphen a/d Rijn, The Netherlands: Samson.

Enríquez, Laura J., and Rose J. Spalding. 1987. "Banking systems and revolutionary change: The politics of agricultural credit in Nicaragua." In *The political economy of Revolutionary Nicaragua*, ed. Rose J. Spalding, 105-25. London: Allen & Unwin.

Erlich, A. 1950. "Preobazhensky and the economics of Soviet industrialization." *Quarterly Journal of Economics* 64:57-88.

______. 1960. *The Soviet industrialization debate: 1924–1928*. Cambridge Mass.: Harvard University Press.

FIDA (Fondo Internacional de Desarrollo Agrario). 1980. *Informe de la misión especial de programación a Nicaragua*. Rome.

FitzGerald, E.V.K. 1982. "The economics of the revolution." In *Nicaragua in revolution*, ed. T. W. Walker, 203-22. New York: Praeger.

______. 1984. *Problems in financing a revolution: The case of Nicaragua 1979–1984*. The Hague, ISS Working Paper, Subseries on Money, Finance and Development 14.

______. 1985a. "The problem of balance in the peripheral socialist economy: A conceptual note." *World Development* 13, no. 1:5-14.

______. 1985b. "La economía nacional en 1985: La transición como coyuntura." Paper presented at ANICS Conference. Managua.

______. 1985c. "Agrarian reform as a model of accumulation: The case of Nicaragua since 1979." *Journal of Development Studies* 22, no. 1 (October):208-26.

______. 1986. *Kalecki on financing development: Elements for a macroeconomics of the semi-industrialized economy*. The Hague, ISS Working Paper, Subseries on Money, Finance and Development 17.

______. 1987. "An evaluation of the economic costs to Nicaragua of U.S. Aggression: 1980–1984." In *The political economy of Revolutionary Nicaragua*, ed. Rose J. Spalding, 195-213. Boston: Allen & Unwin.

______. 1988. "La situación económica en Nicaragua a finales de 1987." In *El debate sobre la reforma económica*, ed. CIERA, 192-9. Managua: MIDINRA.

Frenkel, Veronica. 1988. "El papel del campesinado: Un debate que sigue vivo." *Pensamiento Propio* 6, no. 52 (July-August):24-6.

FSLN (Frente Sandinista para la Liberación Nacional). 1981. *Habla la dirección de la vanguardia*. Managua: FSLN.

Gadourek, I. 1972. *Sociologische onderzoekstechnieken: Inleiding tot de werkwijze bij het sociaal- en gedragswetenschappelijk onderzoek.* Deventer, The Netherlands: Van Loghum Slaterus.

Gatica Barros, Jaime. 1989. Deindustrialization in Chile. Boulder, Co: Westview Press.

Gey, Peter. 1982. "Sozialismus und Industrialisierung." *Leviathan* 10, no. 3:359-76.

Gey, Peter, Jirí Kosta, and Wolfgang Quaisser, eds. 1985. *Sozialismus und Industrialisierung: Die Wirtschaftssysteme Polens, Jugoslawiens, Chinas und Kubas im Vergleich.* Frankfurt: Methuen.

Girling, Robert Henriques. 1983. "Nicaragua's commercial policy: Building a socially reponsive foreign trade." *Latin American Perspectives* 36 (10, no. 1):33-44.

Gorostiaga, Xabier. 1981. "Some aspects of Nicaragua's economy." Excerpts from a talk. *Envío* 5 (October).

______. 1982. "Nicaragua: Los dilemas de la Revolución Popular Sandinista a los tres años del triunfo." *CIDE, Economía de América Latina* 9, no. 2:195-206.

Gregory, Paul R., and Robert C. Stuart. 1974. *Soviet economic structure and performance.* New York: Harper & Row.

Grigsby, Arturo. 1988. "Las implicaciones de un reajuste monetario en el sector agropecuario." In *El debate sobre la reforma económica,* ed. CIERA, 200-22. Managua: MIDINRA.

Groot, Jan P. de, and Ruerd Ruben. 1982. *Politieke ekonomie van de transitie-strategie in Nicaragua: Historische ontwikkeling en strukturele transformatie van de Nicaraguaanse ekonomie.* Amsterdam: Free University, Research Memorandum 1982, no. 10.

Guevara, Elias. 1987. "El sistema estatal de abastecimiento." *Boletín Socio-Económico* 6 (December):19-22.

______. 1988. "Ley de inversiones extranjeras: Análisis comparativo 1955–1987." *Boletín Socio-Económico* 8 (June-July):39-43.

Harris, Richard L. 1985a. "The revolutionary process in Nicaragua." *Latin American Perspectives* 45 (12, no. 2):3-21.

______. 1985b. "The economic transformation and industrial development of Nicaragua." In *Nicaragua: A revolution under siege,* ed. R. L. Harris, and C. M. Vilas, 36-87. London: Zed Books.

Harrison, Mark. 1980. "Why did NEP fail?." *Economics of Planning* 16, no. 2:57-67.

IHCA (Instituto Histórico Centroamericano). 1985a. "Los campesinos dan un giro a la reforma agraria." *Envío* 51 (September):1c-19c.

______. 1985b. "En emergencia." *Envío* 53 (November):1a-24a.

______. 1986. "Crisis económica: Lenta transición a un modelo de sobrevivencia popular." *Envío* 63 (September):1b-24b.

______. 1987. "Empresa privada Nicaragüense; Postura política ante la economía mixta." *Envío* 70 (April):27-36.

______. 1988a. "La reforma monetaria: Inicio de una insurrección económica?" *Envío* 82 (April-May):17-42.

______. 1988b. "The new economic package: Will a popular model emerge?" *Envío* 86 (August):21-63.

______. 1988c. "More on the economy, and more needs to be done." *Envío* 88 (November):13-21.

______. 1989a. "Update: Economy." *Envío* 93 (April):10-7.

______. 1989b. "From a mixed-up economy toward a socialist mixed economy." *Envío* 94 (May):33-54.

______. 1989c. "Update: The economy." *Envío* 95 (June):11-4.

______. 1991a. "Hacia donde nos lleva la política económica de la UNO?". *Envío* 111 (February):19-50.

______. 1991b. "Qué esperar del plan económico: Reactivación o recesión?" *Envío* 117 (July):19-50.

INEC (Instituto Nicaragüense de Estadísticas y Census). 1982. *Encuesta anual industria manufacturera 1980*. Managua.

INIES (Instituto de Investigaciones Económicas y Sociales). 1985. "El nuestro es un proyecto enredado." Interview with Tomás Borge. *Pensamiento Propio* 24 (June-July):7-15.

______. 1987a. "Casa de cambio e inflación." *Boletín Socio-Económico* 5 (August-September):1-7.

______. 1987b. "Resultado de las medidas económicas de junio: Análisis preliminar." *Boletín Socio-Económico* 6 (November-December):13-8.

INIES/SPP (INIES/Secretaría de Planificación y Presupuesto). 1987. *Plan económico 1987*. Managua: INIES.

Irvin, George. 1983. "Nicaragua: Establishing the state as the centre of accumulation." *Cambridge Journal of Economics* 7, no. 7:125-39.

______. 1986. "Como costear la guerra." *Pensamiento Propio* 34 (July):12-7.

______. 1987. "ECLAC and the political economy of the Central American Common Market." *Latin American Research Review* 23, no. 3:7-29.

Janvry, Alain de. 1981. *The agrarian question and reformism in Latin America*. Baltimore: Johns Hopkins University Press.

JGRN (Junta de Gobierno de Reconstrucción Nacional) 1983. Economic policy guidelines 1983–1988. Managua. Mimeo.

Joel, Clark. 1971. "Tax incentives in Central American development." *Economic Development and Cultural Change* 19:229-52.

Jung, Harald. 1980. *Bereicherungsdiktatur und Volksaufstand*. Frankfurt am Main: Vervuert.

Kaimowitz, David. 1989. "La planificación agropecuaria en Nicaragua: De un proceso de acumulación basado en el estado a la alianza estratégica con el campesinado. In *El debate sobre la reforma agraria en Nicaragua*, ed. Raúl R. Ruben and Jan P. de Groot, 47-80. Managua: Editorial Ciencias Sociales/INIES.

Kalecki, Michal. [1967] 1972. *Selected essays on the growth of the socialist and the mixed economy*. Cambridge: Cambridge University Press.

Kornai, J. 1979. "Resource-constrained vs. demand-constrained systems." *Econometrica*. Vol. 47, no. 4 (July):801-19.

______. 1980. *Economics of shortage*. 2 vols. Amsterdam, The Netherlands: North Holland.

Laenen, Arie. 1988. *Dinámica y transformación de la pequeña industria en Nicaragua*. Amsterdam: CEDLA/FORIS.

Lee, N. 1984. "Introduction." In *Industrial structure and policy in less developed countries*, ed. C. H. Kirkpatrick, N. Lee, and F. I. Nixson, 1-11. London: Allen & Unwin.

Little, I., T. Scitovsky, and M. Scott. 1970. *Industry and trade in some developing countries: A comparative study*. London: Oxford University Press.

Lorenz, R. 1976. *Sozialgeschichte der Sowjet Union 1: 1917–1945*. Frankfurt am Main: Suhrkamp Verlag.

Mandelbaum, K., and G. Meyer. 1934. "Zur Theorie der Planwirtschaft." *Zeitschrift fur Sozialforschung* 3, no. 2:228-62.

Marín, José Nicolas. 1971. *Industrial finance in Nicaragua: A study of financial practice in an underdeveloped country*. Managua: INCAE.

Medal, José Luis. 1985. *La revolución Nicaragüense: Balance económico y alternativas futuras*. Managua: CINASE.

______. 1988. *Nicaragua: Crisis, cambio social y política económica*. Managua: CINASE.

Merl, Stephan. 1981. *Der Agrarmarkt und der Neue Okonomische Politik*. Munich/Vienna: Oldenbourg Verlag.

Mesa-Lago, C. 1981. *The economy of socialist Cuba: A two-decade appraisal*. Albuquerque: University of New Mexico Press.

MIDINRA (Ministerio de Desarrollo Agropecuario y Reforma Agraria). 1983. *Informe de Nicaragua a la FAO*. Managua.

MICOIN (Ministerio de Comercio Interior). 1983. Sistemas de comercialización: Productos básicos de consumo popular. Vol. C, Políticas del estado referente a subsidios y precios. Managua (June). Mimeo.

MIND (Ministerio de Industria). 1982. Sector industrial: Evaluación 1981. Managua. Mimeo.

______. 1983a. Estrategia para el desarrollo industrial 1982–1983. Managua. Mimeo.

______. 1983b. Programa industrial 1983. Managua. Mimeo.

______. 1983c. Sector industrial: Evaluación 1982. Managua. Mimeo.

______. 1984a. Programa industrial 1984. Managua. Mimeo.

______. 1984b. Programa industrial 1984: Resultados estimados. Managua. Mimeo.

______. 1984c. Cinco años de gestion. Managua. Mimeo.

______. 1985a. Lineamientos y medidas de la política. Managua. Mimeo.

______. 1985b. Sector industrial: Evaluación año 1984. Managua. Mimeo.

Ministerio de Justicia. 1982. *Leyes de la República*. Vol. 5 (July 1981–January 1982). Managua.

MIPLAN (Ministerio de Planificación). 1980. *Programa económico en beneficio del pueblo*. Managua.

______. 1981. *Programa de austeridad y eficiencia*. Managua.

Myint, Hla. 1972. *South East Asia's economy: Development policies in the 1970s*. Harmondsworth, Middlesex: Penguin Books.

NACLA (North American Congress on Latin America). 1985. "Sandinista foreign policy: Strategies for survival." *Report on the America's* 19, no. 5/6 (May/June):13-57.

Neira, Oscar. 1991. "A las puertas del ajuste." *Pensamiento Propio* 82 (9, July):16-9.

Nove, Alec. 1969. *An economic history of the USSR*. London: Allen Lane/Pen-

guin Press.
Nuti, Domenico M. 1979. "The contradictions of socialist economies: A Marxist interpretation." *Socialist Register* 11: 228-73.
Ortega, Marvin. 1985. "Workers' participation in the management of the agro-enterprises of the APP." *Latin American Perspectives* 45 (12, no. 2):69-81.
Pérez Brignoli, Hector, and Yolanda Baires Martínez. 1983. "Growth and crisis in the Central American economies: 1950–1980." *Journal of Latin American Studies* 15:365-98.
Pilarte, René, Vilma Ubau, and Elias Guevara. 1988. "Evolución y resultados de las políticas económicas en el sector agrícola." *Boletín Socio-Económico* 10 (November-December):9-17.
Pizarro, Roberto. 1987. "The new economic policy: A necessary readjustment." In *The political economy of Revolutionary Nicaragua*, ed. Rose J. Spalding, 217-32. Boston: Allen & Unwin.
PREALC (Programa Regional de Empleo para América Latina y El Caribe). 1973. *Situación y perspectivas del empleo en Nicaragua*. 2 vols. Santiago: ILO.
Preobazhensky, E. [1926] 1965. *The new economics*. Oxford: Clarendon Press.
Ramírez Sánchez, Noel Ernesto. 1982. *The causes of inflation in small developing economies with a fixed rate of exchange: A comparative analysis of Nicaragua and Costa Rica*. Ann Arbor: University Microfilm International.
Ramírez Suárez, C. 1980. *Leyes de la Revolución*. (July 19 1979–March 31 1980). Managua.
Ruben, Raúl, Jan P. de Groot, and Cor Wattel 1989. "El sector socializado en la reforma agraria de Nicaragua." In *El debate sobre la reforma agraria en Nicaragua*, ed. Raúl Ruben and Jan P. de Groot, 155-96. Managua: Editorial Ciencias Sociales/INIES.
Shanin, L. [1925] 1964a. "The nature of the commodity shortage." In *Foundations of the Soviet strategy of economic growth*, ed. N. Spulber, 205-11. Bloomington: Indiana University Press.
______. [1926] 1964b. "Questions of the economic course." In *Foundations of the Soviet strategy of economic growth*, ed. N. Spulber, 212-20. Bloomington: Indiana University Press.
Sjmelev, Nikolaj. 1987. "Voorschotten en schulden." *Intermediair* 23, no. 29 (July 17):3-7.
Solórzano, Arturo and Rebecca de los Ríos. 1984. "Respuesta del sector manufacturero en Nicaragua ante la crisis económica internacional y la agresión imperialista". Paper presented at V Congress of Economists from Central America and the Caribbean. Managua (July).
Steenhuis, Aafke and Jan Joost Teunissen. 1982. "Revolutie en realisme." In *Revolutie en realisme: De ekonomische en politieke uitdaging in Nicaragua*, ed. Aafke Steenhuis and Jan Joost Teunissen, 13-22. Amsterdam/Utrecht, The Netherlands: Transnational Institute/Nicaragua Komitee.
Strachan, Harry W. 1976. *Family and other business groups in economic development: The case of Nicaragua*. New York: Praeger.
Sutcliffe, R. B. 1971. *Industry and underdevelopment*. London: Addison-Wesley.
Szamuely, L. 1974. *First models of the socialist economic systems*. Budapest: Akademiai Kiado.
Toor, Theo van. 1986. "De erfenis van Somoza." In *Nicaragua: De erfenis van*

*Sandino: Een balans van zeven jaar revolutie*, ed. M. van Esch et al., 13-36. Nijmegen, The Netherlands: Stichting Derde Wereld Publikaties.
Torres-Rivas, E. 1980. "The Central American model of growth: Crisis for whom?" *Latin American Perspectives* 7, no. 2/3:24-44.
Utting, Peter. 1987. "Domestic supply and food shortages." In *The political economy of Revolutionary Nicaragua*, ed. Rose J. Spalding, 127-48. London: Allen & Unwin.
Vilas, Carlos M. 1985. "Unidad nacional y contradicciones sociales en una economía mixta: Nicaragua 1979–1984." In *La revolución en Nicaragua*, ed. R. L. Harris and C. M. Vilas, 17-50. Mexico City: Siglo Veintiuno.
______. 1986. *La Revolución Sandinista*. Buenos Aires: Legasa.
Wagener, H.-J. 1979. "De landbouwcollectivisatie en haar sociaal-economische gevolgen voor het platteland van de Sovjetunie." *Internationale Spectator* 23, no. 10:600-5.
______. 1980. *Economische systemen: Theorieën, instituties en doelstellingen*. Alphen a/d Rijn, The Netherlands: Samsom.
Watkins, M. H. 1963. "A staple theory of economic growth." *Canadian Journal of Economics and Political Science* 29, no. 2 (May):141-58.
Weeks, John. 1982. "Impact of changes in import and export prices on Nicaraguan manufacturing: 1960–1977." Washington, D.C. Mimeo.
______. 1985a. *The economies of Central America*. New York: Holmes & Meyer.
______. 1985b. "The industrial sector." In *Nicaragua: The first five years*, ed. T. W. Walker, 281-94. New York: Praeger.
______. 1986. "An interpretation of the Central American crisis." *Latin American Research Review* 21, no. 3:31-53.
Weinert, Richard. 1981. "Nicaragua's debt renegotiation." *Cambridge Journal of Economics* 5:187-94.
Weissenburger, Ulrich. 1983. *Monetärer Sektor und Industrialisierung der Sowjet Union 1927–1933*. Frankfurt/Main: Haak & Herchen.
Wheelock Román, Jaime. 1980. *Nicaragua: Imperialismo y dictadura*. Havana: Editorial de Ciencias Sociales.
______. 1985. *Entre la crisis y la agresión: La reforma agraria Sandinista*. Managua: Editorial Nueva Nicaragua.
Wilber, C. 1969. *The Soviet model and underdeveloped countries*. Chapel Hill: University of North Carolina Press.
World Bank. 1981. *Nicaragua: The challenge of reconstruction*. Washington, D.C.
______. 1982. *Country program paper: Nicaragua*. Washington, D.C.
Zaleski, E. 1980. *Stalinist planning for economic growth: 1933–1952*. London: Macmillan.

# Index


Accumulation, 7-9, 70, 80, 109-111, 113, 184-186, 188
  industrial, 25
  primitive capitalist, 23
  primitive socialist, 23
  private, 25, 31, 87, 104, 105
  process, 177
  rate, 21, 22, 30
  state-directed, 2
Agroindustrialization. *See* Strategy, agroindustrial
Agroindustry, 2, 43, 82, 83, 88, 92, 104, 143, 144, 146-148, 150, 175-177, 183-186, 189
Aid
  foreign, 75, 76, 113, 124, 111, 188, 189, 191, 193
APP. *See* Area of People's Property
Area of People's Property, 77, 127
Assignment
  of foreign exchange. *See* Foreign exchange, assignment of
Balance of payments, 42, 54, 115
  current account of, 40, 53, 112(tab.), 123
Balance of trade, 40, 53, 54, 115, 112 (tab.), 122, 141
Barter, 88, 163
Basic needs, 2, 6, 7, 143, 145, 148, 150, 186
Black market, 132-135
  of foreign exchange 88, 89, 121 (tab.), 122, 137, 160, 178
Bourgeoisie, 62-65, 70-73, 75, 77, 164-180
  comprador, 40
  financial, 110
  patriotic, 73
  vendepatria, 73
Budget constraint
  soft, 105, 136, 189
Budget deficit. *See* Fiscal deficit
Bukharin, 16, 21-24
Business groups, 63-66
CACM. *See* Central American Common Market
Capacity utilization, 42, 49, 50, 52, 154-157, 171
Capital flight, 1, 37, 38, 43(tab.), 55-57, 77, 118, 122
Central American Common Market, 34-56, 61, 118, 120, 153, 161-163, 187
Collectivization, 6, 7, 15, 25, 27-29
Commanding heights, 5, 17, 189
Commercial balance. *See* Balance of trade
Compactación, 83, 84, 139
Confiscation. *See* Nationalization
Contras, 2, 80, 109, 129, 186, 189
  war of. *See* War, of contras
Control
  of domestic trade, 19, 25, 30, 105, 131-136, 187
  of foreign exchange. *See* Foreign exchange, assignment of
  of income distribution, 128-131
  of investment, 17
  of prices. *See* Price policy
  of procurement, 16-18, 24-30, 97, 98, 100, 130
  of sales, 100
  of wages, 100-103, 136, 137, 160, 167
Cooperatives, 19, 20 24-26, 73, 78-82, 86, 87, 89, 93-97, 123, 148, 152
Cooperativization. *See* Cooperatives
Coordinating mechanism, 1, 3-5
COSEP. *See* Superior Council of Private Enterprise

Counterrevolutionaries. *See* Contras
Credit lines, 86, 91, 123, 150, 160, 169
Credits, 18, 20, 25, 52, 60, 62, 65-67, 78, 79, 86, 105, 111, 125-127, 130, 134, 136, 140, 141, 148, 150-152, 176, 192
policy of. *See* Policy, of credits
Current account balance. *See* Balance of payments, current account
Customs union, 35, 40
Debt. *See* Foreign debt
Decapitalization, 57, 77, 78, 111, 148, 153
Deficit
balance-of-payments. *See* Balance of payments
fiscal. *See* Fiscal deficit
global. *See* Global deficit
Dependence, 40, 72
on foreign aid, 32, 152, 193
on imports, 42, 50, 58, 67, 92, 153
on socialist countries, 188
on the government, 177
Devaluation, 89, 122, 137-141, 192, 193
Development strategy. *See* Strategy, of development
Distribution of income. *See* Income distribution
Diversification
agricultural, 33
of export products, 143, 146
Economic integration, 33, 34
Economic order, 3-7, 9, 27, 105
centrally planned, 160, 164
mixed. *See* Mixed economy
state-controlled, 3
Economic system. *See* Economic order
Efficiency, 79, 83, 88, 97, 106, 127, 133, 140, 160, 164
allocative, 105, 136, 185, 189
X-, 105, 185, 187-189
Embargo. *See* Trade embargo
Employment, 20, 42, 49, 111, 139-141, 174, 193
industrial, 50, 53
urban, 29
Enterprises
foreign. *See* Foreign enterprises
Exchange losses
of Central Bank, 115, 122, 123, 125-127, 137, 140
Exchange rate, 60, 88-90, 105, 121 (tab.), 122, 137, 160, 162, 164, 187, 191-193
overvalued, 40, 42, 70, 120, 130, 136, 184
implicit, 106, 120
multiple, 70
Expenditure
defense, 188
investment. *See* Investment, public
government, 61, 123, 139-141, 191-193
Expropriation. *See* Nationalization
First Five-Year Plan, 26-29
Fiscal deficit, 40, 111, 115, 124(tab.), 125-127, 140, 185-187, 192
Foreign capital. *See* Foreign investment
Foreign companies. *See* Foreign enterprises
Foreign debt, 37
of Nicaragua, 37, 112(tab.), 122, 123
of other countries 37, 188
Foreign enterprises, 101, 103, 156-159, 168, 171-175
Foreign exchange, 77, 161, 165
assignment of, 70, 84, 86-93, 103, 104, 127, 157, 162, 166-170, 173-176, 178, 180, 189
use of, 127, 136
Foreign Investment, 21, 34, 35, 40, 54, 55, 58-60, 64, 65, 179
Law, 179
U.S., 34, 35
FSLN. *See* Sandinista Front for National Liberation
GDP. *See* Gross domestic product
Global deficit, 115, 126
Goods famine, 19, 20, 22-26
Government deficit. *See* Fiscal deficit
Grain strike, 18, 20
Gross domestic product
change in, 33, 36, 37, 112(tab.), 113, 115, 123, 140, 189, 192
Guaranteed prices, 87, 88, 98, 104, 106, 120, 122, 187

Import substitution, 41-43, 46-49, 160, 162
Income distribution, 2, 6, 33, 39, 52, 53, 56, 57, 109-111, 128-141
Independence, 2, 21, 143
Industrial policy, 87, 99, 104, 162, 165, 168, 173, 174
Industrialization, 2, 3, 7-9, 27-29, 39-58, 194
  import-substituting. *See* Import substitution
  speed of, 27-29
Industrialization debate, 7, 15, 16, 20-24
Industrialization strategy, 3, 8, 9, 26, 31, 34, 143-152, 160, 186, 188, 191, 194
  in a strict sense, 9, 143
  inward-oriented, 9
  outward-oriented, 9, 148
  socialist, 151
Inefficiency. *See* Efficiency
Inflation, 3, 22, 40, 101, 111, 112(tab.), 115, 127-131, 133-138, 140, 141, 184, 191-193
Informal trade sector, 140, 141, 157
Integration
  economic. *See* Economic integration
  between branches of manufacturing. *See* Linkages
Interest rates, 79, 94, 138, 139, 176, 187
  real, 126, 127, 193
Intermediate regime, 5
Investment, 2, 8, 9, 17, 19, 21, 22, 23, 26, 28, 49, 52, 60-62, 113, 128 (tab.), 139, 145-154, 160, 186, 187
  agricultural, 25
  financing of, 93, 94, 115, 151 (tab.), 178
  foreign. *See* Foreign investment
  industrial, 25, 60, 65, 148-154, 169
  private, 40, 70, 169-171, 174
  public, 120, 125-127, 139, 140, 192
Joint ventures, 54, 64
Land reform, 16, 73, 78-82, 186, 187
Liberalization, 191
  of foreign trade, 194
  of import, 192
  of domestic trade, 134
Linkages, 42, 145, 150, 151
  backward, 39, 45, 50
  forward, 43, 49
Manufacturing exports, 162-164
Market
  black. *See* Black market
  free, 28
  parallel, 89, 121(tab.), 122, 137, 162, 164
  saturation of the, 39, 52, 53
MIND. *See* Ministry of Industry, 173
Minimum wage, 101, 111
Ministry of Industry, 84, 96, 144, 145, 148, 149, 163, 165-168, 173, 174, 179
  relationship with the, 172
Mixed economy, 4-7, 31, 191
  Kaleckian, 5
  Keynesian 4
  late-developing, 5
  Leninist, 5, 17-20, 24-30
  Sandinista, 3, 14, 31
Monetary reform. *See* Reform, monetary
Multinational corporations. *See* Foreign enterprises
Multinational enterprises. *See* Foreign enterprises
Nationalization, 5-7, 16, 66, 73-82, 110, 127, 131, 133-135, 165, 176, 177, 179
NEP. *See* New Economic Policy
NEPmen, 17, 19, 27
New Economic Policy, 15-32, 109
Order. *See* Economic order
Overvaluation. *See* Exchange rate, overvalued
Parallel market. *See* Market, parallel
Pay in kind, 100, 102, 153
Peasants, 1, 5, 16, 18, 21, 23-25, 27, 29, 30, 33, 52, 62, 63(tab.), 70, 73, 74, 78-82, 93-96, 98-100, 105, 111, 139, 186, 187, 192
Planning
  central, 1, 4
  process of, 86, 87
  regional, 34, 50, 51

Policy
of accumulation. *See* Accumulation
of credits, 93-95, 113, 127, 138, 185, 192-194
financial, 93, 126
of foreign exchange. *See* Foreign exchange, assignment of
of income, 110
industrial. *See* Industrial policy
of investment, 103, 146, 150, 162
prices. *See* Price policy
stabilization, 94
Soviet, 187
subsidy. *See* Subsidies
of taxes, 57(tab.), 61, 111, 123, 124
of wages. *See* Wages
Popular shops, 130
Preobazhensky, 21-24, 29
Price policy, 19, 26-31, 70, 96(tab.), 97, 99, 100, 104, 105, 109, 128-137, 141, 160, 168, 184-189
Privatization, 40, 191, 192
Procurement. *See* Control, of procurement
Producer prices, 17, 99, 129-131, 133
Production commissions, 96
Productivity, 8, 20, 78, 79, 85, 118, 136, 156
agricultural, 22, 23, 33
capital, 22
industrial, 23
investment, 151
of labor, 8, 9, 23, 59, 60, 102, 133, 134, 152
Profit transfers, 40, 54, 62, 170-175, 178, 179
Protection, 40-42
effective, 44, 45, 50
Rationing, 131
Reform
economic, 136-141, 178-180, 188, 189
monetary, 121(tab.), 122, 136-138, 153, 164
Requisition. *See* Control, of procurement
Sandinista Front for National Liberation, 1, 71-76, 184
Scarcities, 130, 131, 134
Scissors crisis, 18, 24
Shanin, 21, 22, 24
Shortages, 22-26, 30, 105, 128-130, 132-136
of labor, 131
of raw materials, 118, 153, 156
Small industry, 89, 92, 97
Socialization, 5, 74
Stability
macroeconomic, 30, 31, 110, 135, 184
of the mixed economy, 24, 27-31, 69-71, 109-111, 127, 135, 136, 141, 165, 177-180, 184-189
Stability conditions, 31
Strategy
agroindustrial, 3, 188
development, 2
industrialization. *See* Industrialization strategy
Structuralists, 38-40, 49, 50, 52, 53, 58, 73
Subsidies, 123-125, 129, 130, 133-136, 141, 184-187
export, 188
import, 139, 177
Superior Council of Private Enterprise, 69, 165, 175, 179
Surplus
agricultural, 21, 22, 28, 29
financial, 29
from the private sector, 30, 110, 111, 127, 184
System. *See* Economic order
Terms of trade
external, 36, 39, 51, 54, 56, 120
internal, 28, 29, 70, 100, 105, 131, 134, 187
Trade balance. *See* Balance of trade
Trade embargo, 120, 153, 157
Transition to socialism, 5-7, 183, 186
Transnational companies. *See* Foreign enterprises
Trueques, 163
Trusts, 18
Unemployment. *See* Employment
Unequal exchange, 23, 24, 29, 30

external, 40
Wages, 86, 100-103, 109, 110, 129 (tab.), 130-141, 165, 167, 174, 178, 185-187, 189, 193
historical, 100, 101
War, 36
civil, 16, 37, 57, 58
contra, 31, 71, 80, 114, 115, 120, 168, 175, 184, 187, 188
liberation, 1, 78, 111, 118, 120, 146, 152, 161, 175, 183
propaganda, 133
War communism, 16, 17, 31
War damage, 114(tab.), 115
War economy, 3

## *Series in Political Economy and Economic Development in Latin America*

Series Editor
Andrew Zimbalist
*Smith College*

Through country case studies and regional analyses this series will contribute to a deeper understanding of development issues in Latin America. Shifting political environments, increasing economic interdependence, and the difficulties with regard to debt, foreign investment, and trade policy demand novel conceptualizations of development strategies and potentials for the region. Individual volumes in this series will explore the deficiencies in conventional formulations of the Latin American development experience by examining new evidence and material. Topics will include, among others, women and development in Latin America; the impact of IMF interventions; the effects of redemocratization on development; Cubanology and Cuban political economy; Nicaraguan political economy; and individual case studies on development and debt policy in various countries in the region.